BAR CHEF

Moscow
Margarita
(page 171)

BAR CHEF
Handcrafted Cocktails

**Christiaan Röllich
and Carolynn Carreño**

PHOTOGRAPHY BY ED ANDERSON

W. W. NORTON & COMPANY
INDEPENDENT PUBLISHERS SINCE 1923
NEW YORK   LONDON

For information about permission to reproduce selections from this book, write to
Permissions, W. W. Norton & Company, Inc., 500 Fifth Avenue, New York, NY 10110

For information about special discounts for bulk purchases, please contact
W. W. Norton Special Sales at specialsales@wwnorton.com or 800-233-4830

Manufacturing by Asia Pacific Offset
Book design by Jan Derevjanik
Production manager: Anna Oler

ISBN: 978-0-393-65156-0

W. W. Norton & Company, Inc., 500 Fifth Avenue, New York, N.Y. 10110
www.wwnorton.com

W. W. Norton & Company Ltd., 15 Carlisle Street, London W1D 3BS

1 2 3 4 5 6 7 8 9 0

To my family: Mama, Papa, Melissa, River,
Leaf, Melchior, and Dimitri. Thank you for your
unconditional love. For letting me dream my dreams,
spread my wings, and reach for the stars.

CONTENTS

FOREWORD BY SUZANNE GOIN

It has been both deeply gratifying and a whole lot of fun to watch Christiaan Röllich grow from the eager, personable, and painstakingly precise bartender who first came to Lucques over twelve years ago into a true mastermind and innovator in the world of cocktails. When Christiaan first started working for us, bartending was just a job to pay his bills while he attended school for respiratory therapy. Christiaan was a skilled barman—he brought not only a kind of athletic grace and rigor to the job but also his brand of Old World Dutch charm, and soon he had developed quite a following with our guests. He was also much loved by the staff, so when he finally finished school and said his good-byes, we were all very sorry to see him go. But then, after hardly a week had gone by, he came back and told Caroline and me that he had changed his mind! His time at Lucques, not just working behind the bar but also absorbing what we were doing with the food, had captivated him.

From that moment on, Christiaan threw himself into the world of mixology with a zest I had never seen before, approaching cocktails the way a chef approaches food. He is an adventurous curator who has spread his love of cocktails both new and old and has turned our bars into destinations. Today I cannot imagine my restaurants without Christiaan. The joy, passion, and deliciousness he has brought to our bars over the years is immeasurable and has become an integral part of the Lucques experience.

In retrospect, it shouldn't have been a surprise. Early on in his career with us, Christiaan would always pop into the kitchen before service, snooping around, tasting everything he could, and asking lots and lots of questions. While most servers and bartenders would taste a new dish, ask a few questions, and jot down some notes, Christiaan was always digging deeper: "What gives the Meyer lemon salsa its viscosity?" "How did you get that quince puree to be so silky and almost melting?" "What's the best way to extract the true deep flavor from a beet?" At the time I assumed he liked to cook or was just a particularly curious person, but in fact he had a tangible objective I didn't anticipate: he was soaking up my philosophy and techniques and thinking about how he could apply them to the world of drink. He was beginning to build the bridge from the kitchen to the bar.

Like so many of us in the food world in southern California, Christiaan became obsessed with all the remarkable produce we are so fortunate to have growing in close proximity. Intrigued by the ingredients we were cooking with, he asked if he could come to the Wednesday farmers' market in Santa Monica with me. In the beginning, he diligently followed me around the market, but soon he began shopping there on his own to procure ingredients for the bar. I offered to pick things up for him, but Christiaan wanted to go himself for the same reasons I did: to build relationships with the growers, to discover hidden treasures, to taste and to imagine, to be inspired by and to truly connect with the produce. This affinity for seasonal, locally grown produce became a key driver in Christiaan's development. He was always looking for ways to highlight local treats like Romeo Coleman's strawberry guavas or

Windrose Farm's heirloom apples. I watched with great pleasure as he absorbed the importance of seasonality and supporting local farms that is central to my cooking. Once he had acquired an exhaustive knowledge of what is available when, and who is growing what and why, he was free to go to the next level.

The most joyful part of our collaboration began when Christiaan took over the Sunday bartending duties at Lucques, which is when we serve our Sunday Supper, a three-course prix fixe dinner that changes weekly and has been a signature of the restaurant since its inception. Sunday Suppers often have a theme, and Christiaan came up with the idea of having a special cocktail to pair with the menu. So every week, alongside my planning of the Sunday menu, I would have a dialogue with Christiaan about possible directions for that night's cocktail. Based on our conversations and tasting the dishes, Christiaan would hit the kitchen like it was his science lab. As always, he wasn't shy about asking questions. He would ask me how to infuse the flavor of a pecan into a syrup, the best ways to poach apples, what it means to confit a tomato. He would go off, then come back with a tester. We would taste it and discuss it, and then he would remake and remake that drink until he came up with something that we both loved. By the way, there are worse things than doing due diligence with cocktails . . .

As you can probably tell by now, Christiaan is a perfectionist. He welcomed the critiques and comments because he knew he would learn and improve. I remember making green harissa to serve with a grilled sea bass, and when Christiaan tasted it he said, "That would make a great drink!" I confess, I was a bit skeptical. Really? Oh, yes, really! He took out the garlic and olive oil and created a Green Harissa Syrup, which he combined with rum and kale to create the Leaf and Spear. The Moscow Margarita came about in a very similar way. I was roasting beets and making ras el hanout for a Middle East–inspired salad one Sunday, and next thing I knew it had been incorporated into a wonderful cocktail. As time went on, Christiaan asked me less but showed me more. When I was working the grill, he would come over and offer me a taste of his grapefruit marmalade or excitedly serve me a spoonful of raspberry fennel syrup. He always solicited my opinion and thoughts, even when he knew pretty well that it was amazing.

This is how the drink program and the food program at Lucques came together as one vision. Christiaan makes a cocktail the way I make a dish, with a focus on bold flavors, little surprises, lively spice, balanced acid, and constant mindfulness of texture and mouthfeel. If I had to pick from all his myriad talents, I'd say it's Christiaan's understanding and honoring of texture and mouthfeel that truly sets him apart. He is a master of syrups, liqueurs, tinctures, purees, butters, and more. He is also an avid explorer of flavor, infusing pumpkin, pear, guava, and all manner of nuts and herbs to get their essence into drinks. His cocktails have body and depth and balance that push them over the edge of deliciousness into sublime delectability.

Once Christiaan had mastered the perfect drink, he looked around the bar at all the premade ingredients on the shelf and decided to learn how to make all of these as well. His tinkering began with syrups and liqueurs, and soon he was making his own vermouth, Campari, bitters, even gin. As usual, he was incredibly driven and demanding of himself, making test after test until he finally achieved a product that he loved. Christiaan brings this passion for his work, a respect for ingredients, and an ever-curious palate, along with a splash of love for good times and a jigger of humor, to every single cocktail he creates at our restaurants. What an amazing feat now to have poured all that is in his cocktail soul onto these pages, and what lucky readers we are to have a chance to get inside his mixologist mind and make these drinks ourselves at home. As with my cookbooks, I hope you enjoy making these recipes, but even more than that, I hope you connect with the spirit behind them. My fondest wish is that after following some of Christiaan's recipes and learning his techniques, looking at mixology from Christiaan's point of view inspires you to come up with a signature cocktail of your own. Cheers and happy drinking!

FOREWORD BY CAROLINE STYNE

Some of my most favorite moments at work are when Suzanne and I are sitting in our office and Christiaan pokes his head in the doorway and asks if we have time to taste a few things. Usually he's working on a new seasonal cocktail menu and wants to get our stamp of approval. If it were anyone else asking, I would have to confess that an unexpected tasting like this could actually be a real chore. The intense examination of flavors and nuances can require a great deal of time and attention, as we may be required to find the solution to an issue of balance, taste, or conceptualization. But in the case of an impromptu Christiaan Röllich tasting, this "task" is truly a pleasure, as one after another, he delivers drinks to our desks that are beyond beautiful, rich in flavor, and laden with texture.

Each aspect of Christiaan's cocktails is meticulously conceived, from the house-made ingredients to the ice cubes to the technique and vessel. He realizes that the cocktail needs to provide a multidimensional experience for the drinker, beyond flavor and extending into the visual, aromatic, tactile. He has been deeply influenced by Suzanne, her approach to seasonality, and the inspiration behind her menus. Early on, he decided that our bar program should be in step with her menu and use the same ingredients and flavor combinations, whether it be summer fruits, winter spices, or something as specific as her green harissa. He transformed our bar into a reflection of Suzanne's kitchen.

It should really come as no surprise that Christiaan has achieved so much so quickly.

From the moment he began working behind the bar at Lucques, he became a guest favorite. Always well-groomed and tattooed, he became a genuine barman and entertainer, shaking and stirring each drink with true intent and a good dose of love. At the same time, he developed into a constant caretaker of the culture and values behind our restaurants, providing each guest with a curated dining experience and conveying the meaning and thought process behind our menus, wines, and cocktails. When diners complement me on our staff, they most often call out their experience with "that super knowledgeable bearded guy behind the bar."

Over the years, Christiaan has become a bit of a taskmaster when devising a recipe, and can often be found in the Lucques kitchen alongside the prep and line cooks as he creates his syrups, house-made bitters, and the like. He prefers not to use mass-produced ingredients in his drinks and approaches each recipe with the goal of making each element of the drink himself. The difference this makes is enormous, and clearly worth all of the effort it takes.

Most important, Christiaan approaches each cocktail the way he seems to approach life, with an intense focus on doing things completely, with joy, and with an eye on doing it the right way. He works on his concepts through a thorough understanding of ingredients and flavors, and looks at each element of a drink the way a chef approaches the composition of a dish. In fact, sitting down with him to discuss his ideas for a new seasonal drinks menu can feel very much like it does when I sit down with Suzanne to go over her latest dinner menu. Seasonally inspired produce and spices are listed off in combinations that suggest balance and a deeply intuitive understanding of liquors, produce, herbs, and spices. He doesn't add anything that is superfluous to his recipes. Every ingredient serves a purpose and has a meaningful impact on the cocktail. There is solid reasoning behind each use of a spice, or an infused liquor or syrup. And these elements work together to create a finished product that impacts its consumer the same way great food does, with balance and intensity, and highs and lows on the palate.

The term "mixologist" gets thrown around and tacked on in countless iterations around the country these days. We have always refused to call Christiaan by that moniker as it feels trendy and overused. His talents and work are hard to pin down with merely a title, and though we call him our barman, in truth Christiaan is really a Bar Chef.

INTRODUCTION

My name is Christiaan Röllich, and this is my book of cocktails. I've been mixing up cocktails and serving a wide variety of crowds in Los Angeles for the last twenty years. For the last decade I've worked where I do now, with the Lucques family of restaurants in Los Angeles, one of the most acclaimed restaurant groups in the country.

I love the art and craft of making cocktails, and that's what I want to share with you through the recipes and stories in this book. The kind of cocktails that I make are "craft cocktails." If you've ordered a cocktail in your favorite high-end restaurant or craft cocktail bar in the last decade, you know what I'm talking about. These aren't your usual Manhattans and Martinis. I invent my own drinks, and I give them names, as I did for my children. I make my own liqueurs, vermouths, syrups, and bitters. I squeeze all my fruit and vegetable juices. I often rim a cocktail glass with things beyond the usual salt. Hell, in the world of craft cocktails, even the shape and size of the ice is considered. In the world of the handcrafted cocktail, bartenders are often referred to as *mixologists*, although I prefer *bartender* or *barman*. We have a saying in Dutch, my native language, "Just be normal; that's already crazy enough."

My education as a barman came about through what I learned on the job, from a handful of really great teachers, and, of course, through drinking. I'm not a proponent of excessive drinking, but if you don't know what an ingredient or a mixed drink tastes like, it will be very difficult or even impossible to imagine what that product would do to your cocktail. So tasting, and really paying attention to what you taste, is key. And probably more important: if you don't enjoy the ritual of drinking and the culture of the bar, I can't imagine how you would enjoy making drinks or working in a bar. I like to drink. I enjoy sipping spirits and liqueurs. I like having a beer on a hot day and wine with dinner. I like the ritual of drinking. Drinking is a part of my life, and what I drink and the way that I drink have evolved as I have evolved as a man. I also really like the culture of bars. I like the noise and excitement, the conversations, the general sense that everyone is having fun. I like to talk to people—to strangers as much as to friends—and that, too, comes in handy for a bartender.

My first job as a bartender was at Les Deux Cafes in Hollywood, where I worked from 2000 to 2002 with an old-school barman by the name of Chip Garamella. Chip taught me the basics, the ABCs of bartending. He taught me how to set up a bar, including the order in which to put the bottles in the well. The well refers to the area where bartenders keep the everyday "house" liquors they use in mixed drinks. The way a well is set up is standard; there is a specific order, so that if a bartender steps "into the well" (which is a bartender's term for "behind the bar") of any bar, he or she will be able to reach for a particular spirit and make a drink, no problem. Also key to setting up a bar: Chip taught me how to "flag" bottles, which refers to facing the spout in a particular direction so you can pick it up and pour without having to turn the bottle. And he taught me how to stock a bar: how much ice, how many of each glass, and how much of each liquor I should have on hand. Working alongside the veteran that Chip is gave me the stable foundation I needed to build my future as a barman.

My second "teacher," whom I worked with at the same bar, Les Deux Cafes, was Richard Bairos. Where Chip was the kind of micromanager who kept a close eye on me and let me help him do his work, Richard just threw me behind the bar and let me do his work while he stood smoking cigarettes and holding court with his customers. That was another kind of training altogether—like sink or swim—and equally valuable in a totally different way.

Les Deux Cafes was a real big spender kind of place. Guys would come in, put their black credit cards on the bar, and tell us to buy a drink on them for the entire room. Or they'd pull out a wad of hundred-dollar bills, slap one on the bar to pay for a ten-dollar cocktail, and tell us to keep the change.

Then there is Matt Duggan, whom I still work with, as he is the general manager at Lucques. Matt taught me two things, how to inspire people to rise above themselves and the business of a bar. The latter consisted of invaluable lessons about how a bar program works from a financial point of view. You can't just put a bunch of fancy liquors on a menu and hope to make a profit. You have to have a balance, various price points for different people, and a range of profit margins so that the good profits can make up for the not-so-good but very exciting and hard-to-find specialty liquors. Matt taught me how to take inventory and how to order booze. He also taught me about how to meet with sales reps and distillers who come in wanting me to buy their products: how to talk to them, listen to them, taste their liquors, and ultimately, how to make decisions about what I pass on and what I choose to buy.

One of the most precious things Matt did after I learned how to juggle and play with flavors. He gave me a classic cocktail book to remind me of the foundation and basics of pre-Prohibition beverages.

Last and most important, I learned how to invent and construct cocktails from Suzanne. Suzanne Goin is one of my two bosses; she is the chef of our restaurants and also the owner, along with her business partner, Caroline Styne, who runs the wine programs for all the restaurants. Suzanne has received countless accolades and awards, including Outstanding Chef, the highest honor awarded by the James Beard Foundation. Before opening her first restaurant, Lucques, Suzanne worked at some of the most acclaimed restaurants in the world, including Chez Panisse, Alice Waters's farm-to-table restaurant in Berkeley, California. Suzanne still cooks with that philosophy—using the best-quality ingredients she can find to create the best-tasting food she possibly can. Suzanne and Caroline have seven restaurants in Los Angeles. I run the bar program for everywhere they sell liquor: Lucques, A.O.C., Tavern, and their catering operations. For their other places, the four Larders and the Hollywood Bowl, I am the creative-with-beer-and-soju guy. Their clientele is a mix of young and old, movie stars and directors, up-and-coming creatives, entrepreneurs, and moguls from all over Los Angeles and beyond.

Although I am humbled next to the talent of Suzanne, I like to think that my cocktails mirror the philosophy, quality, and style of the food in the restaurants where they are served. Suzanne is known for her creativity; she has a way with pairing ingredients, adding one last component to a dish that might seem unexpected but that brings the whole thing together. But she never does something creative without having a reason. Her food is based on classics that she tweaks or dresses up in small but significant ways. For example, one of her most iconic dishes is her braised short ribs; by paying careful attention to every last detail and using the very best ingredients in making them, she produces the best damned short ribs you'll ever eat. I like to think that you could say the same for my all house-made Manhattan.

As a boy growing up in a small village outside Haarlem, in the Netherlands, running a huge bar program—or even a single bar—isn't what I thought I would do when I grew up. But looking back, it seems like it was destined. When I was a boy, on special occasions, my parents would take my brothers and me to the local tavern for dinner. I just loved the feeling of being there: the energy, the conversations going on around me, the warm feeling of sitting as long as we wanted, just talking and never having to leave. So one morning when I was fourteen, I walked to the tavern, knocked on the door (since they weren't open yet), and asked the owner for a job. I was a newspaper boy, but working in a tavern seemed like a real grown-up job, and working in a tavern is what I wanted to do. The tavern owner told me I was too young to work there and to come back when I was older. So a few months later, on my fifteenth birthday, I went back and told him I was older now. Could I have a job? I think he appreciated my passion and determination—he hired me as a dishwasher. I worked there for about a year, and I loved every minute of it.

At that time my parents had hopes for me to take over a psychiatric hospital that they owned, in Amsterdam. My father had taken the business over from his mother, who founded it in 1933. Her statue still overlooks the entrance, keeping a close eye on everyone passing by. (I was born two blocks away from the institution, in an old hospital that has since been turned into an addiction clinic, which is another story.) Growing up, I worked in just about every position in my dad's mental hospital except patient care. I cleaned floors, did administrative work, cooked, worked as a telephone operator, and visited with patients. I had been going there for years with my parents, but I remember very clearly the first day my dad dropped me off to work. The weight of the responsibility made it different. One of his employees showed me around and gave me a key that would give me total access to every department. Somehow I lost the key. I figured nobody noticed. After work my dad picked me up and said, "So, I heard you lost your key?" My dad was almighty.

As crazy as it might seem for a boy to be working in a mental hospital, I have to say: I liked it. What I liked most about it was the people. I had a natural connection with the patients. It didn't matter how ill they were; I enjoyed interacting with them. If I had to reintroduce myself every day, I gladly did. I enjoyed talking to them, and I liked the sense that maybe I was making their life better in some small way; I guess you could say that this is the same part of me that likes to work behind a bar. Even though I liked it, taking over my dad's hospital was not going to be my future. I had my own plans. I was going to move to America to become a movie star.

When I was twenty-four, after dropping out of college and doing a short stint as a "carnie" in a traveling carnival throughout the Netherlands, I moved to Los Angeles. I had a thousand dollars in my pocket. Never mind that I had been a kid with glasses the thickness of a Coke bottle and hair that looked like a haystack, I wanted to be the next James Dean. While waiting for my big break, I got a job working as a clown, standing on Melrose Avenue trying to get people to walk into a clothing store. My high point finally came in the form of being a double for Brad Pitt on the movie set of *Ocean's Eleven*. I thought it was the coolest thing. Let me tell you: while standing there, with the helmet and the uniform on and Steven Soderbergh behind the camera, I was like, *Look at me now!* I truly thought I had made it. I was totally naive.

Four years after moving to America, in June 2001, I married Daylani Santos. I was working nights as a club promoter. I was managing the guest list one night at the door when Daylani came in. I saw her, and I just thought she looked so beautiful. I got her number, we started dating, and a few years later we were married. Five months after that, in November of 2001, Daylani went to the doctor with a lump in her breast. When you're twenty-eight and you go to the doctor with a breast lump, the last thing on the doctor's mind is breast cancer. We went to four doctors, and nobody gave us a clear answer. Maybe you have fibroid cysts, some said. Others said it shouldn't be anything to worry about. Finally we went to a breast clinic in Torrance. They did an ultrasound. Normally after these tests, they would say something like "We'll send you results. Have a nice day." But after the ultrasound, the doctor walked into the examining room. I learned that that is never a good thing. She said, "I hope I'm wrong, but I'm pretty sure this is breast cancer." And it was.

From that point, we went through chemo-therapy, radiation, mastectomy, and more chemo. I sat with her to the end and watched as she struggled desperately and, four years after her diagnosis, on February 21, 2006, at the age of thirty-two, she took her last breath.

I was in total despair. I hated the world. When people found out my wife had died and they said, "I'm sorry," I responded by saying, "It's OK." But it really wasn't. We had our whole lives in front of us, and now she was dead. I was angry

at everything and everyone. Life had ended for me; there was no future. It would have been beyond impossible at that time for me to have seen that one day, ten years later, I would have the life I have now and I would be happy.

I met Melissa in 2008. She was managing a boutique in Scottsdale, Arizona. I was working as a wholesaler of designer women's shoes—one of the random jobs I had while bartending, going to school, and a bunch of other stuff. We saw each other for the first time at the New Mart building in downtown Los Angeles during a trade show. She had deep-black shiny hair and pale-blue eyes. It was one of those moments your stomach turns and you wonder what to do. Looking back I have to admit, I was a bit intimidated, she was a babe. I did make sure to hand her my business card before she left, but to be honest I thought that was it. To my surprise I received a text about two weeks later that said, "Your shoes are a bit expensive, but I would love to do business with you." The area code was unfamiliar. I remember thinking "Who is this? And where the hell is this area code?" A quick Internet search found her on Myspace. The girl with the pale-blue eyes. I didn't waste any time and replied, "I would like to do business with you as well." We could not stop talking, in the morning, in the afternoon, at night. I sent her little poems. We were lovebirds. She grabbed me by the hand, and pulled me out of the hole I was living in. She sent me to doctors to make sure I dealt with my past. She stood by me when I went to school and we only had bread and cheese in the fridge. When our first son, River, was born we didn't have money to do anything but take walks at night with our sleeping boy in his stroller. We wandered over Sunset or Hollywood Boulevard. Life was simple but busy. We were happy and in love and nothing else mattered.

When our second boy, Leaf, was born, life got even busier. The boys took over our household with school, swimming, baseball, karate, skate boarding, hockey—it's nonstop. When I come home at night, they are already asleep, and all that's left for me is a kiss and a whisper in their ears, "*Papa houdt van jou. Heel veel*," which means, "Papa loves you a lot" in Dutch. After this Melissa and I will sit down on our patio, looking out over Los Angeles. It is such an amazing feeling to finally get to a place in life where you feel you are where you were meant and want to be. Where you have nothing to strive for or prove, you can just be—enjoying that moment with your best friend and being thankful for it. That's how I feel about my wife, my boys, my job, my craft, and my life.

What does this have to do with a cocktail

book? you're thinking. First, it's *my* cocktail book, and if you're going to read it and use it, and enjoy the cocktails you make from it, I want you to know who I am. At the bar I spend a lot of time hearing about people's lives. It's one of the things I love most about being a bartender. There is a sense of intimacy, but there's also this way in which the relationship is fleeting. People come. They order a drink. We start to talk. They tell me about their day, their sorrows, and their hopes and dreams. I rarely talk about myself except when people hear my accent and want to know where I'm from. And I don't need to tell them about myself. I just need to make them happy with my cocktails. But since you are going to be reading about and making my cocktails, the intimacy is on a different level. I want you to know some things about me, and all of it together is the recipe that brought me to where I am now, to you, standing "behind the stick," as we bartenders say, shaking your drink.

When I started out at Lucques, I was just "making drinks." I was thirty-five years old, and making drinks was a side job and in fact one of *four* that I was working simultaneously. I still sold fancy women's shoes, I mixed drinks at Lucques, I was running a cancer foundation in Daylani's honor, and I was going to school to be a respiratory therapist. I had felt so helpless when Daylani was dying. I wanted to devote myself to trying to save others. I didn't care about making the best possible cocktails. But as I got more and more comfortable at Lucques, I started innovating cocktails whenever the inspiration came. I wasn't responsible for anything; there was no expectation. If I made a cocktail that Caroline and Suzanne liked and put on the menu, great. If not, that was fine too.

But gradually I became more interested in making cocktails. And then I became obsessed. I pushed myself to be more creative, to invent things, and as I did, I started to apply every-thing I was learning from Suzanne's cooking to my own work in making cocktails. Eventually Suzanne and Caroline wanted to turn their entire bar program over to me. I would be in charge of the menu, the ordering, training of the staff, and, ultimately, making sure the bar was profitable. I would be utilizing everything I had learned from my many teachers along the way, which would be great. But I had also just graduated from respiratory school. If I took the job, which would be very demanding time-wise, no doubt I would have to turn my back on what I'd worked so hard to achieve. Save lives? Or run a bar?

Saving lives sounded more noble, but run-ning a bar was, in a sense, my life calling. I had returned to the bar again and again throughout my life from the time I was a boy. And the truth is I just love bars. I love stepping behind a bar when the restaurant is closed and I am setting up. I love the odors of a bar: the mix of booze, beer, and the spilled juices from the night before. I love the feeling of setting up in the peaceful, not-yet-open bar, knowing that the quiet is fleet-ing and precious, the calm before the storm. I love the methodical nature of setting up the bar, the same way, every day. And of course I love the bar when it's running: the noise, the chaos, the rhythm, and most of all, my customers and my interactions with them. Maybe it has to do with the kind of people who like to sit on a bar stool, whether to drink a cocktail or to have dinner and wine, but the people across the bar from me night after night are, for the most part, polite, friendly, open. And being there, standing behind a bar talking with them, is among my favorite places to be. It feels like home.

I gave Caroline and Suzanne's proposal some thought. If I were to run the bar, I told them, I wanted to make everything from scratch, just like Suzanne did with her cooking. This meant I would make my own liqueurs, syrups, bitters, ver-mouth, and cocktail "mixers." And I wanted to juice all of my own fruits and vegetables in house. At the time we were buying fresh juices from a farmer. But by juicing everything ourselves, we would not only save money but also have a fresher product. Plus, there's something special about making things yourself, and it reflects the Lucques philosophy and Suzanne's approach to food and cooking. They loved my proposal. They made me a formal offer, and I took the job.

Today, Lucques is my home away from home. I love my bosses, my co-workers, my customers, my craft, and this profession that I chose—or that seems to have chosen me. I have loyal customers I look forward to seeing on a regular basis; when they drop in, it's like seeing an old friend. And I have the privilege of serving the endless stream of interesting and nice new customers that pass through my bar. Through my job I have also had many amazing experi-ences outside the bars, from developing cocktails for charity organizations to making cocktails for some of the most distinguished and famous people in the country. I've made cocktails for the weddings of Cameron Diaz, Drew Barrymore, and Reese Witherspoon. I've had Jeff Bezos, Conan O'Brien, Elon Musk, and famous chefs from around the world sit at my bars at Lucques, A.O.C., and Tavern. I even had the opportu-nity to meet and shake hands with President Obama. There was a line of people behind me, also waiting to shake his hand, so I had to move along. But I would have loved to be able to have told him, "Thank you. My life is the Ameri-can dream. I came with nothing, worked hard, and now I have everything I could have asked for—and more."

With this book I have one more amazing oppor-tunity: to share my recipes, my stories, and everything I have learned with you. People love cocktails and the ritual of having a drink at the end of the day or with a meal. But—and I hear this all the time from my customers—people believe there is some kind of mystery to mixing drinks. People who might not think twice about whipping up pesto from scratch are intimidated by the thought of a handmade margarita, so they end up buying margarita mix. I will show you that if you can squeeze limes, you're well on your way to a good margarita. And if you can boil water, you can make my sweet vermouth in minutes. Given a good recipe, you should be able to make a great cocktail, even if you have never made a cocktail at home before in your life.

But before we start mixing, on a more sober note, I want to say that, as cool as it is being a barman and making cocktails, there's also a dark side to it. People like to drink alcohol when they're happy, when they're celebrating, or relaxing, getting together with friends old and new. Cocktails often make an occasion festive and fun. But then there can come a point where it's *not* fun. Recently I refused to serve a guy because he came in at 11:30 a.m. and he was already falling off the barstool. That's not fun for me, and I doubt it was for him. I think we all owe it to ourselves and the people close to us to recognize that point when we get there. So drink responsibly. And don't drink and drive. Enough said.

Now, let's have some fun. Get inspired. Invite some friends over. And shake up a cocktail or two to start out the night.

As we say in Dutch, *Proost!* (Cheers!)

MIXING FROM THIS BOOK

RECIPES

There are a lot of cocktail books on the market, and when I decided to write mine, I had to think about what I wanted to do differently. The answer was clear to me; I wanted to write a *cookbook* for cocktails. Many cocktail books consist of a list of formulas: shake this spirit with that juice, pour it into this kind of glass, and garnish with the appropriate garnish. These handbook-type cocktail books are great if you are a professional bartender and someone orders a drink you're not familiar with. But for anyone at home wanting to make a cocktail, it is just not enough information. Not enough teaching.

By contrast, this is not a book of formulas, but of *recipes*, with all the details and explanation you need to take you from beginning to end of each one. It is full of teaching and information. In these recipes, I will tell you how to prep the ingredients, how to shake or stir the cocktail, how *long* to shake or stir, which strainer to use, what kind of ice is best, which glass is ideal, and how to put the garnish on the cocktail. And as in the best cookbooks, I will also tell you how and why I do what I do in the hope that, after making a few recipes, you will begin to understand the fundamentals and mix cocktails more freely on your own.

When making a drink, I start with a flavor I want to work with, whether it's a liquor, fruit, liqueur, or just something I am excited about. Let's say rum. First, I think about the rum. What kind of rum will I be using? Aged rum? Light rum? What kind of feeling do I get from it? Is it warming or refreshing? What is its flavor profile? Is it sweet? Grassy? Woody? From

there, I think about a second ingredient. This ingredient is important, because in essence there are two ingredients that carry every cocktail and the rest is all nuances, layers of flavor. So for that second ingredient, I look for something I think will go with the spirit I've chosen. Back to rum. Let's say I've chosen rhum agricole, which has a grassy, almost black-olive quality, very dominating. There's something summery feeling about rum—it feels like a beach vacation type of drink—and peaches feel the same. So for my cocktail I decide I want rum and peaches. These two flavors just make sense together to me. But now I just have a boozy peach-flavored concoction. Two flavors do not make a cocktail. I start thinking about what kind of acid would be best to cut the sweetness. For me, rum and lime is a classic combo. I try lime. But it's a little too harsh. I try lemon, and it's perfect. Now I need to add sweetness, so I think about the various syrups that I make. Would ginger go with these flavors? Maple? For me, maple and peach go together well. I make another cocktail with the addition of maple syrup. Now I have a really tasty drink. But I work in some of the finest restaurants in Los Angeles, and therefore I don't just want "really tasty." I want something that reaches the next level. I want one more layer of flavor, so I look at my tinctures. I have licorice, sarsaparilla, sassafras bark. I try all of them, making a different cocktail using each one. The cocktail with sarsaparilla tincture turned out to be the best. I've reached the perfect cocktail. Once I've finished a cocktail, I have a few people in the restaurant that I trust taste it; mostly because I am proud of it, not because I want to go back to the drawing board. Finally I give it to Suzanne and Caroline to taste. If they like it, it's on the menu that night.

With few exceptions, the recipes in this book are for one cocktail, because that is how drinks are made in a bar. When you shake or stir a cocktail, you can't do more than two at a time; there isn't room in the shaker or mixing glass. If you're mixing several of the same drink, you will prep enough ingredients for what you need and then mix (shake or stir) the cocktails one at a time. (There's no reason to rush things. The mixing is half the fun. The drinking is the other half.) Punch and blended drinks are the exceptions; the recipes for those make larger quantities because punch is generally served in larger quantities, and the ingredients lists are too long for one cocktail. Also, for some recipes, I give both the single-cocktail recipe and the formulas for making a large batch of the cocktail, which you can keep in the refrigerator to reach for when you want to mix yourself or your friends a quick drink without any fuss. Any of the batch cocktails are good choices for serving a crowd.

I tell you how long each of the components of a cocktail—juices, syrups, liqueurs, bitters, and tinctures—will last in the refrigerator. Sometimes things go bad; sometimes Father Time diminishes the flavor. But this way you can prepare the components in advance, so when you want to mix a particular drink, whether for yourself or for guests, you have everything you need at your fingertips, just like I do when I'm behind the bar. Note that in terms of longevity of ingredients, I erred on the safe side. The true way to know that a concoction has gone bad is that it begins to have a bubbly, champagnelike quality; that means it's fermented, and it's time to throw it out.

In many of the headnotes, I suggest when to make the cocktail—a cold evening by the fire, a hot summer day, a pool party, or a winter holiday party. Like foods, cocktails have a season, a time when they feel most appropriate to drink. Many of my cocktails are also made with ingredients that have fleeting seasons. Working with ingredients at the height of their season is something Suzanne insists on in her cooking, and I do the same with my cocktails. If a drink calls for muddled peaches, make that drink during peach season, when peaches are juicy, sweet, and have lots of peach flavor. If it's winter and juicy peaches are nowhere to be found because it's winter, choose a recipe that calls for apples or pumpkin or no fruit at all. Having said that, note that syrups and liqueurs can be a way to preserve the season. Take Strawberry Liqueur, for example. You'd want to make the liqueur during strawberry season, but since the liqueur lasts for a few months, you can use it to make strawberry-enhanced drinks long after strawberries have come and gone.

ICE

A lot of mixologists and bar books make a big deal out of ice, using several shapes of ice and specifying which shape to use for each drink. While I like the different shapes of ice, such as extra-large ice cubes and ice balls—no doubt they make for pretty cocktails—they are not vital to a great cocktail, and I don't want to intimidate you by asking you to seek out many different shapes and sizes of ice. The reason bartenders use different sizes and shapes of ice has to do with how quickly they melt, and therefore how much they will dilute your cocktail; ice also makes a difference in terms of how the cocktail will feel in your mouth (this is especially true of crushed ice) and, of course, what your cocktail will look like.

For the purpose of these recipes, you really need only two kinds of ice: ice cubes, which just about everyone has at home at all times, and crushed ice, which you have at home only if you have a "crushed ice" option on your freezer door ice dispenser. (I don't.) I describe the various kinds of ice that I use below. Although fancy ice is not practical for my bar program—large cubes require an overly expensive machine, and ice balls have to be made individually, which is unrealistic with the kind of volume I do—they're easy to make at home, using inexpensive silicone trays that you can find online and at bar and beverage supply stores. Have fun with them!

HOTEL ICE is the industry term for the small ice cubes, the ones you find in the buzzing hotel ice machines that stand in the hallways of every kind of hotel. We use a similar machine, and the same ice, at our restaurants. Hotel ice is also what you buy, bagged, at grocery and liquor stores. I use hotel ice for the majority of my cocktails, including my shake-and-dump drinks, shake-and-strain drinks, and stirred drinks. At home, standard ice cube trays make ice cubes that are slightly larger than hotel ice cubes, but they do the trick.

LARGE CUBES, also known as *kold draft*, often used in fancy cocktail bars, are about 1¼ inches square. Large cubes melt more slowly than smaller cubes, so the ice chills the spirits without diluting them, which is a quality appreciated by anyone who orders straight spirits. In a restaurant, large cubes are made using a very expensive machine. I don't have such a machine, so I don't use this ice. The home bartender, however, can make these cubes using silicone ice molds, which you can buy at beverage supply stores and online. I like Tovolo 1¼-inch cubes; use them in any cocktail served on the rocks.

ICE BALLS. I use ice balls on occasion for cocktails that are served on the rocks, especially those that contain only alcohol (and no fruit juices), such as a Negroni or an old fashioned. I make the balls using silicone ice molds, which are widely available.

CRUSHED ICE melts quickly, so I keep this in mind when designing a cocktail that I am going to serve with crushed ice. I love the slushy quality of crushed ice drinks and chew on the ice after it has absorbed all the flavors of the cocktail. For those of you who don't have crushed ice dispensers on your freezer door, rest assured: crushed ice is easy to make using what's called a Lewis Ice Bag, a bag made expressly for this purpose, which is sold along with a mallet for crushing (see Sources, page 277). You put the ice in the bag and then use a mallet or heavy skillet to smash the ice in the bag. If you don't have a Lewis bag, put ice cubes in a large plastic bag (such as a resealable freezer bag), wrap a kitchen towel around it, and beat it with a mallet. If you're making crushed ice for just one cocktail, put 2 cups of ice cubes in a shaker tin and crush the ice with a muddler until it's broken up into pebbles.

GARNISHES

When I started working at Lucques, I didn't garnish my cocktails. None of them. Suzanne wants every plate to look pretty, but she doesn't put things on the plate for decoration. Everything on a plate that she creates is there for a reason, because it adds something to the final taste and experience of the dish. When I started creating cocktails, I wanted to adopt the same principle: I didn't want decoration. So I skipped the garnish altogether. It took me a while to understand that there was a reason for the garnish on a cocktail.

When you are presented with a drink, first you look with your eyes. There has to be no doubt that what you see looks beautiful and appealing. Then you bring the glass to your nose and take a whiff: you may smell a mint garnish, or oil from an orange rind rubbed on the rim, or the smoky whisper of the mezcal in the drink. Assuming it looks and smells appealing, you then take the drink to your lips and take a sip. The garnish plays an important role in all three aspects of this experience: it affects the look, the scent, and the flavor of your drink. Which is why I now garnish my cocktails. But, as Suzanne taught me, every garnish I put on a cocktail has a reason to be there. Following is a list of the garnishes I use most and why.

TWIST (lemon, orange, lime, or grapefruit). A citrus twist is a sliver of citrus peel that you twist over a cocktail. I use a citrus twist when I want the aroma of citrus peel oil to be part of the experience of the drink. The oil is so pungent that it really brightens up the nose (or scent) of a cocktail, so when you bring the cocktail to your lips, you experience the scent of the citrus oil before taking your first sip of the beverage. To optimize the impact of the twist, I squeeze it over the cocktail so the oils release from the skin and drop into the glass, then I drop it, shiny side up, onto the cocktail. Sometimes I start by rubbing the outside of the rind, which contains the oil, on the inside of the rim of the glass; I do this when the cocktail does not reach the rim of the glass. I like to make big, healthy twists, as opposed to thin spiral twists that to me look like they came out of the 1980s. To make a twist, take a good vegetable peeler (preferably a U-shaped peeler), hold the fruit in one hand, and slowly slice the peel from the fruit, being careful not to cut yourself.

WHEEL (lemon, orange, or lime). A wheel is a very thin slice (about ⅛ inch thick) of lemon, orange,

or lime. I don't just stick the wheel on the edge of the glass. Using the citrus this way doesn't do anything for the cocktail except decorate it. (I'll leave that for the beach cocktails served at resort hotels.) To maximize the flavor and the visual appeal of citrus wheels, make a cut in the wheel from the edge, three-fourths of the way to the opposite side of the wheel. Pull both sides of the wheel, stretching the wheel into a spiral, and then drop the spiral onto the cocktail. It is really pretty and festive looking this way, plus you get the fresh scent of the citrus rind in the cocktail, which adds to the overall experience of drinking it.

FRESH HERB SPRIG (mint, basil, rosemary, sage). If you thought a fresh herb sprig was added to a cocktail just for looks, you're wrong. In fact, the fresh herb brings another dimension to your beverage through its scent. Generally speaking, I use herbs as a garnish when the same herb is used in the cocktail, but occasionally the herb garnish is the only way in which the herb is used in the drink. When adding fresh leafy herbs, such as mint, basil, or sage, look for young, small leaves on the top of the plant and pinch off a little sprig with two or three leaves attached. Stick the sprig into the cocktail so only the leaves are visible. For rosemary, use a ½- to 1-inch segment, and I look for the most tender sprigs.

FLOAT (bitters, wine, juice). To "float" something on a cocktail means to drizzle something, such as bitters, wine, or juice, very slowly on a cocktail after it is in the serving glass, so the liquid floats on top of the drink. I do this for two reasons. First, it looks really pretty. And second, adding a "float" means that the first sip of your cocktail will have the intense flavor of whatever is floated on top; after that first sip, the float will begin to seep down and integrate into the cocktail. So the cocktail changes during the process of drinking it, which is really cool. To float something on a

Garnishes I use: basil sprigs; citrus wedges, wheels, and twists; mint sprigs; chile de árbol slices; cucumber slices; star anise; rosemary; sage; minced jalapeño cocktail, drizzle the floater very slowly over the back of the spoon into the finished drink; a thin stream ensures that the liquid won't sink into the cocktail.

FOAM (egg white or beer). You'll notice that some of the drinks in this book are shaken with beer or egg white, both of which result in a cocktail with a layer of foam on top, which gives the cocktail a soft, creamy texture. Occasionally I let the foam be its own statement and don't include a garnish on foamed drinks. Other times, I will drizzle bitters on the foam or stick a fresh herb sprig into the foam. It's not really a double garnish, since the foam is part of the actual drink. To create foam on a cocktail, I go into detail in those recipes calling for beer or egg whites.

TECHNIQUE

SHAKING a cocktail with ice is the typical method you think of when you imagine a bartender making a drink. It's the one you see in the movies that makes a bartender look like a bartender. It's also the method most often used in these recipes and behind my bars. When you shake a cocktail, you don't just move it back and forth lackadaisically. You have to really get into it, which is why I write "shake *hard*" in my recipes. It's an intense, physical action, and you do it for a full seven seconds. Vigorously shaking a cocktail with ice breaks the ice into small shards; the purpose of this is two-fold: it chills the cocktail, and it also dilutes the cocktail. Shake hard, my friends. Shake hard!

SHAKE-AND-DUMP and SHAKE-AND-STRAIN. After shaking a cocktail with ice, you can do one of two things. You can dump it, ice and all, into a glass. Shake-and-dump is considered unrefined, because you're *dumping,* rather than *straining,* a cocktail into a glass. Plus the ice you shook the

cocktail with is also in your cocktail. Personally, I like the casual aspect of shake-and-dump. Plus, when I shake-and-dump, I feel like I am preserving all the flavors of the cocktail that I just carefully constructed, because every last drop that went into the shaker is now going into the glass. The alternative to shake-and-dump is shake-and-strain. To shake-and-strain, you use a Hawthorne strainer to strain the cocktail into a glass. The glass may be filled with fresh ice, or it may be an empty glass; the purpose of using fresh ice rather than the ice you shook with your cocktail is that the fresh ice will be whole, not broken, so it won't melt in the cocktail; it looks neater and keeps the drink colder for longer. Alternatively, the cocktail may be fine-strained over fresh ice or into a Glencairn glass to get a very clean look. Use your Hawthorne strainer as well as your fine strainer at the same time for this.

DRY SHAKING refers to shaking a drink without ice. Dry shaking is done when you don't want to chill your drink with ice at all or when you just want to mix your ingredients at room temperature. And you also dry-shake a cocktail as part of a three-step process used in cocktails that contain egg white or beer, which is done to create foam. First you shake the cocktail ingredients without ice (dry-shake) for seven seconds. Then you add ice and shake again for seven seconds. Next you strain the cocktail, discard the ice, and dry-shake it again, one last time, for seven seconds. The third shake (which is the second *dry* shake) really ensures a solid layer of foam on the drink.

STIRRING is the delicate alternative to shaking a cocktail. I stir a cocktail when I don't want any ice particles in the drink or if for whatever reason I want to treat a drink with a gentler hand. Also, where shaking dilutes a drink by almost 20 percent, stirring allows you to chill a drink without diluting it much. Conventional wisdom is that a drink should be stirred when there is no juice involved, just liquor, such as in a Negroni, Manhattan, or Martini (unless you're James Bond, who prefers his Martini shaken, not stirred) because for these drinks, you want as little dilution as possible so you can taste the pure flavor of the liquor.

SWIZZLING refers to the method by which you insert a swizzle stick (or a long spoon) into a cocktail glass and roll the stick (or the handle of the spoon) between your palms. I swizzle drinks made with crushed ice, where the cocktail tends to stay on the bottom of the glass. Swizzling causes the cocktail to move up the glass through the ice so that the ice and cocktail are evenly distributed.

MUDDLING refers to using a muddler to mash ingredients to a slurry. I muddle limes, cucumbers, herbs—such as mint and basil—and soft fruit—such as peaches. Muddling herbs with ice is frowned upon by many bartenders because they believe it turns the herbs bitter. If this is true, I don't notice it. The amount of sugar that you add to cocktails (via syrups) counters any potential bitterness, and the true essence of the herbs that I get from muddling is worth the trade-off.

LAYERING a cocktail refers to the method of cocktail making where you just pour the cocktail ingredients into the glass, with or without ice, that it will be served in—no stirring, shaking, muddling, or swizzling involved. Layering makes for a pretty drink because you can see the various ingredients in different-colored layers from the side of the glass. It's an especially fun technique when you're dealing with various bold colors, which will stand out on their own in different layers but will turn into a dull brown color when mixed together. That said, after a few minutes or a quick stir, the layers of a layered drink will become integrated, but at least you got that nice first impression.

KITCHEN TOOLS FOR THE HOME BAR

Before you start mixing drinks, you prep your ingredients—and for this, you need some very basic kitchen tools and equipment. There's nothing on this list that isn't part of an average-stocked kitchen. I have listed them in order of importance so you can prioritize on your next trip to the cooking supply store.

ELECTRIC JUICER. A countertop juicer makes easy work of juicing cucumbers, jalapeño peppers, watermelon, pineapple, pomegranate, and other fruits and vegetables that you'll come across in these recipes. If you don't already have a juicer and you are buying one just to make cocktails, at home I use the Jack LaLanne juicer, which is small, inexpensive, and totally does the job.

CITRUS JUICER. Handheld "elbow"-style lemon and lime juicers are such handy tools, and they're really inexpensive. They allow you to squeeze every drop of juice from a lemon or lime without making a mess in the kitchen or getting seeds in your drink. I recommend you make the investment in one of each. That said, if you don't have an elbow juicer, cut the citrus in half and extract the juice by squeezing or by sticking a fork into the fruit and twisting it.

VITAMIX OR ANOTHER GOOD BLENDER. A high-powered blender is such a joy to work with, and for me there is nothing better than a Vitamix. It's one of those fancy machines that can make soup out of potatoes. My first Vitamix was a gift from the company, who gave it to me in exchange for a recipe and some promotion. When I took it home after the event, I felt like such a badass. It was the most exciting kitchen appliance I've ever brought

into my home kitchen. At work I use my Vita-mix daily for making syrups and other cocktail premixes. But you don't have to spend $500 to make a syrup; any blender with a power button will work.

CHINOIS. I call for a chinois, which is a cone-shaped fine strainer, to make the syrups, tinctures, and liqueurs in the book. No worries: it sounds fancier than it is. You can pick one up for under $20 at most restaurant supply stores or cookware stores. If you don't have a chinois, use a fine-mesh strainer or cheesecloth instead to strain out any large bits.

CHINA CAP. I use a China cap, which is a strainer with holes that are slightly larger than the ones in a chinois or fine strainer, when I want to strain out fewer ingredients; this means more small bits make it through, which makes for a more flavorful and thicker end product. I also use a China cap to strain juice. You can find them at kitchen supply stores and online, or use a coarse-mesh strainer instead.

VEGETABLE PEELER. No need to spend your dollars here. The cheap-looking plastic ones that you can buy at the grocery store are awesome. The U-shaped peelers are the best. This is what the guys at our restaurants use. At the bar I use these peelers for peeling citrus zest and ginger, called for in many of my recipes.

Tools I use:
(1) fine strainers, (2) stirring spoon, (3) swizzle stick, (4) elbow juicer, (5) julep strainer, (6) Hawthorn strainer, (7) mixing glass, (8) muddler, (9) Boston shaker, (10) U-shaped vegetable peeler, (11) cocktail tweezers

CHEF'S KNIFE. A lot of food prep is involved in making craft cocktails, so a good, sharp chef's knife is as important to me as it is to the chefs that work around me. Cocktail ingredients and garnishes need to be treated with respect. Having a good, sharp knife allows me to cut the fruits and vegetables that I need for making juices and muddled fruits and to create clean, beautifully cut garnishes. After buying a good knife, keep it sharp by taking it to a knife sharpener or learning to sharpen it yourself.

CUTTING BOARD. At the restaurant, we work exclusively on plastic cutting boards. A wooden cutting board looks sexy, but it is absorbent and not very sanitary, especially when you're in a professional kitchen, where people are cutting all kinds of things—tomatoes, garlic, onions—on the same cutting board. Sometimes bar guys will come to an event and they'll have a cutting board that's six inches wide. I'm like: "Dude, you can't do anything with that." I like a serious cutting board and a serious knife.

BOTTLES are obviously an important piece of "equipment" on a bar. There are so many cool bottles; makers of spirits really get into using different types of glass and different shapes to differentiate their products. If you find one you like, take the label off; sterilize the bottle and lid by washing them in a dishwasher and then plunging them in boiling water and save them to use to store drinks made in batch quantities or to bottle Sweet Vermouth, Dry Vermouth, bitters, Aperitivo, or any of the other delicious concoctions in these pages.

JARS, such as used jam jars and mustard jars, as well as small mason jars, provide a convenient way to store syrups in the fridge. Plus, recycling is a good thing; it's a shame to think that all those pretty, perfectly good jars are used only once.

BAR TOOLS

I don't believe in using fancy bar tools. It doesn't make any difference to the drink. Save the money and buy great booze instead. If you want to spend your money on both, be my guest. But make the bar tools the second most important thing, after the cocktail *ingredients*.

JIGGER. A jigger in bar language refers to a tool used to measure and ensure the correct pour. Most jiggers are hourglass shaped. They have two sides, one that measures a smaller pour (½ or 1 ounce) and another that measures a larger pour (1½ to 2½ ounces). My favorite is a bell jigger. It's a little more expensive than a standard hourglass jigger, but it has lines inside that give you every measure you'll need behind the bar, so if you have this type of jigger, it's the only jigger you'll need.

COBBLER SHAKER. This is a three-part set that consists of a tall shaker, a hatlike lid, and a strainer. It is the type of shaker you'd be most likely to find at a grocery store or cooking supply store or that you'd get as a wedding present or Secret Santa gift. The one convenience of this type of shaker is that you don't need to use a strainer with it, because of the built-in strainer. I do not find this type of shaker very user friendly. After you shake your drink and the shaker is cold, the shaker becomes difficult to open. It is a pain in the ass to open in fact. If this is the only shaker you have, use it, but if you're buying a shaker, skip this and buy a Boston shaker with weighted shaker tins (see below).

BOSTON SHAKER. Your basic shaker, this is a two-part set that consists of a tall shaker and a short shaker or pint glass. The pint glass bottom you mostly see in dive bars. You can buy this shaker at many cooking supply and bar supply sources.

The shaker used by professional bartenders is the one with two weighted metal shakers, one large (28-ounce) and one small (18-ounce). I use this type of shaker exclusively. When shaking cocktails using the Boston shaker, you pour the cocktail into the short side, fill it up with ice to the rim, cover it with the large tin, then flip both so the small tin is on top before you start shaking. The reason being that if, in the process of shaking, the tins come apart, and the large tin is on the bottom, the cocktail will fly all over you and (in my case) the back bar. If the small tin is on the bottom, the cocktail will fly all over your customer. It's a mess either way, but I would rather clean up my back bar than my customers. If you have a Boston shaker, I suggest you use it for all the cocktail recipes in this book; it's especially helpful for recipes where beer or egg whites cocktails are shaken vigorously to create a thick layer of foam.

MIXING GLASS. Used to stir drinks with ice as a means of chilling the drink. A lot of fancy mixing glasses are available, including some with cute measuring lines on the outside and others made of cut crystal. I love the Japanese mixing glasses; they look great, but the downside is they break easily, which is less of an issue at home than in a restaurant, where things can tend to get tossed around. In a bind I use a plain and simple heavy-duty 16-ounce pint glass (aka a beer glass).

HAWTHORNE STRAINER. The iconic bar strainer should be part of everybody's bar kit; it is a flat disk with a coiled spring attached to the underside. It's designed so you can hold the strainer over the top of the shaker to strain a cocktail using only one hand. A Hawthorne strainer is used when you want to strain out ice or other large ingredients, such as fruit. You'll use it a lot in these recipes.

JULEP STRAINER. Traditionally used to strain the ice when making a mint julep, some say to keep the mint from going into your teeth, others say into your beard. I use this strainer any time I am straining from a mixing glass, but you can use a Hawthorne strainer instead. It is not essential to your bar. However, it does look pretty, and when you use it you'll really look like you know what you are doing.

FINE STRAINER. Used when you want to strain out small impurities, such as pulp from fruit, ice particles, or egg whites. It is sometimes used in conjunction with a Hawthorne strainer; the Hawthorne catches the ice while the fine strainer catches the smaller bits. This is called *fine straining*.

STIRRING SPOON. A thin, slender spoon with a long threaded shaft that can be rotated between the fingers. It is used for stirring all kinds of cocktails with ice, most famously Martinis and Manhattans. It is designed so that it can reach the bottom of a tall glass, shaker, or jug. When in a bind I will use it instead of a swizzle stick (see below). When I make a Manhattan at home, I am often too lazy to get out my bar kit, so I have been known to stir my cocktails with chopsticks, a bread knife, or the handle of a fork. I also use my bar spoon as a measuring tool in some of these recipes, where one spoonful is equivalent to 1 teaspoon.

SWIZZLE STICK. Originally swizzle sticks were used to stir up rum swizzles, a rum-based fruity cocktail from Bermuda, and were made from branches of a plant from that island. Later the sticks were made of glass and used to stir some of the bubbles out of champagne for those who claimed the bubbles caused indigestion. I use them to swizzle cocktails made with crushed ice, which helps disperse the beverage throughout the glass. I have a hand-carved swizzle stick that is also a conversation piece. Customers always ask me if I made it myself. (The answer is "No.") A swizzle stick is not essential, as you can use a bar spoon in its place.

MUDDLER. To muddle drinks, you need a muddler, which is a heavy pestlelike tool. Muddlers come in both wood and heavy plastic. I prefer wood because it is more organic, but at the restaurant I use a big black plastic muddler because wood is not permitted by the health department. You can muddle drinks in a shaker, a heavy-duty glass, or directly in the glass you're serving it in; just be careful not to break the glass.

GLASSES

I don't believe that making a good cocktail requires you to serve it in a specific glass. With wine, yes, I understand that if you drink a beautiful burgundy in a special glass, it affects the flavor and the nose and the overall experience of the wine. The same goes for beer. But with a cocktail, whether you pour a Tom Collins into a Tom Collins glass or coupe glass or wineglass, it will taste the same. (At home, my wife and I drink cocktails from short, stemless Spanish wineglasses.) Which isn't to say that the choice of which glass to use is arbitrary. In these recipes, I do specify which glass to use for each cocktail. These recommendations reflect the glasses that I use at the restaurant and that, given the choice, I prefer for each cocktail. If you have the glass called for in a cocktail recipe that you are making, use it. If not, pour the drink into whatever glass you have and love it. Following is a list of the glasses I use most often at my bars and why.

DOUBLE OLD FASHIONED. The glass I use the most behind the bar, besides wineglasses and water glasses, is a double old fashioned. A heavy-bottomed, wide-mouthed glass, it is perfect for rocks drinks; I also sometimes choose this glass to serve drinks that are poured over crushed ice.

TOM COLLINS. A Tom Collins glass, named after the classic cocktail, is the second most common cocktail glass that I use and, with its tall, slim profile, the one I think is the prettiest. It's the typical glass to use for classic refreshing, icy drinks, like a rum and Coke or vodka tonic, and, of course, a Tom Collins. When you're in Europe and you order a spirit and soda pop, it comes with just a little spirit in the bottom of a Tom Collins glass, a couple of ice cubes in the bottom (we are not big on ice Europe) and the soda in a bottle on the side. I love that presentation. A Tom Collins glass looks really pretty when you make a layered drink, meaning its ingredients are poured in layers, directly into the glass in which it will be served.

COUPE. The story behind the coupe glass, a shallow, bowl-shaped stemmed glass, also known as a Marie Antoinette, is that it was named after the shape of Marie Antoinette's breasts. Technically speaking, it's a champagne glass. I use it for champagne as well as for straight-up cocktails, instead of a Martini glass. Cocktails don't spill as easily from a coupe glass as they do from a Martini glass, so it's easier for servers to carry and also for customers to sip out of; when you bring it to your mouth, you don't slosh half of your drink on the table or on yourself. And frankly, I just find a coupe glass to be prettier and more elegant than a Martini glass.

MARTINI. Also called a *cocktail glass*, a Martini glass is a shallow cone-shaped stemmed glass. It is the classic glass for many up cocktails (cocktails without ice), including the cosmopolitan, gimlet, and, of course, the Martini. It has a totally eighties look that I don't love, which is why I serve these and other cocktails that might go in a Martini glass in a coupe glass instead. At Lucques, however, I have a special stash of six Martini glasses for customers who insist on having their Martini in a Martini glass. Use whichever you have or want to use.

SINGLE OLD FASHIONED. A standard on any bar, a single old fashioned glass is a short heavy-bottomed glass with a narrower mouth than a double old fashioned. Despite the name of the glass, I don't use this for old fashioned drinks. I like the larger-capacity double old fashioned for those. I use a single old fashioned glass when serving a single spirit, such as scotch, tequila, gin, or whiskey, on the rocks. I drop two ice cubes into the glass and pour 2-ounces of spirit on top.

GLENCAIRN GLASS. Also called a *scotch glass*, a Glencairn is a pretty tulip-shaped footed glass. It was developed in 2001 and designed to reflect the glasses used as whiskey "nosing copitas" around Scotland. It's meant as a scotch, or whisky (the way it's spelled in Scotland), glass, but I use it whenever I am serving a spirit neat, meaning without ice. Its tapered shape makes it great for "nosing," or smelling a spirit. Do you *need* this glass on your bar? No. You can always use a single old fashioned glass to serve spirits neat. But it's so elegant. Why not?

PILSNER GLASS. Just like wine, beer has a variety of glass styles depending on the beer you are drinking. Wheat beer glass, steins, boots, the generic pint glass. But for cocktails I love the tall, wide-on-the-top, narrow-on-the-bottom Pilsner glass. You can pick it up at your local middle-of-the-road liquor or bar store. The reason I like it for cocktails (even though I drink beer from the bottle) is that it's so narrow on the bottom you can see the different layers you make in a cocktail.

JULEP CUP. Like the name, yes, it is used for serving the famous mint julep: muddled mint with sugar, water, and bourbon. But the tapered silver cup is so pretty, it's a shame to let it collect dust while it desperately waits for that one customer who wants a julep. It's just great for crushed-ice drinks in general, the downside being its size. It doesn't hold a lot of liquid.

IRISH COFFEE GLASS. Of course there are as many different styles of these glasses as there are people claiming to have invented the drink that goes in it. However, we are just using it for a visual, to put pretty drinks and sours in. We don't use the mug-type ones; we use the same ones as Buena Vista Coffee up in San Francisco, the house of Irish coffee.

It's June 2006, and I am traveling through Europe, spending some time here, some time there: Rome, Crans-Montana (a municipality in Switzerland), Hamburg, and visiting my parents in Heemstede, the Dutch village where they live, the village I grew up in. It's a lazy-daisy afternoon. I'm putting away a few Heinekens, reading some emails, and deleting junk mail when I come across an email from a buddy from Los Angeles, Stephen Heath, who tells me he is performing with his two-man band at a bar in Paris.

He tells me to come, and this sounds like a great plan. I mean: Why the hell not? I jump on the bullet train, get drunk on overpriced beer, sleep for a couple of hours, and get sniffed by the drug dogs of the *gendarmerie.* Finally, I arrive at the Gare du Nord, the train station and entrance to the sexiest city in the world: Paris.

Before I left Amsterdam, a friend of my parents pulled me aside. He said, "Christiaan, I collect CDs from the Buddha Bar in Paris." (Yes, the Buddha Bar has, or had anyway, its own collection of CDs. Of course this was before Napster, iTunes, and Spotify changed the world when it came to music.) "I have numbers one, two, four, and five," the friend said. "But I am trying to get my hands on number three. Here is twenty euro for the CD and another twenty so you can buy yourself a drink."

After I enter Paris, my first stop is the Buddha Bar. The first guy I see when I enter is a skinny French dude behind the coat check counter. He is selling memorabilia, including CDs. I ask him for number three. All gone. Oh,

well. I go to get my drink. As I walk inside, I see the beautiful room, decadent, with balconies and tables around the floor, and in the center an enormous Buddha statue. It is full of hipsters and artists hanging out, talking, everything in French. In my imagination they are discussing the great literary works of this world, but in truth they are probably like kids in any bar in any city: trying to get laid. I walk up to the bar, I've got my twenty-euro bill in my hand. "Excusez-moi, excusez-moi, avez-vous de Ketel One?" I speak enough French to get a drink or, rather, to ask him if he has Ketel One.

"Oui."

Yes. He has Ketel One. But he doesn't assume I want to order it. He moves on. Does he think I just want to know if he has it? He doesn't understand I want to order a drink? That's about the extent of my French, but then I remember my mom while on vacation in a French village sending me to the bakery with ten francs to pick up French bread when I was a kid. I totally remember how to say, "Can I have . . . , please." I flash my twenty-euro bill again, which gets the attention of the too-cool barman, and I tell him "Un Ketel One, s'il vous plaît." The guy looks at me, doesn't say a word, and pours a small shot of vodka, neat. "C'est vingt euro," he says. Twenty euro. That comes out to thirty dollars for a vodka neat, and a small one at that. A slurry of vocabulary goes through my head because as a student of the world, at least I know how to curse fluently. But I am not saying any of them because this family friend has bought me the shot. I hand him the bill.

I leave and met my friend who plays rock and roll that night in a hipster club where the drinks are flowing and affordable. And I travel on.

Vodka was the beginning of my cocktail-drinking life, and it's kind of a "gateway" spirit for many. By nature vodka has no distinctive character, aroma, taste, or color, and yet it is the most popular spirit in the world. The majority of vodka is produced in Russia, but both the Russians and the Polish claim to be its inventors; the claim is so intensely fought that the show *Vice* did a documentary called "The Vodka Wars." Russian vodka was originally made from potatoes and later from grains including rye, wheat, and corn. Large manufacturers still make the majority of vodka from those ingredients. But technically speaking, vodka can be made from any sugar-rich plant, and many artisanal vodka producers are making vodka by distilling pears, grapes, strawberries, beets, molasses, soybeans, and rice. These aren't flavored vodka—all vodka is filtered through charcoal to give it the neutral flavor and aroma it's known for—but subtle nuances from these other flavors do come through.

Vodka didn't get popular in the United States until the 1950s, when it kicked gin to the wayside as America's liquor of choice. Today more vodka is sold in the United States than all the other spirits—gin, rum, whiskey, brandy, and tequila—combined. In the vodka belt, which includes Russia, Belarus, Poland, Ukraine, Lithuania, Latvia, Estonia, Sweden, Norway, Finland, and Iceland, vodka is traditionally consumed "neat," often chilled. Here in the United States, vodka is the base for many popular cocktails, including the cosmopolitan, white Russian, Harvey Wallbanger, bloody Mary, Long Island iced tea, sex on the beach, caipiroska, greyhound, screwdriver, Cape Cod, sea breeze, vodka Martini, and Moscow mule.

As popular as vodka is with consumers, vodka is frowned upon in the craft cocktail community for the same reason it's favored by consumers: its lack of flavor. A barman's goal when creating cocktails is to pack as much flavor into a glass as possible, to get as much and as many different, distinct layers of flavor as we can within the four ounces of total liquid that we have to work with. Since vodka has almost no flavor or aroma, by adding it to a drink you are not adding a flavor, as you would if you were pouring, say, whiskey or tequila. You're adding something that has no flavor—like water. So all you are doing is watering down the flavors.

A lot of mixologists might like to eliminate vodka from their repertoire altogether, except for the very important fact that vodka is the engine, the money maker behind the bar. Vodka is inexpensive, and I sell a lot of it. Fifty percent of the drinks I sell are vodka based. It's my bread and butter—and my bacon too. It seems just about everyone (besides mixologists) likes vodka drinks. Professionals, lawyers, agents, investors, and bankers who drink during work lunches often order vodka drinks. "Secret" drinkers drop a ten-dollar bill on the bar on their way to the restroom, request it neat, and drink it in one gulp on the way back to their table. Unseasoned drinkers mix it with fruit juice and sweet syrups. I have such a high profit margin, and sell so much vodka, that it allows me to have slimmer profit margins with the other spirits, which, generally speaking, are more expensive. Special mezcals? Rare whiskeys? Obscure rhum agricoles? I can afford to use them all because vodka is inexpensive, and I sell it all day long. So as far as I'm concerned, vodka is my friend.

In creating my vodka cocktails, I did what I'd do for any friend: I accepted it for what it is. I *embraced* vodka's neutral flavor and, to prevent it from diluting my cocktails, I infused it with other flavors. This way, when I add vodka to the drink, I am simultaneously adding whatever flavors I infused it with: green tea in the case of the green goddess, orange rind for the Country Club and Californication, and Buddha's hand, an Asian citrus, to make the Three Two Three. And those cocktails that do call for straight-up vodka, like the A.O.C. Bloody, I load with layers of intense flavors, so the drink *welcomes* the dilution from the vodka.

In the end, as I did in Paris all those years ago, I think people order vodka drinks because it's what they know. There are many people who don't know anything about cocktails, but they know what a cosmopolitan is, and so they order it—they saw the ladies on *Sex and the City* drinking cosmos—so that's what they order. A lot of customers order a Cape Cod or a sea breeze because they don't want to take the risk of ordering something they don't know and may not like. For me, it's really fun to take the wheel and steer these customers in a slightly different direction. If they order a cosmo or a sea breeze, I have some idea what they like: they like vodka, and they like a cocktail mixed with fruit juice. Very often I tell them, "Let me make this other vodka cocktail for you. If you don't like it, I'll drink it." Of course I wouldn't drink it because I'm working, but I've also never had to fulfill my promise because the customer has always been pleased with the cocktail I made. I find that, in general, people are happy to try something new, as long as it tastes good.

STOCKING YOUR BAR

Following are the vodkas I like, some for infusing and some for cocktails. I also use vodka as a neutral vehicle when making liqueurs including Strawberry Liqueur (page 251), Aperitivo (page 256), and Compound Gin (page 254). As you mix from this book, vodka will be an integral part of your home bar.

KETEL ONE (40% abv), a grain vodka, is my go-to vodka and the one we keep next to the well at the restaurants. I started drinking Ketel One on the rocks when I was a young man traveling around Europe by train. Back then I liked it because it had a mild flavor and was easy to drink. Today, for the bar, I like Ketel One because it manages to straddle both sides of the spectrum—everyone knows it to be a quality vodka, but it still manages to seem unpretentious. And it's totally accessible: you can be in a dive bar in the jungle or some tiny town off a dirt road, and if you look behind the bar, chances are you'll see a bottle of Ketel One. It was widely considered by bartenders to be the number-one vodka, until Tito's came along and gave it a run for its money. Ketel One is the perfect vodka to keep on your bar at home for mixing cocktails and making Martinis.

TITO'S (40% abv) is a corn-based vodka from Austin, Texas, made by a process wherein it is distilled six times; distilling purifies the liquor, so this is a very clean, pure product. If I were to go to a liquor store with the idea of purchasing one vodka, for serving neat, for mixing into cocktails, or for infusing or making liqueurs, this would be it. Besides being a fine-tasting, quality vodka,

the folks at Tito's are really expert at marketing; the two big selling points for Tito's are that it is made in small batches, which is an idea my customers embrace, and it is gluten-free (although some gluten experts claim that there is no trace of gluten left after distilling grains, which would make this fact irrelevant). In recent years, Tito's has replaced Ketel One as my number-one-selling vodka, and my top-selling liquor of any kind. When it first came out, I even used it as my well vodka. But what happened with Tito's, as happens with a lot of liquor brands, is that as it became more popular, the price went up, and it was no longer affordable for the well.

MONOPOLOWA (40% abv). I occasionally get requests for cocktails made with gluten-free vodka. I used to try explaining to customers that once a grain is distilled, it no longer contains gluten, but they didn't seem convinced by me. So now I don't try to convince them. I just steer them toward a potato vodka. Monopolowa is a good, inexpensive (and, yes, gluten-free!) potato vodka from Poland. I use it for mixing cocktails and Martinis, but I don't recommend it for making infused vodka or any of the liqueurs and syrups in these recipes. The potato imparts flavor to the vodka, and when the vodka is being used as a base for other flavors, I prefer something more neutral.

LOFT & BEAR (40% abv). I rotate between our various restaurant bars, but every Monday I work behind the bar at A.O.C. It's my inventory day, my ordering day, my cleaning day, and my tasting day. It's also the day that liquor reps and distillers often drop in. So one such day I was working behind the bar, and this guy came in for lunch. He had a little handlebar mustache, so I assumed he had one of two jobs: either he was a barber, or he was a bartender. It turned out he was a liquor representative, and he was there to try to sell me on a locally made vodka, Loft & Bear. This is pretty unusual in Los Angeles. First, we're a big sprawling city with expensive real estate—not prime distillery country. And also, California is not a make-your-own-booze-friendly state. Hell, because of certain local laws, we were not even allowed to *infuse* vodka until about five years ago. But here he was, telling me his story. I liked the story, and I *really* liked the vodka. So I took some on to see if it would sell. And it did. Our customers are interested in anything locally or artisanally made. If I told them it was from Texas or the Netherlands or Poland, even with the fancy bottle, I wouldn't get much interest. But tell them it's from DTLA (downtown LA) and the maker just dropped it off today, and at least they are willing to try it. It's made from winter wheat, same as Grey Goose, and distilled four times, resulting in a clean, pure product. Local vodkas are being made in New York, Florida, Portland, and I'm sure other places around the country. Search the Internet or ask at your local liquor store for one made where you are. The way I look at it, if someone goes to all the effort to make a local product, the least we can do is give it a try. Use this or other locally made vodka to make Martinis or mixed cocktails.

CHOPIN (40% abv) is a Polish potato vodka that is distilled four times; it's the most popular potato vodka on the market, a market that has grown significantly in recent years as gluten-free has become a popular buzzword for consumers. The glass bottle has a frosted, "frozen" kind of look; it feels heavy in the hand and has a round picture of its namesake, the composer and pianist Frédéric Chopin, on the bottle. It has a fancy feel, and indeed it is also on the pricier side. It has a very clean, velvety potato taste and nose, so for a vodka purist this is a great choice, and it's also perfect for anyone who wants a vodka with the mildest flavor possible. It's great for making a vodka Martini.

BLACK COW (40% abv). This dairy-based vodka is the softest, smoothest vodka I have tasted in a long time. It's not widely available in stores, but you can find it easily on the Internet, and it's worth the effort. The vodka is made from whey, a by-product of cheese making. The folks that make Black Cow found a yeast that allowed them to ferment the lactose sugar in the whey, which is then distilled, turning it into a high-proof spirit. And as if that's not cool enough, they cut the spirit with water that is filtered out of the milk. The taste of the vodka is as special as the process by which it's made.

GREEN GODDESS

green tea vodka and cucumber with arugula, jalapeño, and absinthe

The Green Goddess is the cocktail version of the green juices that Angelenos are obsessed with, and it took Los Angeles by storm. It originated as a nonalcoholic green drink that I created for a celebrity fundraiser, but it became so popular with our catering clients that when we opened A.O.C. Suzanne and Caroline asked me to put it on the cocktail list. "Just add some vodka to it," they said. But you cannot just add vodka to a nonalcoholic cocktail and expect it to taste the same; vodka is virtually flavorless, so adding it dilutes the flavor profile of your drink by half. To counter this, I knew I had to infuse the vodka. I got the idea to infuse it with green tea, which turned out to be delicious. I also coat the inside of the glass with absinthe to give the cocktail another layer of flavor. We serve a nonalcoholic version, too, and we call it a Mock Goddess. To make a mock goddess, eliminate the vodka and absinthe from this recipe and replace it with chilled green tea.

Makes 1 cocktail

GLASS

Tom Collins

PREP

1 Persian cucumber

1 jalapeño, seeds removed

COCKTAIL

2 ounces Green Tea Vodka (page 50)

1 ounce fresh lemon juice (about 1 lemon)

¾ ounce Arugula Simple Syrup (page 50)

½ ounce fresh cucumber juice

1 drop jalapeño juice, plus more to taste

GARNISH

Absinthe rinse

3 thin cucumber slices

A fresh mint sprig

To prep the cocktail, thinly slice half of the cucumber and set aside for garnish. Cut the remaining cucumber into chunks that will fit in your juicer. Pass the chopped cucumber through the juicer and set the cucumber juice aside. No need to clean the juicer. Pass the jalapeño through the juicer and put that aside. You will have enough of each juice to make 4 cocktails.

Combine the cocktail ingredients in a shaker. Fill the shaker with ice cubes, cover, and shake hard for 7 seconds. Pour 1 bar spoon of absinthe into a Tom Collins glass and swish it around to coat the inside of the glass. (This is called "rinsing.") Discard the extra absinthe; fill it up with fresh ice. Use a Hawthorne strainer to strain the cocktail into the glass. Add more jalapeño juice to taste. To garnish, skewer the cucumbers on a bamboo pick and lay it on top of the drink or lay the cucumber slices on top of the drink. Stick the mint sprig into the cocktail, leaving only the leaves visible.

(CONTINUED)

Green Tea Vodka

I use a Chinese green tea called Dragonwell to make this, but any loose-leaf green tea will work.

Makes about 12 ounces (1½ cups)

½ teaspoon loose-leaf green tea leaves
12 ounces grain vodka

Put the tea and vodka in a blender and puree. Pass the vodka through a chinois or fine-mesh strainer and discard the contents of the strainer. Transfer the vodka to a labeled bottle or jar; it will keep, refrigerated, for up to 3 months.

Arugula Simple Syrup

This is simple syrup—sugar and water—but with fresh arugula blended in, which adds a grassy, peppery flavor to the Green Goddess. It lasts for a week in the refrigerator, but after that it loses its bright flavor and color.

Makes about 8 ounces (1 cup)

1 cup plus 2 tablespoons sugar
¾ cup water
1 cup loosely packed arugula

Combine the sugar and water in a small saucepan. Heat over medium-high heat, stirring occasionally, until the sugar dissolves, about 2 minutes. Reduce the heat to medium-low and simmer for about 15 minutes, stirring occasionally, until the liquid is slightly syrupy. Turn off the heat and set aside to cool to room temperature. Combine the syrup and arugula in a blender and blend until the arugula is broken down to tiny flecks. Strain the syrup through a chinois or cheesecloth and discard the solids. Pour the syrup into a labeled bottle or jar and close. The syrup will keep, refrigerated, for up to 1 week.

TAVERN COLLINS

orange-infused vodka and raspberry with lemon and fennel

I designed this drink for Tavern, where I like to stick close to the classics and give them just enough of a twist to make them feel fresh and modern. Where a Tom Collins consists of gin, lemon juice, sugar, and carbonated water, this cocktail starts with orange-infused vodka and includes hints of raspberry and fennel.

Makes 1 cocktail

GLASS
Tom Collins

COCKTAIL
2 ounces Orange-Infused Vodka (page 54)
1 ounce fresh lemon juice (about 1 lemon)
¾ ounce Raspberry Fennel Syrup (recipe follows)
1½ ounces soda water

GARNISH
A fresh mint sprig

Combine the vodka, lemon juice, and syrup in a shaker. Fill the shaker with 2 heaping cups of ice cubes, cover, and shake hard for 7 seconds. Pour the soda water into a Tom Collins glass and dump the cocktail, including the ice, into the glass. To garnish, stick the mint sprig in the cocktail, leaving only the leaves visible.

Raspberry Fennel Syrup

The flavors in this syrup remind me of autumn because the mix of ingredients straddles summer (raspberries) and winter (orange and fennel). The star anise also brings the flavor to a warm place, like mulled wine.

Makes about 8 ounces (1 cup)

¾ cup water
5 ounces fresh or frozen raspberries (about 1½ cups)
3 orange rinds (peeled with a vegetable peeler)
1 teaspoon fennel seeds
1 whole star anise
1 cup plus 2 tablespoons sugar

Combine the ingredients in a small saucepan and bring to a boil over medium-high heat. Reduce the heat to medium-low and simmer for about 15 minutes, stirring occasionally, until the liquid is slightly syrupy. Turn off the heat and set aside to cool to room temperature. Pass the mixture through a chinois or cheesecloth, using the back of a ladle or a wooden spoon to press every bit of juice out from the solid ingredients; discard the solids. Transfer to a bottle or jar and store, refrigerated, for up to 1 month.

Tavern Lemonade

This refreshing nonalcoholic beverage makes great use of the Raspberry Fennel Syrup.

Makes 1 nonalcoholic cocktail

1½ ounces fresh lemon juice (about 1½ lemons)
1 ounce Raspberry Fennel Syrup (recipe above)
3½ ounces soda water

Combine the lemon juice and syrup in a Tom Collins glass. Add soda water to fill the glass halfway and then fill the glass with ice cubes.

CALIFORNICATION

orange-infused vodka and watermelon with cayenne and cucumber

One hot summer evening in Los Angeles, my wife's friend Lauren came over and the two of them wanted to make some cocktails for themselves. They combined watermelon juice and vodka—and that was it. Good times, but not exactly great cocktail inspiration. Still, I took the idea to work with me the next day and created this cocktail in their honor. I added a few layers of flavor, including cayenne, cucumber, and orange, and turned that refreshing summer drink into something sophisticated enough to serve at the restaurants. I'd love to come home one day and find my wife and her friends making this new, improved version of their original cocktail.

Makes 1 cocktail

GLASS
Pilsner

PREP
2 Persian cucumbers
8 ounces seedless watermelon, cut into chunks

COCKTAIL
1½ ounces Orange-Infused Vodka (page 54)
1½ ounces watermelon juice
¾ ounce fresh lime juice (about 1 lime)
½ ounce Simple Syrup (page 59)
Pinch of cayenne

GARNISH
½ ounce cucumber juice
3 thin cucumber slices
A fresh mint sprig

To prep the cocktail, thinly slice half of one of the cucumbers. Cut up the remaining cucumber to fit in your juicer and pass it, skin, seeds, and all, through the juicer. You will have approximately 4 ounces of juice. Put the watermelon in a blender and blend until pureed. Pass the puree through a chinois or cheesecloth and discard the solids. You will have approximately 14 ounces of watermelon juice. (You can refrigerate the juices for up to 3 days. During that time, you could use the extra cucumber juice to make a Green Goddess, page 49.)

To make each cocktail, combine the cocktail ingredients in a shaker. Fill the shaker with 2 heaping cups of ice cubes, cover, and shake hard for 7 seconds. Dump the cocktail, including the ice, into a Pilsner glass. Slowly drizzle in ½ ounce of the cucumber juice to float it on top of the cocktail. To garnish, skewer the cucumber slices on a bamboo pick and lay it on top of the drink or lay the cucumbers on top of the drink. Stick the mint sprig into the cocktail, leaving only the leaves visible.

Pictured, left to right: Californication and Country Club (page 54), both made with Orange-Infused Vodka (page 54).

COUNTRY CLUB

vodka and cranberry with caraway, orange, and lime

I must admit that as a bartender I kind of cringe when someone comes in and orders a cosmo. I offer so many cocktails that I spent a lot of time and thought creating, and of course I'd hope that my customers would be intrigued enough to try them. But many people are creatures of habit, or they simply don't take the time to read the menu and they just order what they know and like. I want my customers to be happy, so I'll make them a cosmo if that's what they really want. But first, when someone orders a cosmo, I try to get them to try this. Instead of the usual cranberry juice, I make my own spiced cranberry syrup. The result is a pink drink that still satisfies the cosmo lover, but that is just more, let's say, twenty-first century.

Pictured on page 53.

Makes 1 cocktail

GLASS
Coupe or Martini

COCKTAIL
2 ounces Orange-Infused Vodka (recipe follows)
1 ounce Cranberry Syrup (recipe follows)
1 ounce fresh lime juice (about 1 lime)

GARNISH
An orange twist

Combine the cocktail ingredients in a shaker. Fill the shaker with ice cubes, cover, and shake hard for 7 seconds. Fine-strain the cocktail into a coupe (or Martini) glass. To garnish, rub the outside of the orange twist on the inside rim the glass. Squeeze the orange twist over the cocktail so the oils release and drop the twist, shiny side up, on the cocktail.

Orange-Infused Vodka

There are two ways to go about making this vodka. At the restaurant I make it the slow way: I cut the orange into thin wheels, submerge them in vodka, and let it sit for a week, shaking it daily. The second way is to put 2 ounces of vodka in your shaker. Twist the rinds of three or four orange peels in there to release the oils, shake it for seven seconds, and that's it. The results of the slow method may be *slightly* better and less bitter, but you'll be amazed by how delicious the quick-shake vodka turns out. It's like a magic trick! If you want to use the vodka to sip on, I suggest you go for the slow version. But if you want to use it in your cocktail tonight, you're going to love this quick version. I use the vodka to make the Tavern Collins (page 51), the Country Club, and the Californication (page 52).

Makes about 8 ounces (1 cup)

½ medium orange
8 ounces vodka

Thinly slice the orange with a chef's knife, submerge it in the vodka, and let it sit for a week, shaking it daily. Strain through a chinois or cheesecloth and the vodka is ready for use. Transfer the vodka to a jar or bottle; it will keep, refrigerated, for up to a month.

Cranberry Syrup

This syrup is infused with orange, lemon, vanilla, and many of the same spices used to make aquavit, including cumin, caraway, fennel, and cardamom. I use a vanilla bean pod scraped of seeds for this. If I used the seeds along with the pod the vanilla flavor would be too strong. If you have a vanilla bean pod saved from another use, that is ideal.

Makes about 10 ounces (1¼ cups)

5 ounces fresh or frozen cranberries (about 1½ cups)

1 cup water

½ teaspoon caraway seeds

½ teaspoon fennel seeds

¼ teaspoon coriander seeds

⅛ teaspoon cumin seeds

1 green cardamom pod

2 wide lemon rinds (peeled with a vegetable peeler)

2 wide orange rinds (peeled with a vegetable peeler)

1 whole star anise

¼ vanilla bean pod, seeds scraped out and saved for another use

1½ cups sugar

Combine all the ingredients in a medium sauce-pan and bring to a boil over medium-high heat. Reduce the heat and simmer until the cranberries pop and split open, about 6 minutes. Turn off the heat and let the syrup cool to room temperature. Strain the mixture through a chinois or cheesecloth into a glass measuring cup, pushing with the back of a ladle or wooden spoon to extract as much liquid from the solids as possible. Discard the solids and transfer to a jar or bottle. Refrigerate for up to 1 month.

Batch of Country Clubs

This "mix" will last for a week, refrigerated.

Makes one 1-liter bottle

GLASS
Coupe or Martini

COCKTAILS
15 ounces Orange-Infused Vodka (page 54)
7½ ounces fresh lime juice (about 7 limes)
7½ ounces Cranberry Syrup (recipe above)
4 ounces water

GARNISH
6 orange twists

Combine the cocktail ingredients in a 1-liter bottle, cover, and give it a quick shake to combine the ingredients. Refrigerate until the cocktail is chilled, about 2 hours, and for as long as 1 week.

Just before serving, remove the bottle from the refrigerator and shake to recombine the ingredients. To make a single cocktail, rub the outside of the orange twist on the inside rim of a coupe (or Martini) glass. Pour 5 ounces of the cocktail mix into the glass and squeeze the orange twist over the cocktail so the oils release. Drop the twist, shiny side up, on the cocktail.

LEBOWSKI

vodka and espresso-infused rum with ras el hanout whipped cream

I named this cocktail after one of my favorite movies, *The Big Lebowski*. If you don't know it, the main character, played by Jeff Bridges, drinks White Russians all day long; he walks around through most of that film in his bathrobe with that drink in his hand. He makes his White Russians with vodka and Kahlúa and whatever kind of milk he can find—half and half, milk, cream, or milk powder, and then he stirs it all together with his finger or the back of a dirty utensil.

This drink, named for that movie, is my version of a White Russian. Instead of being made with milk, it has a thick layer of whipped cream seasoned with ras el hanout, a North African spice blend, on top. It's a really easy cocktail to serve as an after-dinner drink because once you have made the Espresso Rum and the whipped cream, you just layer the ingredients in a glass; no shaking or stirring or straining required. I keep the Ras el Hanout whipped cream in a jar behind the bar, so it's always ready to go. It just needs a quick shake before you lay it on top, so it keeps that nice velvety texture. I serve this drink with a teaspoon so the person drinking it can swirl the cocktail around and also eat a little bit of the whipped cream while enjoying the beverage. It's like an adult dessert and a drink in one.

Makes 1 cocktail

GLASS
Irish coffee

COCKTAIL
1½ ounces grain vodka
1½ ounces Espresso Rum (page 243)

GARNISH
Ras el Hanout Whipped Cream (page 57)

Fill an Irish coffee glass with vodka and Espresso Rum. Spoon 1½ to 2 inches of the Ras el Hanout Whipped Cream on top in a big dollop. Serve the drink with a teaspoon.

Ras el Hanout Whipped Cream

I make whipped cream by shaking it in shaking tins. As much as I'd like to take credit for it, it's a bartender thing. It goes like this: You're behind the bar and someone asks for an Irish coffee or, in my case, a Lebowski. You don't make enough of either to warrant keeping whipped cream in your very tight bar fridge. The kitchen has cream, and you have shaking tins. So you take the spring off the Hawthorne strainer and you put that in the shaker. You're basically using the spring as a whisk. You close your shaking tins and then you shake and shake. You hear the spring rattling as it goes up and down. When this sound becomes muffled, it means that the cream is so thick that the spring is no longer hitting the inside of the jar, which means the whipped cream is ready. It takes a good solid minute of shaking for this to happen, which is about the amount of time it takes for your arm to feel like it's going to fall off. When customers see me shaking the cream like this for them, it's a guaranteed tip. The unusual blend of chile, pepper, and sweet spices in Ras el Hanout Whipped Cream makes this drink multidimensional, instead of being just coffee and cream.

Makes about 16 ounces (2 cups)

1 teaspoon allspice berries

1 teaspoon black peppercorns

1 teaspoon ground cinnamon

1 teaspoon whole cloves

1 teaspoon coriander seeds

1 teaspoon ground ginger

1 teaspoon freshly grated nutmeg (or ground nutmeg)

1 teaspoon ground turmeric

1 cup heavy whipping cream

Put the spices in a spice grinder and grind to a fine powder. Put 1½ teaspoons in a shaker and reserve the rest for another use, such as to make Ras el Hanout Syrup (page 269). (The spice blend will stay fresh for a few months, stored at room temperature in a jar with a tight-fitting lid.)

Remove the spring from your Hawthorne strainer and put it in the shaker. Add the cream, put the shakers together, and shake hard until it is thick and has turned a rich buttery shade of white, about 1 minute. Use or refrigerate for up to several hours. Scoop the leftovers into a jar, so you can use it throughout the night.

LUCQUES GIMLET

vodka and lime with mint

A classic gimlet is a cocktail made with gin, lime, and a little sugar. In the cocktail world, there are many spin-offs on the same formula. For instance, a caipirinha, Brazil's national drink, is essentially a gimlet on the rocks made with cachaça. A daiquiri is the rum version, and the margarita is the tequila version. This cocktail is made with vodka. The neutral flavor of the vodka allows the bright flavors of the lime and mint to shine through. It is a very simple cocktail—sweet, tart, and refreshing. The green flecks from the muddled mint give it a cool rough-around-the-edges look, but in a way that is really pretty.

Makes 1 cocktail

GLASS
Coupe

COCKTAIL
10 fresh mint leaves
2 ounces grain vodka
1 ounce fresh lime juice (about 1 lime)
¾ ounce Simple Syrup (recipe follows)

GARNISH
A lime wheel

Put the mint leaves in a shaker or a sturdy pint glass with 1 or 2 ice cubes and muddle to a green slush. (Purists say to softly press the mint by itself, without ice cubes. Trust me, the sugar will keep it from being bitter.) Add the remaining cocktail ingredients. Fill the shaker with ice cubes, cover, and shake hard for 7 seconds. Use a Hawthorne strainer to strain the cocktail into a coupe glass. To garnish, lay the lime wheel on top of the cocktail.

Simple Syrup

Simple syrup is sugar and water cooked down until it is syrupy. It is used a lot in cocktail making. My simple syrup is a little thicker than some; this way I can sweeten a cocktail without diluting it. You can find simple syrup sold in grocery stores and liquor stores, where the mixers are sold, but in terms of making it yourself, I think you've got this.

Makes about 24 ounces (3 cups)

2¼ cups sugar
1½ cups water

Combine the sugar and water in a medium saucepan and bring to a boil over high heat. Reduce the heat to medium-low and simmer for about 15 minutes, stirring occasionally, until the liquid is slightly syrupy. Turn off the heat and set aside to cool to room temperature. Transfer the simple syrup to a jar or bottle and close. It will keep, refrigerated, for up to 3 months.

THREE TWO THREE

Buddha's hand vodka and kumquat with ginger and jalapeño

I made this cocktail for a party *Saveur* hosted for Suzanne to coincide with a spread the magazine published about her. Suzanne is a Los Angeles native, and her restaurants are all in Los Angeles, so I was asked to create something that was quintessentially Los Angeles for them. I chose fresh kumquats and spicy jalapeño peppers, which definitely fit that description. The magazine crew, which had flown in from New York, was very happy with it. The name of the cocktail, 323, is the area code for the part of Los Angeles where Lucques is located.

You can make this drink as spicy as you want to by adding more jalapeño. Plus, it's easy to make something more fiery but impossible to make it less so. The base of this cocktail is Buddha's hand–infused vodka. Buddha's hand is a fruit in the citrus family that looks like a hand with long, crooked fingers. Farmers' markets in Los Angeles sell it in late fall, and throughout the winter. You can even find it in some grocery stores like Whole Foods.

Makes 1 cocktail

GLASS
Double old fashioned

COCKTAIL
1½ kumquats, roughly chopped
⅛ teaspoon seeded, minced jalapeño, plus more to taste
2 ounces Buddha's Hand Vodka (page 62) or Hangar One buddha's hand vodka
1 ounce fresh lemon juice (about 1 lemon)
¾ ounce Ginger Syrup (page 62)

GARNISH
3 thin jalapeño slices

Combine the kumquats and jalapeño in a shaker and muddle until slushy. Add the remaining cocktail ingredients, fill the shaker with ice cubes, cover, and shake hard for 7 seconds. Dump the entire contents of your shaker into a double old fashioned glass, so you see the kumquats and jalapeño floating around. It gives it that rustic vibe, and leaves you something to chew on. Garnish with the jalapeño slices.

(CONTINUED)

Buddha's Hand Vodka

When you see this fruit for the first time, you wonder what the hell it is. It looks like a crazy fruit-hand hybrid. Yes, it's yellow, with a skin like a lemon, and it also has a citrusy scent. And those fingers! When you cut into it, you notice: there's no flesh inside. It's all pith; solid white with a thin layer of yellow rind on the outside. There are also no seeds. That's a Buddha's hand, a large, hand-shaped Asian fruit in the citrus family.

I got the idea to infuse vodka with Buddha's hand in part because I wanted to see the hand floating, immersed in a jar of vodka. Yes, I'm a grown-up kid: the goriness appealed to me. The rind of the fruit imparts delicious flavor to the vodka; the pithy interior only imparts bitterness. So it's important to use the Buddha's hand whole so that only the exterior of the fruit has contact with the vodka. To make this, you must use a jar in which the Buddha's hand will fit snugly; otherwise you'll have to use too much vodka to cover it, and the resulting infused vodka will have a weaker flavor than it should.

Makes about 16 ounces (2 cups)

1 Buddha's hand, rinsed
2 cups grain vodka

Put the Buddha's hand in a wide-mouthed 1-liter jar (such as a mason jar). Pour in enough vodka to cover the Buddha's hand and let it sit at room temperature for 3 days. That's it. Remove the Buddha's hand from the jar and discard it. You now have a delicious and unusual vodka that will keep, refrigerated, for up to 6 months.

Ginger Syrup

This recipe is nothing more than simple syrup with the spicy zing of fresh ginger added. You can use it in any recipe calling for simple syrup.

Makes about 8 ounces (1 cup)

1½ cups sugar
¾ cup water
2 ounces fresh ginger, peeled and roughly chopped

Combine the sugar and water in a medium saucepan and heat over medium-high heat, stirring occasionally, until the sugar dissolves, about 2 minutes. Turn off the heat and set the syrup aside to come to room temperature. (If you combine the sugar syrup with the ginger when the syrup is warm, the syrup will turn brown. If you wait for it to cool, it turns out a pretty white color.)

Transfer the syrup to a blender. Add the ginger and blend until the ginger is pulverized. Strain through a chinois or cheesecloth and discard the solids. Transfer the syrup to a bottle or jar. It will keep, refrigerated, for up to 1 month.

A.O.C. BLOODY

vodka and tomato with harissa, garlic, Worcestershire, and horseradish

I would be lying to you if I didn't say that dealing with people's hangovers goes hand in hand with serving alcohol, which is why every bar needs a good bloody Mary. I've done my fair share of experimenting, without departing from the bloody Mary concept. I tried substituting fresh ginger for fresh horseradish; I tried adding port and balsamic vinegar. I wanted to have a full-flavored, multiple-layered bloody, and in the end this recipe is what came about. It is a perfectly spicy, intensely tomatoey, refreshing, delicious, and almost addictive bloody Mary. What really sets this bloody apart from all the others is the harissa spices that I add to the mix. Suzanne uses harissa, a Moroccan chile paste—she makes a green version and a red version—often in her cooking. One day she made this amazing chicken paillard dish with red harissa. While I was eating it, lightbulbs went on in my head. This is a tomato-based sauce! How much of a stretch would it be to add harissa spices to a bloody Mary mix? I played with it a lot, tried it, changed the smoked paprika, dropped the olive oil, and used those spices to make the perfect bloody Mary. It sells like crazy. One thing you should know: there isn't a ton of booze in a bloody Mary. People generally drink them because they drank too much the night before. The bloody Mary is based on the theory that they need a little "hair of the dog"—just enough alcohol to make them feel better, to ease them through the day, not to knock them out and make them feel bad the *next* morning too. I don't strain this after blending it because I like the texture and the bits of seeds that you find in this cocktail. I never really got excited about the celery sticks that traditionally garnish a bloody Mary. So instead I garnish mine with a lime wheel and Castelvetrano olives, which are meaty, delicious green olives—and the good news is they're available in jars at regular grocery stores. Also if I have some extra time, I pickle some carrots and jam them into the glass as well.

To make a bloody Maria, substitute tequila or mezcal for the vodka in this cocktail, and if you want to go with gin to make a red snapper, that makes for a delicious cocktail as well.

Makes 1 cocktail

GLASS
Tom Collins

COCKTAIL
1½ ounces grain vodka
4½ ounces Bloody Mix (page 64)

GARNISH
A lime wheel
A Castelvetrano olive

Pour the vodka into the bottom of a Tom Collins glass. Fill the glass half full with Bloody Mix and fill the glass with ice cubes. To garnish, cut the lime wheel three-quarters of the way through from one edge toward the center. Stretch the lime wheel out so it becomes a spiral, and lay it on top of the cocktail, along with an olive.

(CONTINUED)

Bloody Mix

This mix, enough for 5 cocktails or a pitcher, is also delicious on its own, as a refreshing, spicy, and possibly even healthy nonalcoholic meal-in-a-glass type of beverage.

Makes about 24 ounces (3 cups)

2½ cups canned tomato juice

2 ounces fresh lemon juice (about 2 lemons)

2 ounces Worcestershire sauce

¼ plum tomato, seeded

2 teaspoon prepared horseradish (preferably Atomic brand)

½ teaspoon balsamic vinegar

⅛ teaspoon chopped garlic

½ teaspoon celery seeds

½ teaspoon paprika

½ teaspoon kosher salt

¼ teaspoon cumin seeds

⅛ teaspoon caraway seeds

⅛ teaspoon cayenne

4 dashes of Tabasco sauce

Combine the ingredients in a blender and puree until the garlic and tomato are pulverized, about 2 minutes. Pour the mix into a 1-liter bottle. Close the bottle and give it a gentle shake to combine the ingredients. Put it in the refrigerator to chill until you're ready to serve it or for up to 3 days.

Pitcher of Bloody Marys

Makes 1 large pitcher

GLASSES
Tom Collins

COCKTAILS
1 recipe Bloody Mix (recipe above)
8 ounces grain vodka, tequila, mezcal, or gin

GARNISH
5 lime wheels
5 Castelvetrano olives

Fill a large pitcher with ice cubes and pour in the Bloody Mix and vodka; stir. Serve the pitcher with Tom Collins glasses, olives, and limes on the side for people to serve and garnish their own cocktails.

SANCHO PANZA

vodka and ginger with sherry, lemon, and soda

When we get out of work early at the restaurants, the guys in the kitchen always warn each other: "Make sure to call home before you get there." Or "Don't forget to drive around the block and honk the horn, because Sancho might be there." Sancho Panza is the guy who rides the mule next to Don Quixote; our fictional Sancho is the guy who "takes care of" your wife while you are working. The bussers, runners, cooks, bar backs—they all have two jobs. In the morning they work at one restaurant. In the evening they go somewhere else; six hours here, six hours there. They work easily 14-hour days, 70-hour weeks, to take care of their families. Whenever I feel tired, I look at them and know that I don't have anything to complain about. I take the extra step and lead by example.

This cocktail is a play on the famous Moscow mule, a cocktail made of vodka, lime, and ginger beer, traditionally served in a copper mug. The mule supposedly originated right here in Los Angeles, at a long-closed pub called Cock 'n' Bull on Sunset Boulevard. It was developed by a pair of salesmen—one imported vodka, the other imported ginger beer. They got together and wanted to create a drink that would help sell both. It's a very popular drink to this day, and when people request it, I try to steer them toward this variation, which has sherry added to the mix, giving the drink a fuller-bodied flavor, and uses lemon instead of lime. Since sherry is Spanish, I named it after the guy who rides a Spanish mule, Sancho Panza.

Pictured, left to right: Sancho Panza and Quixote (page 95), both made with a ginger syrup

To make this drink, you put soda water in the bottom of the glass and then pour the rest of the cocktail on top. When you do this, the soda and the rest of the cocktail mix together right away, without your even stirring it. That's the effect you want. This is called "bottoming the soda." If you were to pour the soda on top of the drink instead of bottoming the soda, the first sip of your drink would be nothing but soda, and that isn't going to excite anyone.

Makes 1 cocktail

GLASS
Tom Collins

COCKTAIL
2 ounces grain vodka
1 ounce fresh lemon juice (about 1 lemon)
¾ ounce Sherry Ginger Syrup (page 68)
Soda water

GARNISH
An orange wheel

Combine the vodka, lemon juice, and syrup in a shaker. Fill the shaker with 2 heaping cups of ice cubes, cover, and shake hard for 7 seconds. Fill a Tom Collins glass with ½ inch of soda. To garnish, cut the orange wheel three-quarters of the way through from one edge toward the center. Stretch the orange wheel out so it becomes a spiral. Hold it so it hangs down in the glass while you slowly pour the cocktail and ice into the glass; it will stretch out the length of the cocktail, which looks pretty.

(CONTINUED)

Sherry Ginger Syrup

I use amontillado sherry, a medium dry golden-bronze sherry from Montilla Spain. But you don't have to break the bank—any inexpensive dry sherry works perfectly fine. I cool the syrup completely before blending it with the ginger, because adding the ginger while the syrup is still warm will turn the syrup brown. The whitish hue makes for a pretty cocktail.

Makes about 8 ounces (1 cup)

¾ cup amontillado sherry
1½ cups sugar
2 ounces fresh ginger, peeled and roughly chopped

Combine the sherry and sugar in a small saucepan. Heat the liquid over medium-high heat, stirring occasionally, until the sugar dissolves, about 2 minutes; be careful that the flame isn't so high that it can travel around the sides of the pan, as the alcohol in the pan will catch fire. Turn off the heat and set aside to cool to room temperature. Transfer the syrup to a blender. Add the ginger and blend until the ginger is pulverized. Strain the syrup through a chinois or cheesecloth and discard the solids. Transfer to a jar or bottle and refrigerate for up to 1 month.

GREEN HOUND

vodka and grapefruit with lime and cucumber

I definitely felt pressure the first time Caroline asked me to create a cocktail to put on a new menu they were printing for Lucques. I knew I wanted to make something with vodka and cucumber, so I went to the kitchen to talk to the sous chef at the time, Amanda Bacon (she went on to open the Los Angeles juice empire, Moon Juice). I asked her what goes with cucumber. She recommended grapefruit, and it worked like a charm. With those two ingredients in mind, I created this drink. Caroline liked it. It went on the menu. And it really took off. People love it. The recipe evolved over the years into this. It's super easy to make at home. It's also really pretty. The drink is pink, and then I float green cucumber juice on top. I like the flavors together, but I didn't want to stir the colors together. I'm sure the color is one of the reasons it's so popular: had I presented people with a muddled, brownish drink, I doubt it would have become as popular as it has. It's a take on a greyhound, which is grapefruit juice and vodka, which is how it got its name.

Makes 1 cocktail

GLASS
Double old fashioned

PREP
1 Persian cucumber

COCKTAIL
1½ ounces potato vodka

1½ ounces fresh grapefruit juice (preferably Ruby Red, about ¼ grapefruit)

¾ ounce fresh lime juice (about 1 lime)

½ ounce Grapefruit Simple Syrup (recipe follows)

GARNISH
½ ounce cucumber juice

3 thin cucumber slices

A fresh mint sprig

To prep the cocktail, cut up the cucumber to fit in your juicer and pass it, seeds, skin, and all, through the juicer. You will have enough juice for about 5 cocktails.

Combine the cocktail ingredients in a shaker. Fill the shaker with ice cubes, cover, and shake hard for 7 seconds. Fill the glass with ice cubes. Use a Hawthorne strainer to strain the cocktail into the glass. To garnish, skewer the cucumbers on a bamboo pick and lay it on top of the drink. Stick the mint sprig into the cocktail, leaving only the leaves visible.

Grapefruit Simple Syrup

Makes about 10 ounces (1¼ cups)

1 cup fresh grapefruit juice (preferably Ruby Red, about 1 grapefruit)

1 cup sugar

Combine the grapefruit juice and sugar in a small saucepan. Heat the liquid over medium-high heat, stirring occasionally, until the sugar dissolves, about 2 minutes. Turn off the heat and set aside to cool to room temperature. Transfer to a jar or bottle and use or refrigerate for up to 1 month.

Of all the spirits out there, none of them is closer to my heart, and to my heritage, as gin, particularly Holland gin, or genever. Genever is the original gin—the word *gin* is short for genever—but genever is little known outside Holland, mostly only among bar geeks like me. Genever originated sometime during the Rennaissance. It was made by distilling malted wine and infusing it with juniper berries, which were believed to have medicinal properties. Genever became popular in England when William of Orange, leader of the Dutch Republic, occupied the English, Scottish, and Irish thrones. The story of how Holland's own genever got to England, as told to a boy in the Netherlands, to make him proud to be a Dutchman and proud of his national drink, goes like this:

Once upon a time, a long, long time ago, there was the Spanish Inquisition. The Catholic Church, led by a Spanish army, was moving up north, killing everything and everyone who believed differently than they did: Jews, Muslims, Protestants, and atheists. So these people moved north. This led to a long war in the small kingdom of the Netherlands, known as the Eighty Years' War. Even though the Dutch were at the height of their power, they needed a helping hand, and the English offered it. During the fighting, the English soldiers looked on at the Dutch and marveled at their unparalleled courage. They believed that this courage came to the Dutch soldiers via the spirit that these soldiers carried in small flasks on their belts. That spirit was genever, aka "Holland gin," the national drink of the Netherlands. The English took it

home with them and shortened the name to *gin*. Today gin is thought of as an English spirit, and "Dutch courage" has evolved into a term used to describe the (often false) sense of confidence and strength a person derives from drinking alcohol.

Drinking genever is a part of any Dutch person's life. One of my earlier experiences was when Ajax, "my" soccer club, was playing another club, Feyenoord. The two teams and their fans dislike each other with a passion, as with the Red Sox and Yankees or the Giants and Dodgers. The game started at 2:30. Ajax fans, myself included, started drinking at noon in the bar across the street from the Olympic stadium in Amsterdam. We downed shots of genever and lots of beer. At two o'clock a couple of kids came running into the bar: "They're here! They're here! The train is here!" There is one train that goes from Rotterdam to Amsterdam, no stops allowed, and that was the train bringing the opposing team to our stadium in Amsterdam. The train had arrived in the station. There was no time to waste. We all threw down our glasses and rushed outside. We took bricks out of the street and carried them, running toward the train. In front of us was a line of horses with heavy-shielded police riding them. Behind the line of police were the supporters of Feyenoord, the opposing team. As soon as we saw them, we forgot the police and we threw our bricks and shouted at the opposing fans. Undercover cops started moving in and making arrests out of our group. But we continued on, shouting and throwing any loose objects we could find. It wasn't until the police started swinging their heavy batons that we began to move back. This was, for us, just part of the pregame activity. After the good fight, fought well, we set ourselves up in a field behind the goal and lit the fireworks we had smuggled in, ready to watch an amazing game and hoping for our beloved team to win.

We definitely drank genever with abandon, but it was the English, I believe, who gave gin its bad reputation. Today gin is widely believed to have other properties that make people crazy, weepy, and angry as hell and give them the worst hangover of any spirit. You may have heard the phrase "getting 'gin' drunk." Where gin was once considered a poor man's drink and the shortest distance between two points to get a man drunk, today it is considered one of the fancier spirits, with subtle flavor nuances and a sophisticated reputation, for more refined but still *serious* drinkers.

Gin is made from a neutral spirit by adding spices, predominantly juniper berries, so essentially it is a more interesting version of vodka (but don't say that to a gin lover). Today's gins are distilled with as few as three ingredients—juniper berries always being among them and predominant—and as many as the distiller chooses, including ingredients such as lavender, mint, grapefruit, and rose.

Where many spirits, from tequila and rum to whiskey and brandy, are often consumed neat, gin is generally mixed into cocktails or Martinis. Mixing it with other ingredients is said to enhance the flavors infused into gin, and it is the base for more cocktails than any other spirit, including the Martini, gimlet, gin rickey, gin fizz, Negroni, Tom Collins, last word, white lady, French 75, Singapore sling, vesper, and, of course, the national drink of England: the gin and tonic. By contrast, genever, still the pride of Holland, is drunk straight up, from a 1¼-ounce Glencarin glass. The bartender puts the glass in front of you and pours it all the way to the rim. (This is done because the Dutch have a reputation for being cheap, so they want to make sure they are getting their money's worth; when they order a 1¼-ounce drink, they want 1¼ ounces.) To take the first sip, the drinker has to put his mouth to the glass while it's still on the bar or table, or the genever will spill all over him. In Holland, we enjoy our genever with a side of beer, known as a *kopstootje* or "head butt."

STYLES OF GIN

There are many styles of gin, the main categories being Holland gin, or genever, London dry gin, Old Tom gin, and American gin. What they have in common is that they are all distilled grain alcohol—vodka, essentially—flavored predominantly with juniper berries.

GENEVER, which means "juniper" in Dutch, is made with malted wine, and it carries an unmistakable malt flavor. In the Netherlands there are two kinds, Old Genever or Young Genever; basically meaning it's either made with the old recipe or made with the new recipe. The old one uses more malted wine than the young one. But here in the States you pretty much can only find one kind.

LONDON DRY GIN, which is dry in that it does not contain sugar, reflects the style of gin developed after William of Orange brought genever to Great Britain. The majority of London dries have four ingredients in common: juniper berries, coriander, licorice, and angelica root. Beyond that, each manufacturer adds other flavors and nuances to make its version unique. London dry gin is the most popular type of gin there is and the one most people think of when they think of gin.

OLD TOM GIN, whose name refers to a gin recipe from the 1800s, has a flavor profile that falls somewhere between the clean, dry taste of London dry gin and the maltiness of Holland gin. It is sweeter and less floral than London dry gin but dryer than genever. Old Tom gin is the defining ingredient in a Tom Collins (2 ounces Old Tom gin, 2 ounces soda water, ¾ ounce simple syrup, 1 ounce fresh lemon juice) and a Martinez (page 235), one of the iconic cocktails of our grandfathers' and great-grandfathers' generations.

AMERICAN GIN is basically a more adventurous version of London dry. In the free-thinking spirit of America, these gin makers don't believe they need to follow an ancient prescription for gin making. They think outside the box and add whatever flavorings they want: pine, citrus, lavender . . . and *always* juniper berries.

STOCKING YOUR BAR

Here are my favorite gins in all four categories.

BOLS GENEVER (42% abv) comes in a distinct, handsome, square-shouldered bottle. This is my baby; it was my first kiss, in terms of alcohol anyway. The flavor of the malted liquor really shines through. This makes a nice base in mixed cocktails and can also be used in place of whiskey in a classic Manhattan or old fashioned.

BOBBY'S GIN (42% abv). The bottle looks like the little brother of the genever bottle, slightly thinner, softer around the edges, but still the broad shoulders. This combined with the Indonesian pattern painted on the bottle makes it stand out on any back bar. This juice is made by my friend Sebastiaan, in Rotterdam, Netherlands. His grandfather, Bobby, used to take genever with him to Indonesia and infuse it with all the cool and local spices—cloves, lemongrass, cubeb pepper, and so on. Many years later his grandson is doing the same with gin, and the result is an amazing one-of-a-kind spirit. A little harder to find, but definitely in your local specialty store or online.

BEEFEATER (47% abv) is an old-school brand of London dry gin and probably the best-known gin out there. It comes in a tall, slender bottle with the English guard wearing the trademark high hat on the front. (He is a guardian of the Tower of London, and the nickname of those guards is "Beefeaters.") Beefeater is infused with nine different spices—juniper berries, of course, being the predominant one. It's an easy-to-drink gin at a good price point and the one gin I recommend you have on your bar if you are going to have only one gin. If you have Beefeater, you know you can make a proper gin cocktail. Beefeater is the only distiller of London dry gin that remains in London.

TANQUERAY (47.3% abv), which comes in the iconic green bottle, is a longstanding member of my Usual Suspects crew of liquors. Even though it is a London dry gin, today it is produced in Scotland. By its own account, Tanqueray is infused with juniper, coriander, licorice, and angelica root, but another flavor I get from it is lemon. It is produced in pot stills much like the original stills in which gin was made. Tanqueray has a bright, fresh flavor and is the perfect gin for mixed cocktails and Martinis.

WILDER (45% abv), an American gin, is close to my heart, not the least reason for this being that the logo on the bottle is in part designed by Eric Junker, who also designs the posters for L.A. Loves Alex's Lemonade, a charity hosted by my bosses, Suzanne Goin, Caroline Styne, and Suzanne's husband, the Los Angeles chef David Lentz. I was introduced to Wilder gin after I saw a post about it on social media. Something about that post intrigued me, so I contacted Wilder, and the following Monday the whole team was sitting at my bar, talking, of course, about gin. We really hit it off; the owners are such great guys and so into their craft. They were full of questions: Why do you buy this product? Why don't you buy that one? I tasted their gin and loved it. They infuse it with botanicals that are native to Ojai, California, where they make the gin, including sagebrush, purple sage, bay, yerba santa, pixie mandarin peel, and chuchupate, a native medicinal plant. It has such a distinct flavor; I love to use this gin to make a Martini, gimlet, white lady, or any other cocktail where the gin is the star of the show.

ST. GEORGE (45% abv) makes many amazing spirits, including its line of American gin, which includes three types: Botanivor, Dry Rye, and, my favorite, Terroir. The maker describes it as "a forest in a glass," and I would agree. It is very flavorful, with notes of Douglas fir, bay laurel, and sage, and of course the essence of juniper. The distiller, Lance Winters, who has become a friend, told me that he made this gin with an intense pine flavor because he felt like, regardless of where a person is from, everyone can relate in some way to the scent of pine. It's an awesome spirit to use in a Martini, because the piney flavors really shine through.

RANSOM (44% abv). Back in the day, gin was transported in wooden barrels, so if it were distilled in London, by the time it arrived in the United States the gin had been in essence aged in the oak barrel and its flavor affected by the wood. To imitate that accidental aging, and to try to capture the flavor of gin as it was experienced in America, the guys behind Ransom age their Old Tom gin in oak barrels. This gin can be used in any of my recipes calling for genever or in the classic cocktail the Martinez (page 235).

CATERPILLAR

gin and guava liqueur with lime and green Chartreuse

When you stroll the farmers' markets in Los Angeles during the late summer and fall, you can smell guava from many stalls away. Guava has such a sweet, delicious scent, and I love its bold, unmistakable flavor. I wanted to meet that flavor in this cocktail with another bold flavor, which is why I added the Chartreuse, which has a slight Alpine-licorice-like flavor. I call this cocktail the Caterpillar because the ingredients, together, transform into something really beautiful. On second thought, maybe I should have called it the butterfly. It's the perfect fruity cocktail to serve in the fall, before guavas are gone for the year.

Makes 1 cocktail

GLASS
Double old fashioned

COCKTAIL
1½ ounces London dry gin
¾ ounce green Chartreuse (see page 235)
¾ ounce Guava Liqueur (page 249)
1 ounce fresh lime juice (about 1 lime)

GARNISH
A fresh mint sprig

Combine the cocktail ingredients in a shaker and fill it with ice cubes. Cover and shake hard for 7 seconds. Fill the glass with ice cubes and use a Hawthorne strainer to strain the drink over the fresh ice cubes. To garnish, stick the mint sprig in the cocktail, leaving only the leaves visible.

Pictured: guavas

RULE BREAKER

genever and peach with port, maple, and bitters

This is a blended drink I started making several years ago for Alex's Lemonade, a charity event hosted by Caroline, Suzanne, and Suzanne's husband, David Lentz (chef and owner of Hungry Cat restaurants in Los Angeles) to raise money for children's cancer research. Every year, I make a different cocktail for the event. I invite ten to fifteen other bartenders to serve drinks at the event as well. One year I ended up bringing my blender. A blender is generally frowned upon among my fellow bartenders because it conjures images of cheesy resort drinks like strawberry daiquiris and frozen margaritas. That's why I call this the "rule breaker." I felt I was breaking the so-called "rules." Or at least not taking them very seriously. In this case, breaking the rules makes the job of serving a crowd possible. The majority of my cocktails have to be made one at a time, but I can blend as many as eight of these at once.

I made the recipe for the home cook to serve four rather than eight to accommodate a standard-size blender. When I make this for one, I muddle the peach; it's easier, less messy, and faster than using a blender.

Makes 4 cocktails

GLASS

Double old fashioned

PREP

5 ounces ripe peach (about ½ large ripe peach)

COCKTAIL

6 ounces genever

4 ounces fresh lemon juice (about 4 lemons)

3 ounces pure maple syrup

2 ounces port

1 ounce Classic Bitters (page 258)

½ cup ice cubes

GARNISH

4 orange twists

Pit the peach, but don't peel it; cut it into a few chunks. Combine the peach and cocktail ingredients in a blender and blend on high speed for 1 minute (the time will vary depending on the power of your blender), until the ingredients are pulverized and soupy. Fill 4 glasses with ice cubes and pour the blended mix over them. To garnish, squeeze 1 orange twist over the cocktail to release the oils and drop the twist, shiny side up, on the cocktail.

Single Muddled Rule Breaker

GLASS

Double old fashioned

COCKTAIL

3 ounces ripe peach (about ¼ large peach), pitted and cut into a few chunks

1½ ounces genever

1 ounce fresh lemon juice (about 1 lemon)

¾ ounce pure maple syrup

½ ounce inexpensive port

¼ ounce Classic Bitters (page 258)

Muddle the peach in a shaker. Add the rest of the cocktail ingredients and fill the shaker with ice cubes. Close the shaker and shake hard for 7 seconds. Fill a double old fashioned glass with ice cubes. Using a Hawthorne strainer, strain the cocktail into the glass.

COMPANION

genever and cola with lime and bitters

Back in the days when Ernest Hemingway was living in Key West, Florida, he used to go out fishing and drinking in the Gulf Stream with his buddies. One of those friends, Charles H. Baker, was writing a cocktail book called *The Gentleman's Companion*. Of course, they would drink more than they probably should have, on a daily basis. Every morning they woke up feeling horrible, and, yes, ready to start drinking again. So they tried to think of pick-me-up cocktails. Hemingway wanted a cocktail that was strong, sour, and bitter. The cocktail they came up with to fit that bill was one they called "Death in the Gulfstream," which consists of genever, lime, and bitters. This is my version of Hemingway's creation, with the addition of my house-made Cola Syrup, which balances the drink and adds all the layers of flavor that I put into the syrup. You can use another house-made syrup, such as Ras el Hanout Syrup (page 269), Root Beer Syrup (page 120), Ginger Syrup (page 62), or pure maple syrup, in place of the Cola Syrup.

I call this cocktail the Companion, after the cocktail book. For this cocktail, the glass is filled with crushed ice and then angostura bitters are drizzled on top, so it's like a grown-up version of a shaved ice.

Makes 1 cocktail

GLASS
Julep cup

COCKTAIL
3 lime wedges
1½ ounces genever
¾ ounce Cola Syrup (page 271)
¾ ounce fresh lime juice (about 1 lime)
Crushed ice (see page 29)

GARNISH
Angostura bitters

Muddle the lime wedges in a julep cup until they're squashed and have released their juice and oils. Add the genever, Cola Syrup, and lime juice. Fill the cup higher than the rim with crushed ice and top with a couple of dashes of bitters.

CAT'S PAW

gin and oro blanco with Aperitivo and sweet vermouth

Years ago we had a new bartender at Tavern, Jay Culp. Jay and I liked to geek out on cocktails, and one day he mentioned an "old fashioned syrup" that he'd made. "What the hell is old fashioned syrup?" I asked. He explained that it contained the ingredients of a classic old fashioned cocktail, but with some sugar added to turn it into a syrup, he could use it as a sweetener in cocktails and in so doing, get a layer of "old fashioned" flavor in the cocktail instead of just sugar. That sounded like such a brilliant idea that I was inspired to make a syrup out of a classic Negroni cocktail, which is equal parts Campari, gin, and sweet vermouth. That syrup, which is slightly bitter from the Campari, is balanced in this cocktail with oro blanco grapefruit juice. Oro blanco is a California invention; it is a hybrid between a pomelo and a grapefruit. It is sweeter and less acidic than grapefruit. When winter shows up, as soon as I see oro blancos at the farmers' market I put this cocktail on the menu. If you can't find oro blanco, use Ruby Red grapefruit juice instead.

Every gin book you read will have the story of the Cat's Paw, which is a reference to the way gin was sold in London by a bootlegger named Captain Bradley. In front of his house was a statue of a cat. There was an opening in the mouth of the cat, where patrons would put their money, and there was a tube coming from the cat's paw from which the gin would then be dispensed. Once I heard that story I knew I had to have a drink named a Cat's Paw.

Makes 1 cocktail

GLASS
Coupe

COCKTAIL
¾ ounce London dry gin
¾ ounce Negroni Syrup (page 83)
1 ounce fresh oro blanco or Ruby Red grapefruit juice (about ¼ fruit)
¾ ounce fresh lime juice (about 1 lime)

GARNISH
A grapefruit twist

Pour the cocktail ingredients into a shaker and fill it with ice cubes. Cover and shake hard for 7 seconds. Using a Hawthorne strainer in one hand to hold back the ice and a fine strainer in the other hand, fine-strain the cocktail into a coupe glass. To garnish, rub the outside of the grapefruit twist on the inside rim of the glass. Squeeze the grapefruit twist over the cocktail so the oils release into the glass and drop the twist, shiny side up, on the cocktail.

Negroni Syrup

Refrigerated, this syrup should last for up to three weeks. Since we are playing with fortified wine, over time the essence of the syrup diminishes. Just make sure you taste it. I make my own Campari and vermouth, but if you don't feel up to it, you can absolutely use store-bought. If you like the flavor of Campari, make a double batch and use it when you want a sweetener in other cocktails where the distinctive flavor of Campari is welcome. Have fun with it.

Makes 6 ounces (¾ cup)

2 ounces London dry gin
2 ounces Sweet Vermouth (page 240)
2 ounces Aperitivo (page 256)
2 ounces sugar

Combine all the ingredients in a small saucepan and warm over medium-high heat until the sugar dissolves, about 2 minutes; be careful that the flame isn't so high that it can travel around the sides of the pan, as the alcohol in the pan will catch fire. Turn off the heat and set aside to cool to room temperature. Transfer the syrup to a bottle or jar and refrigerate until you're ready to use it.

COMPOUND

Compound Gin and Suze with Bénédictine and Orange Bitters

This is a slightly bitter, lightly sweetened cocktail that gets brightened by a lemon twist. It contains two very old French liqueurs—Suze and Bénédictine—so even though the cocktail itself is something I just invented, it feels like a classic. It has a mild taste, and the alcohol content isn't too high, so I think of it as a great first drink of the evening. The cool thing about this drink is that you make your own compound gin for it. Compound gin is a neutral grain spirit that is infused with spices; it differs from a typical gin where the spices are added to the still in the second distillation. So compound gin is a sort of shortcut. The compound gin is what makes this drink special, but if you really want to make it and don't have a week to make the gin, any American-style gin, such as St. George or Wilder, will work great.

Makes 1 cocktail

GLASS
Coupe or Martini

GARNISH
A lemon twist

COCKTAIL
1½ ounces Compound Gin (page 254)
¾ ounce Suze (see page 86)
¾ ounce Bénédictine (see page 86)
3 dashes of Orange Bitters (page 260)

Rub the outside of the lemon twist on the inside rim of a coupe glass. Set the glass and twist aside while you make the cocktail.

Combine the gin, Suze, Bénédictine, and bitters in a mixing glass, fill with ice cubes, and stir with a bar spoon until the glass is cold, 10 to 15 seconds. Using a julep strainer, strain the cocktail into the prepared glass. To garnish, squeeze the lemon twist over the cocktail to release the oils and drop the twist, shiny side up, on the cocktail.

Suze is a French liqueur, popular in the 1900s in Paris, made from gentian root, which is the bitter agent in Campari, Aperol, and bitters. Pablo Picasso created a collage depicting a bottle of Suze, appropriately named *La Bouteille de Suze*. The liquor was forgotten over the years, and nobody—in the United States anyway—was using it until the recent cocktail movement. Now bartenders and their customers are appreciating unusual old varieties of liquor again, and Suze is back. Still, I suggest you buy a small bottle, as you won't reach for it often.

Bénédictine is a slightly sweet, caramel-colored French liqueur made from different botanicals, the recipe for which the makers are very secretive about. The story that most people believe and tell about Bénédictine is that it's made by Benedictine monks, but a fellow barman corrected me and told me another story, which is that the liquor was given its name to connect it to the monks as a marketing ploy. The marketing ploy evidently worked, as a hundred years later people are still telling the same story—and still buying the liqueur. It's a bit of an obscure liqueur that is nonetheless good to have on hand as it's essential in many classic cocktails, including the following.

Vieux Carré

¾ ounce cognac

¾ ounce rye whiskey

¾ ounce sweet vermouth

1 bar spoon Bénédictine

2 dashes of angostura bitters

2 dashes of Peychaud's bitters

Build the cocktail in a double old fashioned glass filled with ice and stir until the glass is cold. Garnish with a maraschino cherry.

Singapore Sling

2 ounces soda water

1 ounce gin

1 ounce lime juice (about 1 lime)

1 ounce Bénédictine

1 ounce cherry brandy (not to be confused with Cherry Heering)

Bottom a Tom Collins glass with the soda, then add the cocktail ingredients, fill the glass with ice, and top with 3 dashes of angostura bitters.

Monte Carlo

2 ounces rye whiskey

½ ounce Bénédictine

3 dashes of angostura bitters

Build the cocktail in a double old fashioned glass filled with ice, stir until cold, and finish with a lemon twist.

HOLLAND GIN REBEL

genever and blood orange with licorice and egg white

Many moons ago, when I started as a bartender at Lucques, I made a cocktail called the Rittenhouse Rebel, which was a combination of blood orange juice, licorice, and Rittenhouse rye whiskey, shaken with egg whites until foamy. I loved it. And my customers loved it. But, always wanting to push things further, I decided to see what would happen if I switched out the whiskey for another spirit. So I tried a gin version. It worked beautifully, and today that cocktail is equally popular. Blood oranges are a little more sour than regular oranges, and their juice is a really beautiful magentalike color. They're available only during winter. If you can't find them, use navel oranges instead. To make my original Rittenhouse Rebel, switch out the gin in this recipe for Rittenhouse rye whiskey.

Makes 1 cocktail

GLASS
Port or coupe

COCKTAIL
1½ ounces genever
1 ounce fresh blood orange juice (about ½ orange)
¾ ounce fresh lemon juice (less than 1 lemon)
½ ounce Simple Syrup (page 59)
2 bar spoons (2 teaspoons) Licorice Tincture (page 266)
½ ounce egg white (about ½ egg)

GARNISH
Peychaud's bitters

Combine the cocktail ingredients in the short side of a Boston shaker. Put a tall shaker tin on top, flip the shaker around so the tall tin is on the bottom, and dry-shake (shake without ice) hard for 7 seconds. Pour the cocktail into the short shaker and fill to the rim with ice cubes. Put the tall tin on top, flip the shaker again so the tall tin is on the bottom, and shake hard a second time for 7 seconds. Using a Hawthorne strainer, strain the cocktail into the short shaker and discard the ice; don't clean the shaker. Put the tall shaker on top, flip so the tall tin is on the bottom, and dry-shake hard one last time for 7 seconds. Use a fine strainer to strain the cocktail into a port glass. Garnish with a few dashes of bitters.

SPRING NEGRONI

gin and strawberries with Campari and sweet vermouth

I have the luxury of being able to get my hands on exceptionally delicious strawberries from a stand at the Los Angeles farmers' markets called Harry's Berries. When I arrive at the stand on Saturday mornings, there is a long line of people waiting to buy their berries even before they open—and the berries aren't cheap. The line remains until the last of the strawberries are sold. I use those berries in a few different ways, including in this cocktail, which is a Negroni (gin, Campari, and sweet vermouth) with the addition of strawberries and other spices. To make the cocktail, you pour the premade Spring Negroni Mix over ice and garnish with a twist. Super easy, so a super choice for a party.

Makes 1 cocktail

GLASS
Double old fashioned

GARNISH
An orange twist

COCKTAIL
3 ounces Spring Negroni Mix (recipe follows)

Rub the outside of the orange twist on the inside rim of a double old fashioned glass. Fill the glass with ice cubes.

Pour the Spring Negroni Mix into the glass. To garnish, squeeze the orange twist over the cocktail to release the oils and drop the twist, shiny side up, on the cocktail.

Spring Negroni Mix

The next time you see a basket of ripe, delicious berries, make a batch as a way to preserve the season. You can buy rose petals, sold as "rose petal tea," at any tea store.

Makes about 28 ounces (3½ cups)

1 cup American gin
1 cup Aperitivo (page 256)
1 cup Sweet Vermouth (page 240)
1 pound strawberries (about 16 medium to large), hulled and chopped
½ cup water
½ teaspoon whole cloves
¼ teaspoon ground ginger
¼ teaspoon dried rose petals
¼ vanilla bean

Combine all the ingredients except the vanilla bean in a medium saucepan. Using a small knife, cut the vanilla bean in half lengthwise, scrape the seeds out of the pod, and add the seeds and pod to the saucepan. Bring to a simmer over medium-high heat; be careful that the flame isn't so high that it can travel around the sides of the pan, as the alcohol in the pan will catch fire. Reduce the heat to medium and simmer gently until the strawberries become whitish in color, about 10 minutes. Turn off the heat and cool to room temperature. Strain the mixture through a chinois or cheesecloth into a bowl, pushing down on the solid ingredients with a ladle or wooden spoon to extract every last drop of flavor from them, and discard the solids. Transfer to a bottle or jar and refrigerate until chilled, about 2 hours, or for up to 1 month.

HONEYBEE

gin and honeydew with basil, orange blossom honey, and bitters

When I was a kid, my parents used to take me and my two younger brothers, Melchior and Dimitri, to the Greek island of Crete during the summer. Today, Crete is a party destination, but back then it was just idyllic. My brothers and I would drink water from streams, pick fruit from trees, and spend long days on the beach. Often, while Melchior and Dimitri were napping on the sand under the watchful eye of our mom, my dad and I would walk into the village and buy fresh watermelons, honeydew melons, peaches, and other summer delicacies. We would take the fruit back to the beach, where we'd all feast on it. This cocktail, with fresh honeydew melon and muddled basil, is for me the taste of those summers in a glass. It's named after my wife, Melissa, because *melissa* means honeybee in Greek. (I also have a honeybee tattooed on my arm. The tattoos on my arms are all references to things very personal to me: my wife, my sons, my country, flowers from my wedding, and so on.)

To make a nonalcoholic beverage, substitute 2 ounces chilled brewed chamomile tea for the gin in this recipe.

Makes 1 cocktail

GLASS
Tom Collins

PREP
1 pound honeydew melon without rind

¼ cup plus 2 tablespoons orange blossom honey or another neutral-flavored honey

2 tablespoons boiling water

COCKTAIL
1 medium or large fresh basil leaf

1½ ounces American gin

1½ ounces fresh honeydew melon juice

¾ ounce fresh lime juice (about ½ lime)

½ ounce liquefied orange blossom honey or another neutral-flavored honey

Crushed ice (see page 29)

GARNISH
Angostura bitters

A fresh basil sprig

To prep for the cocktail, put the honeydew melon in a blender and puree until it's liquefied. You will have approximately 16 ounces juice. The puree will keep, refrigerated, for up to 3 days. Stir the honey and water together until the honey melts in the water and the mixture is one homogenous diluted mixture; the honey will keep in the refrigerator for up to 1 month.

To prepare the cocktail, put the basil leaf in a shaker with 1 ice cube and muddle until they become a slurry. Add the remaining cocktail ingredients except the crushed ice. Fill the shaker with ice cubes, cover, and shake hard for 7 seconds. Fill a Tom Collins glass with crushed ice. Using a Hawthorne strainer, strain the cocktail over the ice. Insert a swizzle stick (or bar spoon) into the glass and rotate between the fingers of two hands to spread the cocktail throughout the glass. To garnish, float a layer of angostura on top of the cocktail and stick the basil sprig in, leaving only the leaves visible.

WHITE BULL

St. George Terroir gin and sage with Cocchi Americano and wheat beer

The name of this drink is a testament to the long, winding road down which cocktail making often takes me. I started with a blood and sand cocktail (¾ ounce blended scotch, ¾ ounce blood orange juice, ¾ ounce sweet vermouth, ¾ ounce Cherry Heering, shaken with ice cubes, strained into a coupe glass, garnished with a cherry), named after a bullfighting film starring Rudolph Valentino. I changed every aspect of the original to get to this drink, but I still had that one in mind, so I wanted to give it a name that referenced bulls. I settled on White Bull because the drink is white from the beer, which becomes a thick white foam when it's shaken. In addition to the beer in this cocktail, I make the syrup for the cocktail from beer instead of water, which makes for a cocktail with more concentrated flavor. Cocchi Americano, an Italian aperitivo heavy on the botanicals (see page 94), provides the dominant flavor. The gin used in this cocktail, St. George Terroir gin, has a piney flavor. You also have the maltiness of the beer, and fresh sage brings another layer of flavor to the drink. The result of this unusual combination is one of my favorite gin cocktails.

Wheat beer is made of malted wheat instead of the usual malted barley. It has a more structured flavor profile than conventional beer. I use it often in cocktails because it doesn't overpower the other ingredients. Some brands I like are Weihenstephaner, Modern Times, Blanche de Bruxelles, and Sierra Nevada kellerweis. I call for a specific gin to be used in this recipe, St. George Terroir gin. I am not normally so specific, but this gin has a distinct Alpine flavor; there truly is no substitute.

Makes 1 cocktail

GLASS
Double old fashioned

COCKTAIL
1 ounce St. George Terroir gin
1 ounce Cocchi Americano (see page 94)
¾ ounce Sage Beer Syrup (page 94)
1 ounce fresh lemon juice (about 1 lemon)
1 ounce wheat beer

GARNISH
2 fresh sage leaves

Combine the cocktail ingredients in the short side of a Boston shaker. Put the tall shaker tin on top, flip the shaker around so the tall tin is on the bottom, and dry-shake (shake without ice) hard for about 7 seconds, until the tins feel like they are pulling apart from the pressure of the CO_2 in the beer expanding. Pour the cocktail into the short shaker and fill to the rim with ice cubes. Put the tall tin on top, flip the shaker again so the tall tin is on the bottom, and shake hard a second time for 7 seconds. Using a Hawthorne strainer, strain the cocktail into the short shaker. Discard the ice, put the tall tin on top, flip so the tall tin is on the bottom, and dry-shake hard one last time for 7 seconds. Fill the glass with ice cubes and fine-strain the cocktail into the glass. Garnish with the fresh sage leaves.

(CONTINUED)

Sage Beer Syrup

For me hefeweizen, or wheat beer, screams summer, hot weather, patios in Amsterdam, living without a care in the world. I created this beautifully fragrant syrup for the White Bull cocktail, because I knew the sage, which pairs well with beer, would also play nicely off the piney flavor of the St. George Terroir gin in that drink.

Makes about 8 ounces (1 cup)

¾ cup wheat beer
¾ cup sugar
4 fresh sage leaves

Combine the beer, sugar, and sage leaves in a small saucepan. Heat the liquid over medium-high heat, stirring to dissolve, about 2 minutes; be careful that the flame isn't so high that it can travel around the sides of the pan, as the alcohol in the pan will catch fire. Turn off the heat and set aside to cool slightly. (If you put ingredients in a blender while they are still very hot, the heat will expand and explode out of the blender.) Transfer the mixture to the jar of a blender and puree until the sage leaves are as small as grains of sand. Strain the liquid through a chinois or fine-mesh strainer and discard the solids. Transfer the syrup to a bottle or jar. It will keep, refrigerated, for up to 1 month.

Cocchi Americano

Cocchi Americano is an Italian aperitivo wine with botanical and citrus flavors. It contains cinchona bark, a source of quinine, which was used to prevent malaria in the nineteenth century. Cocchi Americano became popular among makers of craft cocktails in recent years with the resurgence of hand-built cocktails, when barmen like me became interested in how things used to be made. Cocchi Americano is often compared to the more widely known quinquina (quinine-containing liquors), Kina Lillet. That product was discontinued. (Lillet was introduced to replace it, but that liqueur lacks the distinct bitterness of Cocchi and Kina Lillet.) Kina Lillet was originally used to make a vesper, a classic cocktail featured in James Bond's *Casino Royale*. Today a classic vesper is made of 1½ ounces gin, 1 ounce vodka, and ½ ounce Lillet, but I use Cocchi in place of Lillet, which makes the cocktail closer to the original. You can also use Cocchi as you would Campari, combining it with a splash of soda and an orange wheel to make a simple, refreshing aperitivo. All that being said, Lillet is more widely available than Cocchi and makes an acceptable substitute.

QUIXOTE

gin and grapefruit with Aperol and ginger

The Aperol spritz, a classic cocktail of Italy, has become really popular in the United States in recent years. This is my twist on an Aperol spritz, which is also a riff on the Sancho Panza (page 67), my cocktail named after Don Quixote's side-kick. There's a 1955 drawing of Sancho Panza and Don Quixote by fellow Spaniard Pablo Picasso that I love. I had that image in mind when I gave this cocktail its name.

Makes 1 cocktail

GLASS
Tom Collins

COCKTAIL
1½ ounces London dry gin
1 ounce fresh grapefruit juice (from about ¼ grapefruit, preferably Ruby Red)
1 ounce fresh lemon juice (about 1 lemon)
½ ounce Aperol
½ ounce Honey Ginger Syrup (recipe follows)
Soda water

GARNISH
An orange wheel

Pour all the cocktail ingredients except the soda into a shaker and fill with ice cubes. Cover the shaker and shake hard for 7 seconds. Pour a splash of soda into a Tom Collins glass. To garnish, cut the orange wheel three-quarters of the way through from one edge toward the center and stretch the orange wheel out so it becomes a spiral. Hold it so it hangs down in the glass while you slowly pour the cocktail and ice into the glass and keep holding the orange so it doesn't fall into the cocktail.

Honey Ginger Syrup

Ginger and honey make such a delicious combination. Use leftovers of this syrup to make a penicillin, a famous cocktail invented at the legendary Milk & Honey by New York barman Sam Ross (2 ounces blended scotch, 1 ounce fresh lemon juice, and ¾ ounce of this syrup, shaken with ice cubes and fine-strained into an Islay-coated double old fashioned glass filled with fresh ice, garnished with a lemon twist). This syrup can be used instead of plain honey in a Bee's Knees or Gold Rush.

Makes about 8 ounces (1 cup)

¾ cup orange blossom or another neutral-flavored honey
¼ cup hot water
2 ounces fresh ginger, peeled and roughly chopped

Combine the honey and hot water in a blender and stir until blended. Allow the mixture to cool slightly. (If you add the ginger to the blender while the liquid is hot, the syrup will turn an unappealing shade of brown.) Add the ginger and blend until the ginger is pulverized. Strain through a chinois or mesh strainer and discard the contents of the strainer. Let the syrup cool to room temperature, transfer to a small bottle or jar, and refrigerate for up to 1 month.

BRIXTON SOUR

gin and Peychaud's bitters with Orgeat and egg white

After my first wife died in 2006, at the age of twenty-eight, I was an angry man. I trained in Thai boxing six days a week just to take it all out on the leather bags. I had just started working at Lucques, and in those days a group of us would go out and drink every day. Often we drank like tomorrow was not a guarantee.

One day some guys at the bar started talking to us, pushing buttons, challenging us. We were all a bunch of punk kids not knowing when to stop. At the end of the night I was walking alone to my car, when two guys came up to me and asked: "Hey. Were you the guy talking trash to us in there? Where did your friends go? You're not so tough now, huh?" The first guy came in toward me and lifted his hands to swing, but before he could even throw a punch, I threw a right cross and dropped him. He went out cold, fell unconscious on my chest. I grabbed his head and threw in some knees for insurance. His friend meanwhile was screaming "What did you do? What did you do?" I have to admit, I was a bit scared too. It's an eerie feeling to see someone stop moving after you hit him. I lifted my hands in the air and said, "Sorry I don't want to fight," and walked off.

Driving home that night, the song that was my anthem during those angry days came on, "Guns of Brixton," written by Paul Simonon, sung by the Clash. Years later I was making a gin cocktail and I thought of the phrase "gin drunk," which refers to getting so drunk you get into trouble. I remembered that night and that song.

The drink is a beautiful orange or pink from the bitters, but don't let the color deceive you: this is no cosmopolitan.

Makes 1 cocktail

GLASS
Coupe or Martini

COCKTAIL
1½ ounces London dry gin
¾ ounce Peychaud's bitters
1 ounce fresh lemon juice (about 1 lemon)
¾ ounce Orgeat (page 274) or store-bought
½ ounce egg white (about ½ egg)

Combine the cocktail ingredients in the short side of a Boston shaker. Put a tall shaker tin on top, flip the shaker around so the tall tin is on the bottom, and dry-shake (shake without ice) hard for 7 seconds. Pour the cocktail into the short shaker and fill to the rim with ice cubes. Put the tall tin on top, flip the shaker again so the tall tin is on the bottom, and shake hard a second time for 7 seconds. Using a Hawthorne strainer, strain the cocktail into the short shaker and discard the ice cubes; don't clean the shaker. Put the tall shaker on top, flip so the tall tin is on the bottom, and dry-shake hard one last time for 7 seconds. Use a fine strainer to strain the cocktail into a coupe (or Martini) glass.

McINTOSH

genever and poached apple with pecan and pale ale

When I was growing up in the Netherlands, our neighbors had an enormous apple tree in their backyard, and they shared the tree's apples with the neighborhood. Every fall my brothers and I would pick as many apples as we wanted, and my mother would make applesauce and other treats that would preserve the apples. Today, when I return to the Netherlands in the summer with my own sons, I take them to the petting zoo, which has an apple orchard where my boys can grab the apples off the trees and throw them to the reindeer. It's not quite as idyllic, but at least they get to see how apples grow. To make this juice, I poach the apples before juicing them; cooking apples makes them much sweeter and changes their flavor (think about the flavor of apple pie), and that's what I wanted for this fall-feeling drink. The Pecan Liqueur in this drink takes it into true Thanksgiving/winter holiday territory. Even though the apples and pecans are classic holiday pie ingredients, this isn't by any means a sweet cocktail.

This cocktail is made with pale ale, which has all the notes of an IPA (India pale ale), but it is lighter and less bitter. I look for pale ales made by small producers, such as Craftsman Brewing Company here in Los Angeles (Pasadena, specifically), Eagle Rock, Strand Brewing Company, and the more widely available Sierra Nevada. Choose one that you like or that is produced near where you live.

Makes 1 cocktail

GLASS
Tom Collins

COCKTAIL
1 ounce genever
1 ounce Poached Apple Juice (page 99)
1 ounce fresh lemon juice (about 1 lemon)
¾ ounce Pecan Liqueur (page 248)
1½ ounces pale ale

GARNISH
Three ⅟₁₆-inch slices sweet apple, such as Fuji or Gala

Combine the cocktail ingredients in the short side of a Boston shaker. Put the tall shaker tin on top, flip the shaker around so the tall tin is on the bottom, and dry-shake (shake without ice) hard for about 7 seconds, until the tins feel like they are pulling apart from the pressure of the CO_2 in the beer expanding. Pour the cocktail into the short shaker and fill to the rim with ice cubes. Put the tall tin on top, flip the shaker again so the tall tin is on the bottom, and shake hard a second time for 7 seconds. Using a Hawthorne strainer, strain the cocktail into the short shaker. Discard the ice, put the tall tin on top, flip so the tall tin is on the bottom, and dry-shake hard one last time for 7 seconds. Fill the glass with ice cubes and fine-strain the cocktail into a Tom Collins glass. To garnish, spear the apple slices on a bamboo pick and lay the pick on top of the cocktail.

Poached Apple Juice

I poach the apples before juicing them, which keeps the juice a pretty, clear color, whereas raw apples turn brown when they're juiced. The texture of the juice is thicker than apple juice but thinner than applesauce; this thicker juice adds nice body to the cocktail.

Makes about 10 ounces (1¼ cups)

1 large sweet apple (such as Gala or Fuji), peeled, cored, and cut into ½-inch cubes (about 1¼ cups)

½ cup dry white wine (such as chardonnay), plus more as needed

1 short cinnamon stick

1 dried bay leaf

Combine all the ingredients in a small saucepan and bring to a boil over medium-high heat. Reduce the heat to medium and simmer for 20 minutes; be careful that the flame isn't so high that it can travel around the sides of the pan, as the alcohol in the pan will catch fire. Turn off the heat and set aside for about 5 minutes to cool slightly. Transfer the contents of the saucepan to a blender and puree. (If you put ingredients in a blender while they are still very hot, the heat will expand and explode out of the blender.) Strain the puree through a chinois or cheesecloth and discard the solids. Add more wine if necessary to achieve the consistency of thick, viscous juice. Transfer to a bottle or jar and cool to room temperature. Cover and refrigerate for up to 2 weeks.

HILO

gin and pineapple with Luxardo and bitters

The cool thing about this drink is that I use the bitters as an alcohol ingredient. This gives the cocktail a robust bitterness, which, along with the almost medicinal flavor of the maraschino cherry liqueur, provides the perfect contrast to the sweetness of the pineapple syrup. This is a fruity drink but also feels like a serious cocktail because it is not *too* sweet—and there's a bunch of booze in it. You can replace the gin with tequila, mezcal, or rhum agricole. Hilo is a variety of pineapple. I have to use a more mainstream variety because that's all that is available in California. The Hilo, like living on the beach in Hawaii, is more like a dream.

Makes 1 cocktail

GLASS
Double old fashioned

COCKTAIL
1½ ounces London dry gin
½ ounce Classic Bitters (page 258)
½ ounce Luxardo maraschino cherry liqueur
1 ounce fresh lime juice (about 1 lime)
½ ounce Pineapple Syrup (recipe follows)

GARNISH
An orange twist

Combine the cocktail ingredients in a shaker. Fill the shaker with ice cubes, cover, and shake hard for 7 seconds. Fill a double old fashioned glass with ice cubes and fine-strain the cocktail into the glass. To garnish, squeeze the orange twist over the cocktail to release the oils and drop the twist, shiny side up, on the cocktail.

Pineapple Syrup

Makes about 8 ounces (1 cup)

1 cup fresh pineapple juice (about ½ pineapple)
1 cup sugar

Combine the pineapple juice and sugar in a medium saucepan and heat over medium-high heat, stirring constantly, until the sugar dissolves, about 2 minutes. Remove from the heat and cool to room temperature. Transfer to a bottle or jar. It will keep, refrigerated, for up to 2 weeks.

Batch of Hilos

Makes one 1-liter bottle

GLASS
Double old fashioned

COCKTAILS
12 ounces London dry gin
4 ounces Classic Bitters (page 258)
4 ounces Luxardo maraschino cherry liqueur
8 ounces fresh lime juice (about 8 limes)
4 ounces Pineapple Syrup (above)
3 ounces water
8 orange twists

Combine the cocktail ingredients in a 1-liter bottle. Close the bottle and gently shake to combine. Refrigerate until chilled or for up to 1 week. To serve, pour 4 ounces into each double old fashioned glass filled with ice cubes. Squeeze an orange twist over each cocktail and drop the twist, shiny side up, on the cocktail.

G & G

gin and strawberry liqueur with Galliano L'Autentico and Orange Bitters

G & G stands for the Gaviota strawberries and the Galliano liqueur (see box below) that this is made with. Gaviota is a delicious, intensely flavored variety invented in Oxnard, California, north of Los Angeles, that we buy from Harry's Berries, a stand at the Santa Monica farmers' market. It would be an injustice to compare this cocktail to strawberry lemonade, especially considering the layers of vanilla and anise flavors you get from the Galliano, but it is, essentially, a form of "gin and juice," like the Snoop Dogg song "Gin and Juice."

Cocktail purists would argue that, with the amount of juice this cocktail contains, it is supposed to be shaken, not stirred. According to those cocktail purists, you're supposed to stir a cocktail if it consists strictly of liquor, such as a Negroni, and you can shake a drink only if it contains juice. But I don't want to follow a rule just because somebody made it 100 years ago. Stirring makes for a less diluted drink. (Which is why gin lovers order their Martinis stirred: in order not to dilute the gin, so they can really taste the flavor of the booze.) But this is such an elegant drink that I didn't want to do something so forceful as shaking it. Stick with me, break with tradition, and stir. You'll be fine. And so will your cocktail.

Makes 1 cocktail

GLASS
Coupe or Martini

COCKTAIL
1½ ounces Compound Gin (page 254) or American gin
¾ ounce Strawberry Liqueur (page 251)
1 ounce fresh lemon juice (about 1 lemon)
½ ounce Galliano L'Autentico
4 dashes of Orange Bitters (page 260)

GARNISH
An orange twist

Combine the cocktail ingredients in a mixing glass, fill the glass halfway with ice cubes, and stir with a bar spoon for about 15 seconds, until the glass feels cold. Using a julep (or Hawthorne) strainer, strain the cocktail into a coupe (or Martini) glass. Rub the outside of the orange twist on the inside rim of a coupe glass. Squeeze the orange twist over the cocktail so the oils release into the drink and drop the twist, shiny side up, on the cocktail.

Galliano L'Autentico

Galliano L'Autentico is an Italian liqueur; it comes in a distinctive, tall, steep-shouldered bottle. It has a bright, almost fluorescent yellow color and a sweet vanilla and anise flavor, which, despite the color, is actually really nice. It's not the most popular liqueur on any bar; you'll likely find it on an out-of-reach shelf somewhere collecting dust. Galliano's claim to fame is the Harvey Wallbanger, a famous cocktail from the late 1970s of vodka, orange juice, and Galliano. I'm not a fan of the Harvey Wallbanger, but I do like Galliano and use it in a few cocktails. I pair it with strawberry liqueur in the G & G and cherry liqueur in the Raoul Duke (page 198).

CHRISTIAAN'S G&T

Compound Gin and grapefruit with lemongrass and tonic

In the last several years, the gin and tonic—especially in Spain but also in the Netherlands—has changed from the very simple drink of our parents' generation into something really festive and fun. The "new" G&T is served in a big goblet and garnished with tons of fruit and sometimes whole spices. For a while I resisted serving a fancy G&T at the restaurants. I just didn't feel good about charging cocktail prices for something so basic. But then the wheels started spinning, and I thought, "What if I make my own gin for my G&T? What if I make my own tonic?" Then I started to get excited about it. I can count on one hand the restaurants in Los Angeles serving G&Ts made from house-made gin and house-made tonic: Lucques, A.O.C., and Tavern. Even though it was on the menu, I didn't include it in the book until the very end, when my editor, Melanie Tortoroli, came from New York City to visit me at Lucques. She saw the big goblets of G&Ts flying out of my bar into the dining room and asked me if they were in the book. When I told her they weren't, she insisted that we add it. We had had to cut some recipes, because we ran out of pages in the book, so I didn't know how we were going to have room for this one. As you can see, she made the space.

Calling it Christiaan's G&T was Caroline Styne's idea; I felt a little uncomfortable, but I was also flattered, so I let it go. I'm glad I found a way to include it on the restaurant menus and in the book, because everyone *loves* it—even people who don't like gin and people who don't like tonic. So I guess it's kind of a "gateway" cocktail to gin and tonic. I should have called it The Gateway.

Makes 1 cocktail

GLASS
Burgundy wineglass

COCKTAIL
1 lime wedge
2 ounces Compound Gin (page 254)
1 ounce Tonic Syrup (page 272)
4 ounces soda water
5 juniper berries
5 whole cloves
1 star anise
1 cucumber slice
1 fresh sage leaf
1 fresh bay leaf
½ orange slice

GARNISH
A grapefruit twist

Squeeze the juice of the lime wedge into the bottom of the glass and drop in the lime wedge. Add the remaining ingredients and fill the glass with ice cubes. Squeeze the grapefruit twist on top.

**When I came out of high school,
I went on to university** with the goal of
finding the study that would yield the most
opportunities for me to become wealthy. This
thought, however, was short-lived. After I had
been at university for six months, I saw an ad
in the newspaper that read "Clean young man
wanted to travel with the carnival." This sounded
more exciting to me than school, and in fact it
sounded about as exciting as anything could. I
picked up the phone and called the number in
the ad. I got the job, dropped out of school, and
started traveling as a "carnie." So much for university. I was the only guy on the fair with a high
school diploma.

Being a carnie turned out to provide exactly
the kind of life experience I had been searching
for—adventurous and free. My bosses were a
husband and wife; the husband came from a
real gypsy family, from Romania. The three of
us, plus one other guy, traveled from city to city
throughout the Netherlands. In each city we
would meet up with a bunch of other carnies
that were on their own journey. I stole my first
bicycle, drove a car once that we started with
a screwdriver. There were knife fights and the
more than occasional death threat. I learned
a lot during that time, about trust and about
standing up for what is right and for myself.
One life-altering moment that really sticks
with me was one afternoon in the north of the
Netherlands. We had set up the carnival and
had a rare day off. Some guys from our camp
were going into town, so I decided to join them.
Next thing I knew, there I was, with a bunch
of real badass grown-up carnies sitting in a bar,

far from home. The guys were ordering beer. I
wanted to seem tough, and like one of the guys,
so I decided to order *bacootje*, which translates
as "little Bacardi and Coke." It was one of the
few cocktails you saw in the Netherlands back
then, and even a fairly naive young man like
me would have heard of it. The Coke masked
the flavor of the alcohol, and it was easier for
me to drink than beer, which is why it was my
drink of choice. Throughout that day and into
the night, each time the guys ordered another
beer, I ordered another *bacootje*. I didn't want
to look like a weakling. Suffice to say that that
was the beginning of a long and drunken night.
I got so smashed that I had to call it quits while
they went on drinking. I pretty much crawled
home on my own. I would walk five steps and
then fall down, hammered off my ass, but I
managed to make it back to the trailer. I woke
up the next morning on the floor of our carnie
trailer. One of the guys walked in with stitches
all over his face from his chin to his forehead;
he told me he had been stabbed in the face
with a broken beer bottle. That night definitely
marked the loss of my drinking innocence, and
for many years this is just what I thought a rum
night looked like.

The rum that I drank that night, and that is
behind most of our collective memories of rum,
comes from the Caribbean and the northern
part of South America, but in fact, rum, which
is made from sugarcane, is produced all over the
world, from the Caribbean to Germany, Spain,
Scotland, and Guyana; nowadays, there are even
awesome artisanal rums and rhum agricoles
being made in the United States.

Americans generally don't think of rum as a sipping beverage. Here rum is most often associated with sweet, fruity cocktails, many of which are likely to come with an umbrella or a wedge of pineapple and a fluorescent cherry sticking out of the top, such as the mai tai, piña colada, and hurricane. But in their countries of origin, many rums, especially aged rums, are enjoyed on their own, neat or on the rocks.

Today, when I use rum in cocktails, I look for a balance that you don't typically think of in rum drinks. Unlike the *bacootjes* of my youth, I try to create drinks that are a little less sweet, and I try to bring out the flavor of the rum. To do this, I use less sugar than one might normally see in rum drinks, and I create my own syrups infused with various herbs and spices to produce cocktails that are less cloying and that offer many layers of flavor and nuance, resulting in cocktails that are more balanced and sophisticated. And that might not leave a young man crawling home alone.

TYPES OF RUM

The rules and regulations around rum production are very inconsistent and loosely interpreted; they are different depending on what nation is producing the spirit. This makes it complicated to divide rum into distinct groups, but for my purposes, in terms of how I look at rum when I am serving and mixing drinks, there are four types of rum: light rum, aged rum, navy-strength Jamaican rum, and, a fourth category that includes rhum agricole and cachaça.

LIGHT RUM is a clear, distilled, barely aged spirit. It has a soft, smooth, sugary palate to it, with occasional hints of vanilla. Light rum is the one you get in a rum and Coke. Standard-issue Bacardi is a light rum. I use light rum in a cocktail

when I don't want the rum to overpower the other flavors. I use Havana Club or SelvaRey light rum when I am infusing it.

Here is the catch: Most light rums have been aged and carbon filtered, leaving a slightly tanned, see-through color. This color is what people refer to when talking about a light rum.

AGED RUM, which is rum that has been aged in oak barrels for three months and up, is one of my favorite spirits. The aging process gives the rum a distinctive amber color and a warm, oaky, vanilla-forward flavor profile similar to bourbon. I use aged rum in cocktails when I want the beautiful wood and vanilla flavor that you get from something that has been aged in oak. I often suggest aged rum as a sipping beverage to those who like bourbon, and aged rum can be used in place of bourbon in recipes if you want a softer undertone, such as in the Kingbird (page 188) or Kentucky Sour (page 183). Aged rum is not what I would call a new thing, but its presence on the American market has been growing, especially in the last 10 years.

SPICED RUM is aged rum to which molasses, spices, and possibly color have been added. When many people think of rum, spiced rum is what they imagine, including brands such as Captain Morgan and Sailor Jerry. Spiced rum is generally inexpensive and low-quality. I use it exclusively for making Eggnog (page 125), where the spices in the rum add to the experience. If you must drink spiced rum, try the El Dorado.

JAMAICAN RUM. After the British Royal Navy invaded Jamaica in 1655, the British Navy gave its sailors a daily shot of domestically produced spirit for its so-called health benefits. The rum was very high in alcohol, and its alcohol content was tested on the ships by whether or not it was flammable; a small amount of the spirit was mixed with gunpowder to form a paste. If the rum was above a certain strength, it would ignite; if it was below that strength, it wouldn't ignite. No matter what you call it, this is a high-octane rum with an unmistakable funk, which comes from what is called *dunder*. Dunder is the liquid left in a boiler after distilling a batch of rum. When making Jamaican rum, the dunder is left in the potstill to add that distinct flavor to the next batch. Jamaican rum comes in both white and aged varieties.

The last type of rum includes **RHUM AGRICOLE** and **CACHAÇA**. These rums are made from sugarcane juice instead of molasses. Ten years ago my customers couldn't seem to wrap their head around the idea of rhum agricole. First, with its flavors of green grass and black olives,

it didn't taste anything like what they expected rum to taste like. And on top of that, they didn't care for the aggressive vegetable funk of rhum agricole. But these days, with the ongoing cocktail revolution happening in the United States and around the world, I am finding that people are more and more open to trying rhum agricole and more likely to like it when they try it. I use it when I am looking for a spirit that will stand up to other bold flavors I am using in a cocktail. The most well-known drink using rhum agricole is ti' punch, which is a simple cocktail popular in the French-speaking Caribbean islands consisting of rhum agricole, lime juice, and cane syrup. It is almost identical to a caipirinha, the national cocktail of Brazil made with cachaça, lime juice, and sugarcane. I enjoy sipping both rhum agricole and, as the Brazilians do, cachaça.

STOCKING YOUR BAR

HAVANA CLUB AÑEJO BLANCO (40% abv) is a one year-aged light rum originally produced in Cuba. Bacardi makes Havana Club rum in Puerto Rico, using the original Cuban recipe. Rum aficionados and bar geeks like me like to debate about which one is better, the original Cuban Havana Club, which is still made there, or the Bacardi-made Havana Club. The truth is that they are almost indistinguishable from one another—and it's a moot point anyway, since, because of sanctions, the Cuban rum is not sold in the United States. No matter where it is produced, Havana Club is white in color because it is filtered through charcoal.

SELVAREY RUM (40% abv). What's not to like? Made by the legendary maestro ronero (rum blender) Francisco "Don Pancho" Fernandez in the Panamanian rainforest, it's a blend of a three-year-old and a five-year-old rum. Pineapple yeast is used in the fermentation process, after which it's distilled in its copper column stills and finally laid to rest in bourbon barrels. The last step is carbon filtration, after which the juice is left with a beautiful vanilla-like winter spice flavor, making it great for sipping as well as cocktails.

EL DORADO 12-YEAR (40% abv) is the rum I would buy if I could stock my bar with only one rum. It is distilled in Guyana, where demerara sugar, the gourmet brown sugar, is produced. It is not as widely available as some other rums, but it's worth seeking out. It carries the beautiful flavors of baking—soft vanilla, fruit, and sweet spices—combined with the woody flavor of the used bourbon barrels in which it is aged. I like this as a sipping rum, but price-wise, you can also use it in cocktails that call for aged rum without breaking the bank.

FLOR DE CAÑA 7-YEAR (40% abv) is a great everyday rum; it has all the flavors you want and expect from aged rum: vanilla, caramel, molasses, leather, and a little bit of oak. It is made by the same distiller as SelvaRey, Francisco "Don Pancho" Fernandez. It is also economical, making it good for sipping and equally useful to keep on hand for mixed cocktails. It's not as sweet as some rums on the market, which I appreciate. I always have this rum on my home bar for mixing cocktails and sipping. You can find this rum at any basic liquor store or grocery store.

SMITH & CROSS (57% abv) is my preferred brand of Jamaican navy-strength rum. The amazing, funky flavor characteristic of Jamaican rum shines in this rum. Sip on it; this is definitely not a rum to do shots with—you'd be falling over if you did! If you use it to make mixed drinks or punch, use cautiously.

ST. GEORGE CALIFORNIA AGRICOLE RUM (40% abv). Years ago, when I started buying liquor for the restaurant, I set up a meeting with my general manager, Matt Duggan, and the distiller for St. George Spirits, Lance Winters. St. George is an artisanal spirit producer based in Alameda, in the San Francisco Bay area. Lance and I started geeking out, talking syrups, liquors, and so on. I was looking for a funky rum, not the average run-of-the-mill stuff, but something special. He looked at me and said, "Hold on. Give me a minute!" He ran out to his car and came back with a prototype bottle and label he had been working on for a new rhum agricole. He gave me a taste, and here was this grassy, black olive, funky-ass flavor, and I fell in love. What I was tasting was this rhum agricole, which is now in production and widely available. I sometimes add half an ounce or an ounce of this to a rum cocktail, and sometimes I make the whole drink with it. There are many spirits that come from the mind of this distiller, but this rhum agricole is one of my favorites.

RHUM J.M AGRICOLE BLANC (40% abv) has a complex flavor, with grassy notes reminiscent of the sugarcane juice from which it is produced, as well as banana and dried fruit. It is not too pricey, and when I am building a cocktail, I am much more excited to add these flavors to the cocktail than to use a plain light rum, which doesn't taste like much of anything.

LEBLON CACHAÇA (40% abv) is one of the fancier cachaça brands; it's made especially for the American market and is probably the easiest to find of the cachaça brands in the United States. Cachaça is a spirit that you don't want to go too cheap with because there are a lot of low-quality cachaça brands out there and you can really taste the difference; pick one that is in the middle price range or above. And don't worry: none of them are terribly expensive. After distillation, the juice for this cachaça is rested for up to six months in cognac barrels, giving it a subtle oaky flavor without overpowering the flavor of the sugarcane. This is the cachaça I use for all cocktails I make containing that spirit, the most popular, of course, being the caipirinha, the national drink of Brazil, as well as a custom cocktail, the Black on Black (page 116), which is a refreshing summer drink that contains blackberry compote and fresh lime juice.

EVENING STORM

rum and pineapple with Calvados and champagne

Several years ago I was behind the stick (barman speak for "behind the bar," referring to the stick, or handle, that you pull to pour draft beer) at A.O.C. during a busy lunch shift. I was winding down, setting up for the night crew, when a woman sat down to chat while she waited for her date, who was using the restroom. We started talking about what I do and what she does. She was a writer. She wrote about food. She was really nice and so excited about everything concerning food. Then the man returned and she went to the restroom. He started telling me more about her, that she was a journalist, published author of five books, contributing editor to the *Wall Street Journal, Elle Decor,* and so on. I would have been intimidated by her credentials, but she had been so friendly before I knew she was this big deal. When she returned, they both decided to have a cocktail with me. At that point she started telling me about her book, a book about southern cuisine, called *Julia Reed's South.* "Do you have cocktails in your book?" I asked. Nope, she didn't. We went on to have a really fun conversation, and by the end Julia had convinced me (or maybe I'd convinced her!) to include a punch recipe—my punch recipe—in her book. During our conversation she'd told me about a friend of hers, a painter, and a particular painting he'd done called *The Evening Storm.* So that is how

this punch came to be and how it got its name. I hope to have the chance someday to drink it on a stormy summer evening, under a covered porch not far from the Mississippi River.

One of the requirements—or requests, I should say—was to use Flor de Caña 7-year, which coincidentally beautifies my back bar. I started with the classic mai tai recipe (1 ounce Martinique rum + 1 ounce aged Jamaican rum + 1 ounce lime juice + ½ ounce orgeat + ½ ounce orange liqueur, shaken and strained over fresh ice) and started adding, subtracting, and building from there.

I got the idea to serve the punch in coffee cups from the New York City–based chef Gabrielle Hamilton, who asked me to serve her recipe for caipirinhas that way when I made them for a party we hosted at Lucques to celebrate her cookbook, *Prune.*

This recipe makes a big batch, because punch is meant as a party cocktail. Heck, it's served in a giant punch bowl. Besides, the way the recipe is constructed, using a lot of fresh fruit and fruit juice and more than the usual number of ingredients, it would be impossible (or at least a big pain) to make just one. Make it for a party. Or have a party just so you can make it.

(CONTINUED)

Makes about 12 servings

GLASSES

Punch glasses, teacups, or small coffee cups

PREP

1 ripe pineapple

PUNCH

1 cup fresh pineapple juice (about ½ pineapple)

1 cup chopped pineapple

1 pint strawberries, hulled and quartered

3 cups aged rum

2 cups champagne (or other dry sparkling wine such as dry prosecco)

1 cup Calvados

¾ cup Velvet Falernum (page 242)

¾ cup Orange Liqueur (page 245)

1½ cups fresh lemon juice (about 12 lemons)

1 cup brewed black tea, at room temperature

1 cup fresh blackberries

1 orange, sliced into thin half-wheels

1 lemon, sliced into thin half-wheels

1 lime, sliced into thin half-wheels

To prep, cut the skin off the pineapple. Cut half of the pineapple into chunks, put them in your juicer, and juice them. Core the remaining pineapple half and cut it into ¾-inch pieces.

To make the punch, pour 1 cup of the pineapple juice into a punchbowl or another large vessel and reserve any remaining pineapple juice for another use. Add the chopped pineapple and the remaining ingredients to the bowl and give them a good stir to combine. Fill the bowl with ice cubes. Ladle the punch into punch glasses, teacups, or small coffee cups.

VAQUERO

rhum agricole and peach with sarsaparilla and maple

I originally designed this cocktail for an article for the *Los Angeles Times*, about St. George Spirits' rum. Peaches, maple and sarsaparilla—I know. It sounds weird. You usually hear about peaches and cream, but I promise, this combination works magically well. I got an idea for using cracked coffee beans mingled in from Coffee Bean & Tea Leaf, of all places; they garnish some of their blended drinks with cracked coffee beans. I was looking for one more addition to perfect this cocktail, which is an unusual combination of rhum agricole, maple syrup, sarsaparilla, and peaches, and those beans came to mind. It turned out to be the perfect pairing. You want to make this with super flavorful, ripe, juicy peaches, so that means summer, when peaches are in season.

When you fine-strain a cocktail, you take out all the texture. For a drink like this where I want to be sure to preserve the flavor of the fruit, I use a Hawthorne strainer. I strain out the ice or other large ingredients but still get all the pulp and flavor of the fruit.

Makes 1 cocktail

GLASS
Double old fashioned

COCKTAIL
3 ounces ripe peach (about ¼ large peach), unpeeled, cut into a few chunks

1½ ounces rhum agricole

1 ounce fresh lemon juice (about 1 lemon)

¾ ounce pure maple syrup

2 bar spoons (2 teaspoons) Sarsaparilla Tincture (page 267)

3 coffee beans, cracked with a mortar and pestle or the bottom of a heavy skillet

Crushed ice (see page 29)

GARNISH
3 thin peach slices

Put the chopped peaches in a shaker and muddle them to a slurry. Add the remaining cocktail ingredients except the ice; cover and dry-shake hard for 7 seconds. Fill a double old fashioned glass over the rim with crushed ice. Use a Hawthorne strainer to strain the cocktail into the glass. Insert a swizzle stick or bar spoon and rotate the stick between the fingers of both hands to help the cocktail move up the ice. Garnish with the peach slices.

BLACK ON BLACK

cachaça and blackberry with orange, vanilla, and amaro

I'm often inspired to create a cocktail by the ingredients and components of dishes I see the cooks working with at the restaurants. For example, one day I was in the walk-in (refrigerator) looking for some vegetables that I needed, when my eye caught a jar labeled "Blackberry Compote." I asked our then pastry chef, Christina Olafsun, about it, and if I could "borrow" some, and of course she said yes. I took the compote to the bar and started playing with it until I came up with this beautiful black and purple cachaça cocktail. This is a fruity, summery drink; think of it as a sort of twist on a margarita. The bright sugarcane notes of cachaça gives it a summery feeling, and blackberries, which have a short season, are also a summertime treat. I coat the rim with a combination of sugar and Himalayan black salt, which has a really intense mineral flavor. You can find black salt in specialty food stores and health food stores.

Makes 1 cocktail

GLASS
Double old fashioned

FOR THE GLASS
1 teaspoon sugar
1 teaspoon black salt
A lime wedge

COCKTAIL
1 ounce cachaça
1 ounce Averna amaro
3 dashes of Classic Bitters (page 258)
1 ounce fresh lime juice (about 1 lime)
¾ ounce Spiced Blackberry Syrup (page 117)

GARNISH
An orange twist

To prep the glass, combine the sugar and salt on a small plate. Rub the lime around the rim of a double old fashioned glass and dip the glass into the sugar-salt to coat the rim; discard the lime. Set the glass aside while you make your cocktail.

Combine the cocktail ingredients in a shaker and fill it with ice cubes. Cover and shake hard for 7 seconds. Fill the prepared glass to the rim with ice cubes. Using a Hawthorne strainer, strain the cocktail into the glass. To garnish, squeeze the orange twist over the cocktail to release the oils and drop the twist, shiny side up, on the cocktail.

Spiced Blackberry Syrup

In Los Angeles we see blackberries almost year-round, even at farmers' markets, but they never taste as good as they do in the summer, when they're plump and sweet, with a lot of blackberry flavor. That's when I make this syrup. Like jam, it lasts for a long time, so you can use this recipe as a way to preserve the delicious flavor of blackberries and enjoy this refreshing fruity cocktail even after summer has passed, like during our hottest days in Los Angeles, September and October. If you feel the urge to use it in other cocktails, you can use the classic cocktail formula to mix this syrup into a cocktail of your invention: 2 ounces spirit (vodka, gin, tequila, or whiskey) + 1 ounce fresh lemon juice + ¾ ounce Spiced Blackberry Syrup. The syrup is also delicious drizzled over ice cream.

Makes 9 ounces (1⅛ cups)

1½ cups blackberries
½ cup fresh orange juice (about 2 oranges)
¼ cup port
¼ cup red wine
½ cup sugar
1 ounce inexpensive brandy
2 fresh thyme sprigs
¼ teaspoon freshly ground black pepper
¼ vanilla bean or ½ teaspoon vanilla extract

Combine all the ingredients except the vanilla bean in a small saucepan. Using a sharp knife, split the vanilla bean down the middle, scrape the seeds out of the pod, and add the beans and pod to the saucepan. Bring the liquid to a boil over medium-high heat; be careful that the flame isn't so high that it can travel around the sides of the pan, as the alcohol in the pan will catch fire. Reduce the heat to medium-low and simmer for 15 minutes. Turn off the heat and set aside to cool to room temperature. Pass the compote through a chinois or cheesecloth and discard the solids. Transfer to a bottle or jar and refrigerate for up to 1 month.

CHARLES E. HIRES

Jamaican rum and root beer with lemon and Aperol

My first experience with root beer was on my son River's first birthday. Melissa and I were living in a little one-bedroom near Sunset Boulevard, in the heart of Hollywood, with strip clubs all around us and a needle exchange program around the corner. It was not the best place to raise a kid, so we got out of there pretty soon after, but that day we were there, sitting around the kitchen table with an eclectic, international group of friends, drinking wine, eating cheese, tasting liquors, and celebrating River. All of us were from different countries. There was a French guy, a Swedish girl, an English girl, along with me, from the Netherlands, and all of us with our American partners. Suddenly Melissa goes to the kitchen and comes back and announces: "Root beer floats!" She was holding a tray of glasses filled with soda and vanilla ice cream that was foaming up and out of the glasses. I was flabbergasted. Why would anyone put ice cream in soda? My fellow Europeans and I all looked at each other and back at the bubbling concoctions. None of us had ever seen such a thing. Unlike many American sodas, root beer didn't make its way to Europe. I tasted my float, and the flavor of root beer was nothing like anything I'd ever tasted before. Now, especially as a barman, I can appreciate all the spices and flavorings it takes to get such an unusual-flavored soda, but it's really a wild thing, tasting it for the first time.

The warm flavors of cinnamon, vanilla, and sarsaparilla in the root beer syrup called for something bright and summery to contrast, so I add lemon and Aperol to this cocktail, which gives it a pretty red hue and makes it into something almost like a tiki cocktail. I feel like this cocktail has one leg in the summer and one leg in the fall. It goes down really easy—I would say *dangerously* easy, since it is made with navy-strength rum, in addition to the alcohol in the Root Beer Syrup. The cocktail is named after Charles E. Hires, the guy who commercially brought root beer to the American market; you have probably seen it as Hires Root Beer.

Makes 1 cocktail

GLASS
Double old fashioned

COCKTAIL
1 ounce aged navy-strength Jamaican rum
1 ounce Aperol
1 ounce fresh lemon juice (about 1 lemon)
¾ ounce Root Beer Syrup (page 120)

GARNISH
An orange wheel

Pour the cocktail ingredients into a shaker. Fill the shaker with ice cubes, cover, and shake hard for 7 seconds. Fill a double old fashioned glass with ice cubes and fine-strain the cocktail over the ice. To garnish, cut the orange wheel three-quarters of the way through from one edge toward the center. Stretch the orange wheel out so it becomes a spiral and lay it on top of the cocktail.

(CONTINUED)

Root Beer Syrup

Commercial root beer syrup has a chemical taste to it, so I make my own. My syrup has a very bold flavor, which stands up to the Jamaican rum in the Charles E. Hires cocktail.

I use shredded licorice to make this; if all you can find are licorice sticks, shred it yourself by smashing the stick two or three times with a meat mallet or the mallet you use for crushing ice. Once the stick is broken up a bit, you can shred it by hand.

Makes about 6 ounces (¾ cup)

1 whole star anise
¼ teaspoon dried lavender
¼ teaspoon ground cinnamon
1½ teaspoons sassafras root
1 teaspoon shredded licorice root
1 teaspoon sarsaparilla (preferably Indian)
¼ teaspoon burdock root powder
1 cup water
Rind of ½ lemon (peeled with a vegetable peeler)
Rind of ½ orange (peeled with a vegetable peeler)
½ cup packed light or dark brown sugar
½ cup granulated sugar
¼ vanilla bean

Put all the ingredients except the vanilla bean in a medium saucepan. Use a sharp knife to split the vanilla lengthwise. Scrape the seeds from the bean and put the seeds and bean in the saucepan. Bring the liquid to a boil over medium-high heat. Reduce the heat to medium-low and simmer for 15 minutes. Turn off the heat and set aside to cool to room temperature. Put the mixture in a blender and give it a quick, 30-second spin. Strain through a chinois or fine-mesh strainer, pushing on the solids with a ladle or wooden spoon to extract as much liquid from them as possible; discard the solids. Transfer to a bottle or jar and refrigerate for up to 1 month.

Batch of Charles E. Hireses

Makes one 1-liter bottle

GLASS
Double old fashioned

COCKTAILS
8 ounces aged navy-strength Jamaican rum
8 ounces Aperol
8 ounces fresh lemon juice (about 8 lemons)
6 ounces Root Beer Syrup (recipe above)
4 ounces filtered water

GARNISH
8 orange wheels

Combine the cocktail ingredients in a 1-liter bottle, cover, and give it a quick shake to combine the ingredients. Refrigerate until the cocktail is chilled, about 2 hours, and for as long as 1 week. Just before serving, remove the bottle from the refrigerator and shake to recombine the ingredients. Pour into double old fashioned glasses filled with ice cubes. To garnish each cocktail, cut an orange wheel three-quarters of the way through from one edge toward the center and stretch the orange wheel out so it becomes a spiral, then lay it on top of the cocktail.

MOCAMBO

aged rum and vermouth with horchata de arroz negro

My wife's grandmother, Grandma G.G., loved to talk to Melissa and me about the golden days in Hollywood, which she lived through. She talked about the bars and restaurants and the people who lived it. She told us about all the glamorous clubs of the 1940s and '50s: the Trocadero, Cio's, and the Mocambo. And then she he talked about moving to Hawaii with legendary cocktail maker Don the Beachcomber. *What!?* Grandma G.G. moved to Hawaii? With a *guy?* And the guy was Don the Beachcomber? Indeed he was a legend, and of course I know all about him. I asked her so many questions about Don the Beachcomber, and she loved going back in time to remember those days. After Grandma G.G. passed in 2016, Melissa and I found postcards and photos of her in all these nightclubs and one of her in Hawaii, standing at Don the Beachcomber's bar, which of course was called Don the Beachcomber. I named this cocktail the Mocambo, but really I was naming it after Grandma G.G.

The idea behind this cocktail was to start with an horchatalike syrup but without the additions of cinnamon, vanilla, and condensed milk. I wanted it to be clean. Once I developed the rice syrup, my natural inclination was to pair it with tequila, since horchata is so popular in Mexico, but the flavor of the rice was so subtle that all I tasted was the tequila. I decided to go with aged rum, which has a subtler flavor. Because the horchata syrup is made from black rice, the drink is a dark, moody color, like a dark, stormy sky. Maybe that's why I see it as a fall or winter drink.

Makes 1 cocktail

GLASS
Double old fashioned

COCKTAIL
2 ounces aged rum
1 ounce fresh lime juice (about 1 lime)
¾ ounce Horchata de Arroz Negro Syrup (page 122)
½ ounce Sweet Vermouth (page 240)

GARNISH
An orange wheel
Berries, such as blackberries and raspberries
A mint sprig

Combine the cocktail ingredients in a shaker and fill with 2 heaping cups of ice cubes. Cover and shake hard for 7 seconds. Dump the cocktail, including the ice, into a double old fashioned glass. To garnish, cut the orange wheel three-quarters of the way through from one edge toward the center. Stretch the orange wheel out so it becomes a spiral and lay it on top of the cocktail. Add skewered berries and a mint sprig.

(CONTINUED)

Horchata de Arroz Negro Syrup

When summer descends on Los Angeles, the days get longer, the sun gets higher in the sky, and our restaurant kitchens are so hot they feel like ovens themselves. At this time the cooks and prep cooks get busy making horchata, a refreshing milky rice drink flavored with cinnamon and vanilla—and a *lot* of sugar—from their native Mexico. There are many variations of horchata, some including walnuts, almonds, and some made with milk or sweetened condensed milk, others made with just the milk extracted from the rice. When I went to make horchata for the first time, I found black rice in the pantry at Lucques. It has an unusual, nutty flavor and turns a beautiful shade of deep purple when cooked. I use black rice to make this horchata syrup. It doesn't have the milky quality or the cinnamon usually identified with horchata, just the clean flavor of rice.

Makes about 9 ounces (1 cup plus 2 tablespoons)

1 cup black rice

1 cup water

2 ounces light rum

1 cup sugar

Combine the rice, water, and rum in a blender and puree until the rice is very fine, like grains of sand. Transfer to a jar, cover, and refrigerate overnight to steep the rice. Remove the puree from the refrigerator, add the sugar, and heat the liquid over high heat, stirring occasionally, until the sugar dissolves, about 2 minutes; watch that the flame isn't so high that it can travel around the sides of the pan, as the alcohol in the pan will catch fire. Also be aware you do not want to cook the rice—as soon as the sugar is dissolved, strain it through a chinois and set aside to cool to room temperature. Be careful—it's burning hot. Pour the cooled syrup into a labeled bottle or jar and close; it will keep, refrigerated, for up to 1 month.

Batch of Mocambos

Makes one 750-ml bottle

GLASS

Double old fashioned

COCKTAILS

11 ounces aged rum

5½ ounces fresh lime juice

4½ ounces Horchata de Arroz Negro Syrup (recipe above)

2¾ ounces Sweet Vermouth (page 240)

2 ounces water

GARNISH

6 orange wheels

Berries, such as blackberries and raspberries

6 mint sprigs

Combine the cocktail ingredients in a 750-ml bottle. Close the bottle and give it a gentle shake to combine the ingredients. Refrigerate the cocktail mix until chilled or for up to 1 week. Just before serving, remove the bottle from the refrigerator and shake to recombine the ingredients. Pour into double old fashioned glasses filled with ice cubes. To garnish each cocktail, cut an orange wheel three-quarters of the way through from one edge toward the center and stretch the orange wheel out so it becomes a spiral and lay it on top of the cocktail. Add skewered berries and a mint sprig.

Pictured: a batch of Mocambos for a party

EGGNOG

rum and cream with vanilla, brandy, ginger, nutmeg, and egg

One year at Christmastime, my wife, Melissa, came home from the grocery store with a jug of eggnog, and I thought, How cool would it be to offer eggnog at the restaurant! The closest thing I ever had in the Netherlands is *advocaat*, some kind of eggnog but minus the cream. Looking back at it, it was really nothing like eggnog. It was all about the American style for me.

After I played around with some ideas, I ended up with this rich, thick, super delicious eggnog. I keep it in flip-top glass bottles behind the bar during holiday season. My customers like it so much that some have bought bottles of it to give to their friends as holiday gifts. Others asked me for the recipe so they could make it and bottle it themselves. Because it has enough alcohol in it, if refrigerated, the eggnog lasts for up to a month, so if you want to put this on your holiday gift-giving list, you can plan ahead.

Makes one 750-ml bottle

GLASSES
Coupe, double old fashioned, or punch

EGGNOG
6 large egg yolks
½ cup plus 2 tablespoons plus 1 teaspoon sugar
2 cups heavy (whipping) cream
1½ cups whole milk
¾ teaspoon freshly grated nutmeg
¾ teaspoon ground ginger
¾ teaspoon ground cinnamon
¾ teaspoon ground cloves
¾ cup spiced rum
⅓ cup inexpensive brandy

GARNISH
A whole star anise

(CONTINUED)

Combine the egg yolks and 2 tablespoons plus 1 teaspoon of sugar in the bowl of a stand mixer. (You can also use a mixing bowl and handheld mixer.) Fit the mixer with the whisk attachment and whip on high speed until the mixture is pale yellow and fluffy and nearly double in size, about 5 minutes. Turn off the mixer.

Combine the cream, milk, and remaining ½ cup sugar in a large saucepan and warm over medium heat, stirring occasionally, until it reaches 180°F on a candy thermometer, about 6 minutes.

Gradually add the whipped egg and sugar mixture to the pot with the hot milk and cream, whisking constantly to prevent the hot milk

from cooking the eggs. Add the spices. Cook over medium heat, stirring constantly with the whisk, until the mixture reaches 180°F and is thick enough to coat the back of a wooden spoon, about 5 minutes. Turn off the heat and set aside to cool to room temperature. Add the rum and brandy and transfer to a 1-liter bottle. You will have a little leftover; transfer it to another bottle or jar. (I think of the small portion as the barman's bonus.) Refrigerate until chilled or for as long as 1 month.

To serve, shake the bottle to recombine the ingredients. Pour the eggnog into a coupe or double old fashioned glass and garnish with a whole star anise.

From top to bottom: Add the cinnamon to the eggnog (recipe on pages 125–26). Grate in the nutmeg. Keep stirring, making sure the spices are evenly distributed.

LEAF AND SPEAR

rum and cilantro with kale, harissa, and jalapeño

When you work for an acclaimed chef as I do, the media is always looking at what you do. This can add pressure, but it's also really fun. For instance, when *Saveur* magazine called to ask me to develop a recipe for them, I was excited like a little boy. I wanted to scream it off the rooftops. But then I still had to come up with the cocktail—and the magazine still had to approve it. When I started brainstorming, I knew that I wanted something that was very L.A. and also reflected A.O.C. I started with green harissa, which is a spice blend that I was introduced to through Suzanne. I turned it into a syrup to use in cocktails. I wanted to add kale to the drink, which I did by making a kale-infused rum. I sent the recipe to *Saveur*. They made it in their test kitchens, and they told me they loved it. This is that recipe. I named the drink for a variety of kale called Leaf and Spear, because my son's name is Leaf. He wasn't born yet, but we already knew that we were having a boy, and we had already decided what we were going to name him. Despite the name, I make this drink with *cavolo nero* or black kale, because we always have it at the restaurant. Use whatever variety of kale you like. This drink is super green and almost opaque, like a healthy juice and a cocktail in one. What could be more L.A.?

Makes 1 cocktail

GLASS
Tom Collins

COCKTAIL
2 ounces Kale-Infused Rum (page 129)
1 ounce fresh lime juice (about 1 lime)
¾ ounce Green Harissa Syrup (page 129)

GARNISH
2 blackberries

Pour the cocktail ingredients into a shaker and fill it with ice cubes. Cover and shake hard for 7 seconds. Fill a Tom Collins glass with ice cubes and use a Hawthorne strainer to strain the cocktail into the glass. To garnish, skewer the blackberries on a bamboo pick and lay it on top of the drink or lay the blackberries directly on the drink.

Kale-Infused Rum

This infused rum is so easy to make: just blend, strain, and that's it. You want to use this within two days of making it, because after that the color turns from a really vibrant rich and beautiful shade of green to a not very pretty brown color. I make this with *cavolo nero,* a flat-leaf kale variety with blackish-green leaves. It's also called Tuscan kale, black kale, and dinosaur kale. Any variety of kale will work. You can also use this recipe to make kale-infused tequila, gin, or vodka instead of rum and use that infusion to make a different version of the Leaf and Spear.

Makes about 14 ounces (1¾ cups)

2 cups light rum
1 cup packed kale leaves (stems removed and discarded)

Combine the rum and kale in a blender and blend until the kale is pureed. Pass the liquid through a chinois or fine-mesh strainer, using the back of a ladle or wooden spoon to extract as much liquid as possible from the kale. Discard the solids. Transfer the infused rum to a bottle or jar and refrigerate for up to 2 days.

Green Harissa Syrup

This syrup is definitely spicy from jalapeño juice, but in my opinion it adds just the kick you want to the Leaf and Spear.

Makes about 9 ounces (1 cup plus 2 tablespoons)

1 cup sugar
⅔ cup water
1 cup fresh cilantro leaves and stems
½ teaspoon cumin seeds
½ teaspoon caraway seeds
½ cup fresh parsley leaves and stems
1 jalapeño, seeded

Combine the sugar and water in a small saucepan and heat over medium-high heat, stirring occasionally, until the sugar dissolves, about 2 minutes. Reduce the heat to medium-low and simmer for about 15 minutes, stirring occasionally, until the liquid is slightly syrupy. Turn off the heat, let the syrup cool to room temperature, and transfer to a blender. (If you put the ingredients in a blender while they are still very hot, the heat will expand and explode out of the blender.) Add the remaining ingredients and blend until the ingredients are pulverized. Pass the mixture through a chinois or fine-mesh strainer and discard the contents of the chinois or strainer. Transfer to a bottle or jar and refrigerate for up to 1 week, after which both the spicy flavor and the beautiful green color will start to go downhill.

PISTACHIO COLADA

rhum agricole and passion fruit with lime and pistachio

Despite the name, this drink is only vaguely related to a piña colada. It's shaken with ice instead of blended like its namesake, it contains homemade pistachio syrup instead of coconut, and fresh passion fruit replaces the pineapple. But the main difference, which is why this is such an awesome drink, is the addition of lime juice. I know this sounds insignificant, but the piña colada is quite a sweet drink. Still, I call it a "colada" because I felt the festive connotation of that word fit with this drink. Passion fruit is so naturally sweet and flavorful; the first time I tasted it I had a glass of passion fruit juice on vacation in Hawaii. It was kind of an orangey color, and I wasn't sure what to make of it, and when I took a sip I wondered how anything so average looking could taste so good. The rim for this cocktail glass is dressed with pistachios, sugar, and cayenne. It's so festive. I make it in late September and October, when I find passion fruit and pistachios at the farmers' market, so it feels like a late summer vacation in a glass.

Makes 1 cocktail

GLASS
Double old fashioned

FOR THE GLASS
2 teaspoons finely chopped toasted unsalted shelled pistachios (to toast the nuts, see Pistachio Syrup on page 132)

2 teaspoons sugar

¼ teaspoon cayenne

A lime wedge

COCKTAIL
2 ounces rhum agricole

½ passion fruit, flesh scooped out of skin, skin discarded

1 ounce fresh lime juice (about 1 lime)

¾ ounce Pistachio Syrup (page 132)

To prepare the glass, put the pistachios, sugar, and cayenne on a small plate and stir to combine. Rub the rim of a double old fashioned glass with the cut side of the lime and dip the glass into the pistachio-sugar mixture on the plate. If it doesn't stick, rub the rim with a little simple syrup instead of the lime; it's a bit messier but guaranteed. Discard the lime and set the glass aside while you make the cocktail.

Combine the cocktail ingredients in a shaker and fill it with 2 heaping cups of ice cubes. Cover and shake hard for 7 seconds. Dump the cocktail, including the ice, into the prepared glass.

(CONTINUED)

Pictured, left to right: Pistachio Colada and Dr. Common (page 217), both made with Pistachio Syrup (page 132)

Pistachio Syrup

Once I learned how to make orgeat, which starts with toasted almonds, I knew that the sky was the limit and I applied the method for making it to just about every nut (and some seeds, too) that I could find. Turning pistachios into a syrup adds such a concentrated pistachio taste to a cocktail because the liquor—in this case vodka—pulls out more of the flavor from the nuts than water would. When you're toasting the nuts for this recipe, toast extra to use for rimming the glass for the Pistachio Colada.

Makes about 12 ounces (1½ cups)

1 cup shelled unsalted pistachios

¾ cup water

¼ cup inexpensive vodka

1 cup sugar

Adjust the oven racks so one is in the middle position and preheat the oven to 350°F.

Spread the pistachios out on a baking sheet and toast them in the oven until they are golden and fragrant, about 10 minutes. Remove the nuts from the oven and set aside to cool to room temperature.

Combine the pistachios, water, and vodka in a blender and blend until the nuts are broken down into coarse pieces. Transfer to a bottle or jar and refrigerate overnight. Add the sugar and heat over medium-high heat, stirring occasion-ally, until the sugar dissolves. Set aside to cool to room temperature. Strain the nut mixture through a chinois or cheesecloth into a labeled bottle or jar and refrigerate for up to 1 month.

RIOJA LIBRE

rum and cola with orange and red wine

I love Spain, the way that it is a land of hills and mountains, horses and bulls, wine and food, artists and architects, history, and, most important, my favorite "football club," as we call soccer teams in Europe: Barcelona. I remember being a kid and my parents taking my brothers and me to Mallorca. They wanted us to see it all: the beaches and the culture, which of course included a bullfight. It was pretty gory, as you can imagine. I love my memories of that trip and wanted to create a drink that captured that experience, but in an adult way. This Spanish version of a rum and Coke is what I came up with.

Spain has a drink called the *kalimotxo*, which is equal parts red wine and Coke. It is without a doubt the preferred drink of Spanish teenagers. They take a 1½-liter bottle of Coke, pour out half of it, and fill it with cheap red wine. I took that idea, crossed it with a Cuba Libre—which is rum and Coke with a squeeze of lime—and turned it into this cocktail. It's flavorful from the Cola Syrup and orange juice; it's almost like a sangria, especially when you think that some people put Coke in their sangria. I garnish this cocktail with mint and cucumber, which makes for a really fresh and fresh-looking drink.

Makes 1 cocktail

GLASS
Tom Collins

COCKTAIL
1½ ounces light rum
1 ounce fresh lime juice (about 1 lime)
¾ ounce Cola Syrup (page 271)
½ ounce fresh orange juice (about ¼ orange)

GARNISH
½ ounce dry red wine (preferably Spanish)
2 thin cucumber slices
A fresh mint sprig

Combine the cocktail ingredients in a shaker. Fill the shaker with 2 heaping cups of ice cubes, cover, and shake hard for 7 seconds. Dump the cocktail, including the ice, into a Tom Collins glass. To garnish, slowly drizzle red wine to float on top of the drink. Skewer the cucumbers on a bamboo pick and lay it on top of the drink or lay the cucumbers on top of the drink. Stick the mint sprig in the cocktail, leaving only the leaves visible.

SHAOLIN PUNCH

rhum agricole and lime with Lapsang Souchong

Beau du Bois, fellow cocktail man, turned me on to a drink popular in the Caribbean called ti' punch, consisting of rhum agricole, lime, and sugar. The name is short for the French petit punch. Beau and I like to go back and forth on how this beverage was intended to be served, with or without ice. According to Beau, the original was supposedly served at room temperature. For this cocktail, I go the opposite way and serve it over crushed ice, so it's almost like a slushy.

Shaolin monks invented kung fu. The punch in the name of this drink is a reference to punch the beverage, not a punch in the face, but since I'm obsessed with martial arts, I thought it would be fun to use the word both ways. To make my version, I started with petit punch, added a syrup made of smoky black tea, and made a few other twists and turns to create this refreshing reinvention.

Makes 1 cocktail

GLASS
Double old fashioned

COCKTAIL
3 lime wedges
1½ ounces rhum agricole
¾ ounce Lapsang Souchong Syrup (recipe follows)
¾ ounce fresh lime juice (about 1 lime)
Crushed ice (see page 29)

Muddle the lime wedges in a double old fashioned glass until they have released all their juice. Add the rum, syrup, and lime juice and fill the glass with crushed ice so it piles over the rim of the glass.

Lapsang Souchong Syrup

Lapsang Souchong is a Chinese black tea that is dried by smoking it over pine, so it has a really nice toasty, woody flavor that adds another unusual and really delicious element to a cocktail.

Makes about 6 ounces (¾ cup)

2½ tablespoons loose-leaf Lapsang Souchong tea
¾ cup sugar
½ cup water

Combine the tea, sugar, and water in a small saucepan and heat it over medium-high heat, stirring occasionally, to dissolve the sugar, about 2 minutes. Reduce the heat to medium-low and simmer for about 15 minutes, stirring occasionally, until the liquid is slightly syrupy. Turn off the heat. Pass the ingredients through a fine-mesh strainer or cheesecloth and set aside to cool to room temperature. Transfer to a jar or bottle and refrigerate for up to 1 month.

IL LAVORO

aged rum and amaro with strawberry liqueur

I love this cocktail; it's elegant, beautiful, and complete, with great flavor, great aroma, and wonderful texture. I was introduced to Amaro Meletti, the Italian amaro that I use in this drink, by a very well-known Los Angeles bartender, Eric Alperin, during a fundraising dinner we were hosting at Lucques. He was making the drinks for the event and requested this particular brand of amaro, which he had used in a cocktail at Osteria Mozza, a popular L.A. restaurant where he'd been the opening bartender. I had tried many amaro brands over the years, but never Meletti. When I tasted it, I could see why Eric liked it so much; it's a lot softer than many amaro brands and slightly sweeter, so it's easy to drink on its own, and it doesn't overpower the other flavors when you add it to a cocktail like this one.

Makes 1 cocktail

GLASS
Double old fashioned

COCKTAIL
1 ounce aged rum
¾ ounce Strawberry Liqueur (page 251)
¾ ounce Amaro Meletti
1 ounce fresh lime juice (about 1 lime)

GARNISH
An orange twist

Combine the cocktail ingredients in a shaker and fill with ice cubes. Cover and shake hard for 7 seconds. Rub the outside of the orange twist on the inside rim of a double old fashioned glass. Fill the glass with ice cubes and fine-strain the cocktail over the fresh ice. To garnish, squeeze the orange twist over the cocktail to release the oils and drop the twist, shiny side up, on the cocktail.

THAMES STREET

Jamaican rum and ras el hanout with lemon and amontillado

Try this cocktail the next time you want to sip something refreshing on a warm afternoon, instead of, say, a daiquiri. I make it with Smith & Cross rum, but any funky Jamaican rum will do. You'll notice it calls for only one ounce of alcohol; this particular Jamaican rum has a high alcohol content, and trust me: one ounce will do the trick. Amontillado is a variety of medium-colored sherry. It has a slightly sweet, nutty flavor with oaky notes from the barrels in which it is aged. It mellows out the funkiness of the rum and the intense flavors of the North African spice blend ras el hanout.

Makes 1 cocktail

GLASS
Double old fashioned

COCKTAIL
1 ounce aged navy-strength Jamaican rum
1 ounce fresh lemon juice (about 1 lemon)
¾ ounce Ras El Hanout Syrup (page 269)
1 ounce amontillado sherry

GARNISH
A lemon twist

Combine the cocktail ingredients in a mixing glass, fill with ice cubes, and stir with a bar spoon for 10 to 15 seconds, until the glass feels cold. Rub the outside of the lemon twist on the inside rim of a double old fashioned glass. Fill the glass with ice cubes. Use a julep strainer to strain the cocktail into the prepared glass. To garnish, squeeze the lemon twist over the cocktail to release the oils and drop the twist, shiny side up, on the cocktail.

THREE SISTERS

aged rum and pumpkin with ginger, cloves, orange, and pepitas

The first day I served this cocktail at A.O.C., I had tons of people—regulars and new customers—coming in just to taste it. We'd sent out a press release, and the cocktail was written about in many publications all on the same day. Everyone loved it. I made so many that I ran out of the spiced pumpkin mix that is the essence of the drink. It was a nice problem to have.

The name "three sisters" refers to the three crops—corn, beans, and winter squash—that are traditionally grown together in Native American culture. The Spiced Pumpkin Mix that is the base of the cocktail, which is actually made from butternut squash, contains the spices associated with pumpkin pie: ginger, cinnamon, cloves, and nutmeg. The cocktail is balanced with pepita, or pumpkin seed, syrup, so it's like pumpkin two ways. I garnished the drink with fresh sage leaves. With those autumnal flavors, this lovely, fragrant cocktail is the ideal way to start Thanksgiving or any chilly fall dinner.

Makes 1 cocktail

GLASS

Tom Collins

COCKTAIL

2 ounces aged rum

1½ ounces Spiced Pumpkin Mix (recipe follows)

1 ounce fresh lemon juice (about 1 lemon)

¾ ounce Pepita Syrup (page 140)

GARNISH

2 fresh sage leaves

Combine the cocktail ingredients in a shaker and fill with ice cubes. Close and shake hard for 7 seconds. Fill a Tom Collins glass with ice cubes and use a Hawthorne strain to strain the cocktail into the glass. Garnish with the sage leaves.

Spiced Pumpkin Mix

I make this "pumpkin" mix with butternut squash, which has more flavor and is also easier to find year-round than cooking pumpkin (which, yes, is a different variety from the one you use for jack-o'-lanterns at Halloween). It is made with all the sweet spices—ginger, cloves, cinnamon, and nutmeg—that Americans typically put in pumpkin pie, and the mix has the same texture and color as it would if I'd made it with pumpkin. To me pumpkin pie is as much about those spices as the pumpkin itself. Unlike pumpkin pie, this mix is not sweet; it contains no sugar, because the cocktail it's used in is made with pepita syrup. This recipe makes enough for a big batch, but if you try to make less, there isn't enough to blend in your blender.

Makes about 12 ounces (1½ cups)

¾ cup diced peeled butternut squash (about 4½ ounces)

1 cup fresh orange juice (about 4 oranges)

½ teaspoon ground ginger

½ teaspoon ground cloves

½ teaspoon ground cinnamon

½ teaspoon freshly grated nutmeg

½ vanilla bean

(CONTINUED)

Combine all the ingredients except the vanilla bean in a medium saucepan. Using the back of a sharp knife, scrape the vanilla seeds out of the bean and add the seeds and bean to the saucepan. Bring the liquid to a boil over medium-high heat. Reduce the heat to medium and simmer for about 10 minutes, until the squash is tender when pierced with a fork. Turn off the heat, set aside to cool slightly, and transfer the contents of the saucepan to a blender. (If you put the ingredients in a blender while they are still very hot, the heat will expand and explode out of the blender.) Puree to a smooth, creamy texture, a little less thick than a butter.

Transfer the pumpkin mix to a small jar, cover, and refrigerate for up to one week.

Pepita Syrup

Suzanne often uses pepitas in her dishes, but as much as I liked them, I didn't think about using them behind the bar until I was making a pumpkin drink. I was watching the Netflix series *Chef's Table,* with René Redzepi, who was then the chef of the famed Copenhagen restaurant Noma, which at that time was named "best restaurant in the world" by many sources. Redzepi was explaining how he went about creating his dishes by foraging for vegetables around him, which meant that the vegetables all grew near one another and were therefore related to each other in some way. I had that thought in my mind when I was making my Spiced Pumpkin Mix, which gave me the idea to use the mix in combination with pumpkin *seeds*. How much closer could you get to pumpkin! It made total sense; however, I still needed to try it. I made this syrup, and the flavor exceeded my expectations. I tried it together with the Spiced Pumpkin Mix,

and that resulted in one of the most delicious and acclaimed cocktails I have ever made. I start with raw pepitas and toast them, but if you wanted to save a step by starting with toasted pepitas, that works, too.

Makes about 16 ounces (2 cups)

1 cup shelled unsalted pepitas (pumpkin seeds)
1¼ cups water
¼ cup inexpensive vodka
1½ cups sugar

Adjust the oven racks so one is in the middle position and preheat the oven to 350°F.

Spread the pepitas on a baking sheet and toast them for 5 to 7 minutes, until they are golden and fragrant. Remove the seeds from the oven and set aside to come to room temperature.

Combine the pepitas, water, and vodka in a blender and blend until the nuts are coarsely chopped. Transfer the mixture to a container, cover, and refrigerate overnight. Remove from the refrigerator and add the sugar. Heat over medium-high heat, stirring occasionally, until the sugar dissolves, about 2 minutes; be careful that the flame isn't so high that it can travel around the sides of the pan, as the alcohol in the pan will catch fire. Turn off the heat and set aside to cool the syrup to room temperature. Strain the mixture through a chinois or cheesecloth into a labeled bottle or jar and close. It will keep, refrigerated, for up to 1 month.

Pictured: ingredients for Spiced Pumpkin Mix (page 139)

WHITE ELEPHANT

rhum agricole and coconut with cilantro and Thai chile

There's one vendor at the Santa Monica farmers' market that I look forward to visiting every week: Kong. He brings produce from his dad's Thao Farm and is so excited about everything he sells that he gets me equally excited. I walk up and he's like: "Hey, Christiaan! I grew this ginger! You have to try it!" "Hey, Christiaan! I have Thai chiles today! You won't believe them!" "Hey, Christiaan! Are you interested in sugarcane? Check this out!" Armed with fresh ginger and Thai chiles that I'd bought because of Kong's enthusiasm, I came up with this drink.

In Thailand, where I have spent a lot of time traveling, they believe white elephants to be very sacred. They aren't a separate species—they're albino elephants, so they're very rare. They are generally kept by royalty and rulers of nations. If you look at old-school Southeast Asian artwork, they often include depictions of white elephants, all dressed up with jewels and other decorations. Since this drink is white, and has Thai influences, the name White Elephant seemed perfect.

Makes 1 cocktail

GLASS
Tom Collins

COCKTAIL
2 ounces rhum agricole
1½ ounces Thai Coconut Syrup (recipe follows)
1 ounce fresh lime juice (about 1 lime)

GARNISH
A lime wheel

Combine the cocktail ingredients in a shaker and fill with 2 heaping cups of ice cubes. Cover, shake hard for 7 seconds, and dump the cocktail, including the ice, into a Tom Collins glass. To garnish, cut the lime wheel three-quarters of the way through from one edge toward the center. Stretch the lime wheel out so it becomes a spiral and lay it on top of the cocktail.

Thai Coconut Syrup

This delicious syrup combines some of my favorite Asian flavors—coconut, spicy chile, ginger, and cilantro. I intentionally make it only slightly sweet so I can add more coconut flavor to a cocktail without making the drink too sweet.

Makes about 12 ounces (1½ cups)

1 cup well-shaken canned coconut milk
1 cup sugar
1 ounce fresh ginger, peeled and roughly chopped
1 tablespoon fresh cilantro leaves
¼ red Thai chile or chile de árbol

Combine the coconut milk and sugar in a small saucepan and heat it over medium-high heat, stirring occasionally, until the sugar dissolves. Turn off the heat and set aside to cool to room temperature. (If you proceed before the syrup has cooled, the heat will change the color of the syrup from beautiful light green to a not at all pretty brownish green.) Transfer the milk to a blender and add the remaining ingredients. Blend until the ginger, cilantro, and chile are pulverized. Transfer the syrup to a labeled bottle or jar and close; refrigerate for up to 1 month.

RUBIN CARTER

Jamaican rum and pomegranate with orange and passion fruit

Several years ago Suzanne and Caroline were hosting a dinner for the famous New Orleans restaurant Commander's Palace to celebrate that restaurant's latest cookbook. Suzanne and her kitchen were cooking from the book, and of course we wanted to serve cocktails to go with the meal. New Orleans has many classic cocktails, so I had a lot to choose from. I decided to serve three cocktails: a Sazerac using house-made Orange Bitters, a Vieux Carré with house-made Sweet Vermouth and house-made bitters, and a hurricane, which is one of the more famous rum cocktails of all time (after the mai tai and the daiquiri). When you drink a hurricane in New Orleans, you get a very sweet, very strong version in a larger-than-life glass. It'll knock you over, like a hurricane would. This is my version of that favorite, with house-made grenadine and fresh passion fruit in place of passion fruit syrup, which is typically used to make a hurricane. These touches—both of which reduce the sugar content in the cocktail considerably—take the hurricane to a whole new place. Bob Dylan wrote a beautiful song about the real-life "Hurricane" Rubin Carter, a middleweight boxer who was wrongfully convicted of homicide. I decided to name this drink after him. This cocktail can be made individually or as a punch. I give you recipes for both.

I use Smith & Cross rum for this, which has great flavor. But at over 100 proof, it's too strong on its own, so I use half an ounce of Smith & Cross and one and a half ounces of Havana Club, a light rum. If you don't want to buy two rums, just use two ounces of the Havana Club or your choice of light rum. Whatever you do, don't use two ounces of the Smith & Cross. It'll knock you out. No, really. The idea when making any cocktail is to combine flavors that work together in a glass, so that the resulting cocktail is pretty, delicious, and enjoyable. It is not to get someone hammered.

Makes 1 cocktail

GLASS
Pilsner

COCKTAIL
½ passion fruit, flesh scooped out of skin, skin discarded
1½ ounces light rum
½ ounce navy-strength Jamaican rum
1 ounce fresh lime juice (about 1 lime)
1 ounce fresh orange juice (about ½ orange)
¾ ounce Grenadine (page 145)

Combine the cocktail ingredients in a shaker. Fill the shaker with ice cubes, cover, and shake hard for 7 seconds. Fill a Pilsner glass with ice cubes and use a Hawthorne strainer to strain the cocktail into the glass.

Grenadine

Makes about 12 ounces (1½ cups)

1 cup sugar

1 cup pomegranate juice

Rind of ¼ medium orange (peeled with a vegetable peeler)

⅛ teaspoon dried lavender

One 1–inch segment of a vanilla bean

Combine the sugar, pomegranate juice, orange rind, and lavender in a medium saucepan. Use a paring knife to split the vanilla bean down the middle. Scrape out the seeds and throw the beans and seeds into the saucepan. Heat over medium-high heat, stirring occasionally, until the sugar dissolves, about 2 minutes. Turn off the heat and let the syrup cool to room temperature. Strain it through a chinois or cheesecloth and discard the solids. Transfer the grenadine to a labeled bottle or jar and close; it will keep, refrigerated, for up to 3 months.

Batch of Rubin Carters

Punch is a great thing to make in a big batch because of the number of ingredients involved. When I make a batch of Rubin Carters, I add brewed tea and red wine, which I don't do in the single cocktail because there is simply not enough room in the glass.

Makes 12 servings

GLASS
Punch glasses or small coffee cups

COCKTAILS
4 passion fruit

1½ cups fresh orange juice (about 6 oranges)

2 cups light rum

½ cup aged navy-strength Jamaican rum

1 cup fresh lime juice (about 8 limes)

1 cup cold brewed rooibos tea

1 cup dry red wine (such as pinot noir or merlot)

½ cup Grenadine (recipe above)

½ cup Luxardo maraschino cherry liqueur

¼ cup Orange Liqueur (page 245)

1 cup hulled, sliced strawberries

1 cup sliced peach, unpeeled

Cut the passion fruit open, scoop out the flesh, and put it in a small bowl, discarding the skins. Add half of the orange juice and whisk until the seeds are released from the flesh.

Combine the remaining ingredients except the strawberries and peach in a punch bowl or another large serving bowl. Add the passion fruit mixture and stir to combine. Add the sliced strawberries and peach. Ladle the punch into punch glasses or small coffee cups.

When I was growing up in the Netherlands, there were not a whole lot of choices when it came to tequila. You could find either Cuervo or Sauza, and margaritas were made with a shitty, bright green sour mix. So we did the only thing a bunch of rowdy young guys wanting to drink tequila could do. We drank Tequila Slammers, which is equal parts tequila and 7UP. We would put a coaster on top of the glass, slam it on the bar so it would fizz up, and drink it down before it all spilled out of the glass. When I moved to the States, all too often tequila meant trouble for me, the end of the line on many nights—the kind of nights you don't remember or don't want to remember. By the time I started working behind the bar, I hadn't touched tequila in years. When I was reintroduced to tequila as a barman, I was excited to see how much it and its reputation had changed. Tequila had grown up. And so had I.

Tequila is a distilled juice made from the agave plant. The first tequila was produced in the sixteenth century on the outskirts of Tequila, a city near Guadalajara. Before tequila, there was *pulque*, an indigenous beverage made from fermented agave. Tequila was invented after the Spanish conquistadores applied their distillation methods to the fermented beverage.

Technically, tequila is a type of mezcal. The difference between tequila and mezcal is that tequila is made exclusively from blue agave, whereas mezcal can be made from any of the nearly forty varieties of agave. Tequila also has protected designation of origin status, which means that true tequila can be produced only in particular regions, including the state of Jalisco, where 95 percent of tequila is made, and a few other areas in the surrounding states of Tamaulipas, Michoacán, Nayarit, and Guanajuato.

The production process between the two is also different. To make both spirits, first, the inside core, or *piña*, of the agave plant is harvested. There is one piña per agave plant, and each piña yields about four bottles of tequila. Mezcaleros often work with wild agave, which are a lot smaller and therefore yield a lot less, which is why mezcal can tend to have a high price tag. For tequila, the *piña* is baked in brick *hornos*, or ovens. For mezcal, the *piña* is roasted in below-ground clay mesquite-burning ovens, which imparts a smoky flavor, similar to that in scotch, that is unique to mezcal. In both cases, once cooked, the agave is shredded and then fermented. Finally, the fermented juice is distilled.

Not until I started buying liquor for the restaurants did I become aware of the enormous variety of agave-made spirits. Of course, there is the stuff that's made for big markets throughout the world, where the agave is cooked in an autoclave—a heated, vacuum, microwave oven type of thing—which imparts a faint chemical flavor. You know those brands. But there are many small producers of tequila and mezcal, which even today are still made as they have been for centuries, by hand, using primitive tools and age-old techniques, where the agave is still crushed by a *tahona,* a stone that is pulled by a donkey.

Traditionally, in Mexico, tequila and mezcal are both sipping beverages, enjoyed "neat" (no ice, no other ingredients). But outside of Mexico, tequila and mezcal are often served with lime or salt. Traditional cocktails made with tequila are few and far between. There's the margarita, of course, the bloody Maria, the tequila sunrise, and Mexican coffee. Since tequila wasn't born out of a cocktail culture, classic tequila drinks are riffs on cocktails traditionally made with other spirits, such as the bloody Maria (a bloody Mary made with tequila instead of vodka), Oaxaca old fashioned (mezcal instead of whiskey), and Jalisco mule (a Moscow mule with tequila). I love the flavors of tequila and mezcal, so I approach cocktails made with these spirits with the mindset that I want the flavor of the spirits to shine through. So my agave cocktails are not, by and large, sweet and fruity. They are sophisticated and nuanced, and, in my opinion, destined to become classics.

TYPES OF TEQUILA

Tequila is divided into three aging categories, tequila blanco, reposado, and tequila añejo. Blanco is the original, where aged tequilas are an attempt to be contemporary, or to "upgrade." They are made by applying techniques usually applied to other spirits, such as brandy or rum, to tequila. Although aged tequila is not as authentic, it is delicious, and it still has its place on the bar.

TEQUILA BLANCO (white) or *plata* (silver) is clear tequila, fresh from the still, aged no more than two months. A blanco never lies; you can taste the true essence of the agave, the pure, unadulterated spirit. I love tequila blanco for this reason, both as a sipping spirit and for mixing in cocktails. It is the original tequila.

REPOSADO, which means "rested," is tequila that has been aged between two months and one year in oak barrels, giving it a faint oaky flavor and light caramel color. Reposado is often aged in used barrels purchased from American whiskey makers, which softens the agave flavor and imparts hints of vanilla to the tequila. I use reposado in cocktails when I don't want the aggressiveness of pure agave that you get in blanco.

TEQUILA AÑEJO, which means "aged tequila," is aged from one to three years in oak barrels, giving it an even woodier flavor than reposado. I use añejo occasionally in cocktails, when I want the oaky flavor that comes from its having been aged it in oak. **Extra-añejo** is a relatively new subcategory of tequila añejo, of tequila that is aged over three years. This is very expensive, and I would never use it in a cocktail; it is meant to be savored, neat, like a fine cognac.

MEZCAL

Where many tequilas are made by large-scale producers in an industrialized way, almost all **mezcal** is made in small villages, according to traditional methods that date back hundreds of years. Mezcal is not for everyone, and that is how the *mezcaleros* (those who make mezcal) want it. They want mezcal to be complex and for the consumer to have to understand it to appreciate and like it. Mezcal is also not cheap and, in fact, by the price tag, you know that most mezcals are sipping spirits. I use mezcal in many cocktails because I love the hint of smoke it brings to the glass. In my recipes, you can substitute tequila for mezcal. If you want to sip mezcal but the taste is just too much for you, cut it with tequila to mellow out the flavor. And if you try mezcal and you find that it just is not your jam, there is no need to feel ashamed. But do try it again in a year (or two or three) to see if your palate has changed. You may begin to appreciate how beautifully complex and wild it tastes; I think you will be glad you tried it again.

STOCKING YOUR BAR

ESPOLÒN BLANCO TEQUILA (40% abv) is the perfect white tequila for the home bar. It is readily available and economical: you can make cocktails with this all day long without breaking the bank or sacrificing taste. The flavor of Espolòn tequila, which is double-distilled, is vegetal, with warm citrus notes; the flavor of the agave really shines through.

DON JULIO (40% abv) is the Johnny Walker Black of tequila, meaning you can wander into a dive bar in the middle of Anytown, USA, and you are likely to find a bottle of Don Julio behind the bar. It's not the most spectacular tequila, but it's totally decent. It is light on the nose with faint citrus notes; it is super easy to drink. Whether you're buying tequila to drink neat or to use in cocktails, I recommend the blanco, reposado, and añejo.

TEQUILA OCHO (40% abv) is the bartenders' tequila. If someone claims this is their favorite tequila, I'm going to guess he or she has the same job I do. One of the cool things about Tequila Ocho is that it is the first to designate the year and the field from which the agave is harvested. The makers believe that, like wine, tequila has a different expression every season depending on the rain, the sun, and the land. The flavor is very agave-forward; it's very vegetal, and it's not for everyone. I like the blanco and the reposado for both sipping and mixing cocktails.

1 2 3 TEQUILA (40% abv). So, I am working at Lucques and in comes a guy, larger than life, riding an old motorcycle, with a beard at least two weeks old, smoking a cigar, and wearing an Indiana Jones hat. His name is David Ravandi. He sat down and introduced himself and then introduced me to his Uno, Dos, Tres tequila: all three are in hand-blown recycled glass bottles with vintage-looking labels. I love them all, but the Uno is my favorite, because I am biased toward blancos. He also makes an extra-añejo that is phenomenal—it maintains the unmistakable flavor of agave but with the added complexity from the wood in which it is aged. What's more: Uno Dos Tres is widely available.

EL SILENCIO MEZCAL (43% abv) is my first-choice mezcal for making cocktails. Brought to the United States by its owner, Fausto Zapata, this is a smooth, smoky mezcal, liked by anyone who is ever going to like mezcal. In developing this mezcal, Zapata's idea was to take the mystique out of mezcal and slowly but surely build a global, affordable brand. In it, you will taste sweet ripe fruit, some banana, and of course the unmistakable flavor of smoked mesquite over which the agave is roasted. Besides its rich flavor profile, it is also economical. What's not to like?

DEL MAGUEY MEZCAL (42% abv) is brought to us by Ron Cooper, who is arguably the most important person in the American mezcal industry. Cooper began importing mezcal made by small manufacturers, and he also included with his sales pitch an education on the product for the barmen he was selling to. He was passionate and knowledgeable about this ancient spirit, and he wanted to share that passion and knowledge with anyone who would listen. Del Maguey is a single-village mezcal, and what's really cool is that, on every bottle, the village where it is made is named. There are fifteen different "expressions" of Del Maguey, ranging from low-priced to very expensive. I think of them all as sipping beverages. It's fun to do "tastings" with various expressions, as they are all awesome in their individual way.

EL JOLGORIO BARRIL MEZCAL (48.2% abv) is my number-one sipping mezcal. It is on the pricier side, so absolutely not for making cocktails. Where the majority of mezcals are made with Espadín, the easiest to find of all the agave varieties, this mezcal is made with an agave variety called Barril, which is a subset of the more common Karwinskii agave. To harvest this specific agave, someone has first to climb a mountain in search of the plants, then return to the plants periodically to find out when the agave is ready to be harvested, harvest it, and bring it down off the mountain to turn it into mezcal. This mezcal has a soft, smoky flavor with light fruit and vegetal qualities. I consider it an honor to be able to serve and drink this mezcal. It is a bit pricey, but it is widely available; reserve it to serve as a sipping beverage.

BEAUMONT

tequila and guava with lime and aquavit

In Hawaii about fifteen years ago I ordered a glass of guava and orange juice for breakfast. I had never tasted guava before, so I didn't know what to expect. The juice came to the table and . . . it was *yellow*! I loved it, but I forgot all about guava after drinking the juice. A couple of years later I was in the kitchen at Lucques and I smelled a sweet, fruity fragrance. I looked around and—you guessed it—guava! I picked one up and bit into it. Man, it tasted so good! Of course, I knew I had to start using it in cocktails. There are many varieties of guava, including Beaumont. Guava is a tropical fruit, and one of the few fruits, besides citrus, that you find in the markets in California in the winter. If you can't find guava, substitute kumquats or strawberries for the guava in this recipe.

Makes 1 cocktail

GLASS
Double old fashioned

COCKTAIL
¼ small to medium guava
2 ounces tequila blanco
1 ounce fresh lime juice (about 1 lime)
1 ounce Aquavit Syrup (page 275)

GARNISH
A fresh rosemary sprig

Muddle the guava in a shaker until it's a slurry. Add the rest of the cocktail ingredients, fill the shaker with ice cubes, and shake hard for 7 seconds. Fill a double old fashioned glass with ice cubes and use the Hawthorne strainer to strain the cocktail into the glass. Garnish with the rosemary sprig.

Batch of Beaumonts

At the restaurant, of course, I make all my cocktails one at a time, but this cocktail also works great made in a big batch. Then when you're ready to serve it, you just pour it over a glass of ice. Because it's so refreshing—and easy to like—it's the perfect cocktail to serve at an outdoor pool party or, say, after a ball game when you invite your team over.

Makes one 1-liter bottle or 8 cocktails

GLASS
Double old fashioned

COCKTAILS
14 ounces tequila blanco
7 ounces Aquavit Syrup (page 275)
7 ounces fresh lime juice (about 7 limes)
2 small to medium guavas, cut into quarters
4 ounces water

GARNISH
Fresh rosemary sprigs

Combine the cocktail ingredients in a blender and blend until the fruit is pureed. Strain the drink through a China cap into a 1-liter bottle. Close the bottle and give it a quick shake to combine the ingredients. Refrigerate for a minimum of 2 hours and up to 1 month. To serve, remove the bottle from the refrigerator and give it a quick shake to recombine the ingredients. Pour it into double old fashioned glasses filled with ice cubes. Garnish each cocktail with a fresh rosemary sprig.

FIRE AND SMOKE

mezcal and blood orange with chile de árbol and licorice

Before we reopened A.O.C. in 2013, I got busy playing with a lot of different cocktail ideas for our debut, and this cocktail was one of my favorite outcomes. I've always liked licorice, but outside my native Holland, where it is very popular, it seemed to be difficult for people to wrap their heads around the idea of licorice in a cocktail. I was sure that once people tried this drink, they'd like it. So in the description, instead of *licorice*, I wrote *sweet wood*, which is a literal translation from the Dutch. I guess it was a good idea, because this cocktail became a big success. It's been written about in so many magazines and blogs that I have never been able to take it off the menu. The original version is made with blood oranges, which are in season only during the winter; I make variations on it throughout the year using other fruits that are in season: orange juice muddled with fresh blackberries; pomegranate juice; or watermelon juice. Try this instead of a margarita the next time you want to serve a tequila-based cocktail. It's really easy to make and just as easy to like. You have to prepare a few different tinctures for this cocktail, but all of them are very simple and fun items to keep in your repertoire for future cocktails.

Makes 1 cocktail

GLASS
Double old fashioned

COCKTAIL
1½ ounces mezcal

1½ ounces fresh blood orange juice (about 1 blood orange)

¾ ounce fresh lime juice (about 1 lime)

½ ounce Simple Syrup (page 59)

1 scant bar spoon (3 dashes or about 1 teaspoon) Chile de Árbol Tincture (page 265)

1 scant bar spoon (3 dashes or about 1 teaspoon) Licorice Tincture (page 266)

GARNISH
An orange twist

Pour the cocktail ingredients into a shaker and fill it with ice cubes. Cover and shake hard for 7 seconds. Fill a double old fashioned glass with ice cubes and use a Hawthorne strainer to strain the cocktail into the glass. To garnish, squeeze the orange twist over the cocktail to release the oils and drop the twist, shiny side up, on the cocktail.

CHUPACABRA

mezcal and pumpkin with maple and tequila

When I invent a new cocktail, the first thing I do is "taste" my bosses on it—restaurant speak for having them taste and give me their feedback on it. Once they approve it, I take a cocktail that uses the same spirit off the menu, and onto the menu goes the new cocktail. The next thing I do is teach the individual bar crews that will be serving that cocktail how to make it. And then I add it to the production schedule. Making one drink for your *jefes* to taste is all fine and dandy, but try prepping enough ingredients so that you are prepared for a busy night where you might have three hundred people passing through the restaurant, and you have to have every possible ingredient ready; this is another thing altogether. And this is where Ignacio Murillo comes in.

Ignacio started at Lucques as a busser. He asked one of the managers if he could sit in on a cheese tasting. They said he could, and he did, and after awhile he knew more about the cheeses we serve than anyone else at the restaurant. Next he asked if he could sit in on the wine tastings, and he did that until he knew the wines better than the waiters. Then he came to me. "Can I learn about liquor from you?" Of course, I told him. Yes. Today, Ignacio is my right-hand man. He is the one responsible for making all the juices, tinctures, and syrups so that I have everything I need at my fingertips to make all the cocktails on my menu. Ignacio knows my cocktails better than anyone else except me. This is his favorite drink.

Many people say there are no seasons in Los Angeles. But as someone who works with food, I can tell you: there are *definitely* seasons. In the summer I work a lot with melons and peaches,

and when fall comes around, I start thinking of fall flavors, like pumpkin. I make this every year around Halloween. It even has a spooky name. *Chupacabra* means "goat sucker" in Spanish. It refers to a legendary blood-sucking cryptid that supposedly sucked the blood of livestock, in particular goats. The sweetness of the spiced pumpkin mix, the sour of the lime, and the smokiness of the mezcal make a really balanced and tasty drink. Make it for your grown-up friends at your next Halloween party. I like the depth of flavor I get from combining tequila and mezcal as it is in this cocktail, but doubling up on one or the other will also result in a delicious drink.

Makes 1 cocktail

GLASS
Double old fashioned

COCKTAIL
¾ ounce tequila blanco
¾ ounce mezcal
1 ounce Spiced Pumpkin Mix (page 139)
1 ounce fresh lime juice (about 1 lime)
¾ ounce pure maple syrup

GARNISH
A fresh rosemary sprig

Combine the cocktail ingredients in a shaker and fill with ice cubes. Cover and shake hard for 7 seconds. Fill a double old fashioned glass with ice cubes and use a Hawthorne strainer to strain the cocktail into the glass. Garnish with the rosemary sprig.

PISTOLERO

mezcal and ginger with honey and chile de árbol

Once, working behind the stick at Tavern, I was asked the age-old question: "Can you make me a spicy margarita?" Typically, if you order a spicy margarita, you get a margarita with jalapeño added. But although a jalapeño adds a lot of flavor, the heat is difficult to control, and often what you end up with tastes so strongly of jalapeño that it should be called a *jalapeño* margarita. When that request came in, I had recently concocted a syrup with honey, ginger, and chile de árbol. I added the syrup to a margarita, and the customer was thrilled. That was the inspiration for this cocktail. Unlike a margarita, I use lemon instead of lime, and I don't salt the rim of the glass.

I named the drink for one of the guys at work, Reuben. Every Sunday we have what is called Sunday Supper at our flagship restaurant, Lucques, where we serve a set menu, including wine pairings. I often create a special cocktail to go with the meal. One Sunday every year, the Sunday Supper has a BBQ theme. The entire staff dresses up in western gear with cowboy hats, boots, western shirts, the whole bit. Reuben—he comes to work, works his ass off, leaves, and goes to his next job. He doesn't come to parties, and he doesn't dress up for events. So here I come, strutting in with my cowboy shirt on, a belt with a big fancy buckle, and cowboy hat. And he goes, "Hola, pistolero!" which means "gunslinger" in Spanish. I thought it was a cool name, so I had to let it live on in a cocktail. With the smokiness, acid, and spice, this is the perfect refreshing drink to serve at a barbecue. The smokiness complements any food coming off a wood-fired grill.

Pictured on page 205.

Makes 1 cocktail

GLASS
Tom Collins

COCKTAIL
2 lemon wedges
2 ounces mezcal
1 ounce fresh lemon juice (about 1 lemon)
¾ ounce Honey Árbol Ginger Syrup (page 159)

GARNISH
A lemon wheel

Squeeze and drop the lemon wedges into a shaker. Add the rest of the cocktail ingredients, fill the shaker to the rim with ice cubes, and shake hard for 7 seconds. Dump the cocktail, including the ice and lemon wedges, into a Tom Collins glass. To garnish, cut the lemon wheel three-quarters of the way through from one edge toward the center. Stretch the lemon wheel out so it becomes a spiral and lay it on top of the cocktail.

Honey Árbol Ginger Syrup

Makes about 8 ounces (1 cup)

¾ cup orange blossom honey

¼ cup boiling water

2 ounces fresh ginger, peeled and roughly chopped (about ½ cup)

½-inch piece of chile de árbol, plus more to taste

Put the honey and water in a blender and stir until the honey dissolves. Add the ginger and chile and blend on high speed until the ginger is pulverized. Strain through a chinois or cheese-cloth and discard the solids. Let the syrup cool to room temperature. Transfer to a small jar or bottle and refrigerate for up to 1 month.

Batch of Pistoleros

This is a great make-ahead cocktail for any time of year. Serve the bottle of cocktails along with glasses, ice, and lemon wheels at your next backyard barbecue or picnic.

Makes one 1-liter bottle

GLASS
Double old fashioned

COCKTAILS
12 ounces mezcal

6 ounces fresh lemon juice (about 6 lemons)

4½ ounces Honey Árbol Ginger Syrup (recipe above)

3 ounces water

2 lemons, each cut into 8 wedges

GARNISH
6 lemon wheels

Combine the cocktail ingredients in a bottle. Close the bottle and give it a gentle shake to combine the ingredients. Refrigerate until the cocktail is chilled, about 2 hours, or as long as 1 week.

To serve, cut the lemon wheels three-quarters of the way through from one edge toward the center. For each cocktail, squeeze and drop 2 lemon wedges into a double old fashioned glass and fill it to the top with ice. Pour 4 ounces of the cocktail mix into the glass. To garnish, cut the lemon wheel three-quarters of the way through from one edge toward the center. Stretch the lemon wheel out so it becomes a spiral and lay it on top of the cocktail.

MONK'S DREAM

tequila and kumquats with Orgeat and Luxardo

I got the name for this drink from one of the first barmen I worked with at Lucques, John McPherson, who had a real gift for the art of naming a cocktail. I would come up with a drink, not knowing what to call it, I'd tell him the ingredients, and five seconds later he would have a couple of options. He got the name for this one from the 1963 jazz album of Thelonious Monk. There is no correlation between the drink and the record, as far as I remember, but the name just seemed right. I mean, fruit and tequila: that's *anyone's* dream.

This recipe calls for kumquats, but you can swap them out for just about any seasonal fruit, including blackberries, passion fruit, strawberries, nectarines, or peaches. You muddle the fruit, which is kind of fun to do, and then it's just a shake and dump kind of cocktail. It's so quick and easy; there's not even any straining involved.

Makes 1 cocktail

GLASS
Double old fashioned

COCKTAIL
2 kumquats, cut into quarters
1½ ounces tequila blanco
½ ounce Luxardo maraschino cherry liqueur
¼ ounce Orgeat (page 274)
1 ounce fresh lime juice (about 1 lime)

Muddle the kumquats in a shaker until they are mushy. Add the rest of the cocktail ingredients. Fill the shaker with 2 heaping cups of ice cubes, cover, and shake hard for 7 seconds. Dump the cocktail, including the ice, into a double old fashioned glass. To garnish, lay some kumquat wedges on top.

Pictured: Monk's Dream made with strawberries (left) and kumquats (right)

MOLOKA'I

tequila and pineapple with blood orange and bitters

I first made this cocktail for Drew Barrymore's fortieth birthday party, which Lucques catered. When I was thinking up the drink, I remembered a movie Drew had made called *50 First Dates*, which was set in Hawaii, so I decided to make a pineapple cocktail with a Hawaiian name and took it from there. This calls for blood oranges, which are in season in the winter, so I think of it as a winter vacation kind of drink. Moloka'i is one of the Hawaiian islands, known for its sugar and pineapple production, the only island that I have never visited. The limes are like a garnish; they're placed at the bottom of the cocktail, like the jewels on the ocean floor that you forget exist until you put your head under the water with a snorkel and mask. If you can't find blood oranges, use fresh Cranberry Juice (page 230) or fresh pomegranate juice instead. It has to be something red, because this drink is built in layers, so it has a beautiful, fiery color. The bitters add a warm fragrance to an otherwise clean, refreshing cocktail.

Makes 1 cocktail

GLASS
Pilsner

COCKTAIL
3 lime wedges
½ ounce blood orange juice
1½ ounces tequila blanco
1 ounce fresh lime juice (about 1 lime)
¾ ounce Pineapple Syrup (page 100)

GARNISH
Angostura bitters
A fresh mint sprig

Toss the lime wedges into the bottom of a Pilsner glass. Add the blood orange juice and set aside. Combine the tequila, lime juice, and pineapple syrup in a shaker and fill it with 2 heaping cups of ice cubes. Cover and shake hard for 7 seconds. Dump the cocktail, including the ice, into the glass with the limes and juice. To garnish, slowly pour the bitters to float in a thin layer on top of the cocktail and finish with the mint sprig.

SHANGRI-LA

mezcal and pomegranate with lime and pale ale

One evening Yifat Oren came in for Sunday Supper with her husband and children. Yifat is the party planner for many of the celebrity weddings and high-end parties for which we do the catering—and of course I do the beverages—and through working together, Yifat has become a friend. That evening, Yifat mentioned that she had some extra pomegranates on her tree in Ojai and asked if I would like some. I told her that I would love some. Her husband and I got to talking about the best ways to take the seeds out to juice them when Yifat interrupted and said, "No, no, no! Just cut them in half, put the halves in a juicer, and that's it." Her husband and I looked at each other, thinking this cannot be true. I'd spent years going through the messy job of picking out the seeds and passing them through a juicer. The next day, after I picked up the pomegranates at her office, I came back to the restaurant and tried it first thing. I cut the pomegranate in half and put the half on the juicer just like you would half an orange, and, *voilà!* It worked perfectly. Out came the beautiful, ruby-red juice, no mess involved. It was a life-changing moment.

This cocktail is made with pale ale, which has all the notes of an IPA (India pale ale), but it is lighter and less bitter. I look for those made by small producers, such as Craftsman Brewing Company here in Los Angeles (Pasadena, specifically), Eagle Rock, Strand Brewing Company, and the more widely available Sierra Nevada Pale Ale. Choose one that you like or that is produced near where you live.

Makes 1 cocktail

GLASS
Coupe

COCKTAIL
1½ ounces mezcal
¾ ounce fresh pomegranate juice
1 ounce fresh lime juice (about 1 lime)
¾ ounce Orgeat (page 274)
1 ounce pale ale

GARNISH
Edible flower, such as nasturtium or Johnny-jump-up

Combine the cocktail ingredients in the short side of a Boston shaker. Put the tall shaker on top, flip it around, and dry-shake (shake without ice) hard for 7 seconds, until the shakers feel like they are pulling apart from the pressure of the CO_2 in the beer expanding. Pour the ingredients into the short shaker, fill it to the rim with ice cubes, and shake hard for 7 seconds. Using a Hawthorne strainer, strain the cocktail again into the short shaker. Discard the ice, close the shaker again, and dry-shake hard one last time for 7 seconds. Fine-strain the cocktail into a coupe glass. Garnish with edible flowers.

THE INITIAL

tequila añejo and Luxardo with lime and Calisaya

I made this cocktail for the first time for a fashion event on Rodeo Drive in Beverly Hills. We've done events for Chanel, Prada, and what seems like just about every fashion house represented on Rodeo Drive, and we always get the same request: the cocktail has to be clear—no red cocktails, no green cocktails—so that if it spills, it doesn't damage the carpet or the clothing. For the same reason, this cocktail works well if you're having a big party indoors, where your guests might be likely to slosh their drinks around. Even though the Luxardo is made from cherries, it's transparent. Calisaya is an uncolored bitters made in Oregon. For another uncolored bitters, you can also use my house-made Aperitivo (page 256). This is a great drink for your party's first drink of the evening. Except for the lime, it's all alcohol, so it's really easy to make, and there is nothing seasonal in this drink, so you can serve it year-round. I made this for a party for Bottega Veneta, whose slogan is "When your initials are enough." Thus the name.

Makes 1 cocktail

GLASS
Double old fashioned

COCKTAIL
1 ounce tequila añejo
¾ ounce Luxardo maraschino cherry liqueur
¾ ounce Calisaya
1 ounce fresh lime juice (about 1 lime)

GARNISH
An orange wheel

Pour the cocktail ingredients into a shaker and fill it with ice cubes. Cover the shaker and shake hard for 7 seconds. Fill a double old fashioned glass with ice cubes and fine-strain the cocktail into the glass. To garnish, cut the orange wheel three-quarters of the way through from one edge toward the center. Stretch the wheel out so it becomes a spiral and lay it on top of the cocktail.

TRES GARANTIAS

mezcal with Punt e Mes and absinthe

I developed this cocktail recipe for El Silencio Mezcal. The company was hosting a party at A.O.C. to celebrate a new mezcal production and asked me to come up with four different drinks using its mezcal to accompany the meal. I made one shaken, one stirred, one foamy (shaken with egg whites), and this stirred, boozy, thank-you-for-coming cocktail to finish off the evening.

Since this cocktail is all alcohol—no juice or syrup involved—it's very easy to make. Tres Garantias, or "Three Guarantees," was the name of the Mexican army whose purpose was to defend religion, independence, and unity (the three guarantees) after Mexico gained its independence from Spain. There are *no* guarantees when you introduce a new cocktail, especially one as boldly flavored as this one, which combines the smoky flavor of the mezcal, the aggressive, licorice-like flavor of absinthe, and the slightly sweet, slightly bitter taste of the Italian liqueur Punt e Mes. Granted, nobody really says no to free alcohol at a party, but empty glasses are still a sign of a successful cocktail, and that's what I saw after serving these. If you're planning ahead, you can mix the three liqueurs together, bottle it, and keep it on your bar. Then just pour and stir each cocktail in 3½-ounce pours as you want them.

Makes 1 cocktail

GLASS
Coupe

GARNISH
A lemon twist

COCKTAIL
1½ ounces mezcal
1 ounce Punt e Mes (see box below)
½ ounce absinthe

Rub the outside of the lemon twist on the inside rim of a coupe glass. Set the glass and twist aside while you prepare the cocktail.

Combine the cocktail ingredients in a mixing glass, fill with ice cubes, and stir with a bar spoon until the glass is cold, 10 to 15 seconds. Using a julep strainer, strain the drink into the prepared glass. To garnish, squeeze the lemon twist over the cocktail to release the oils and drop the twist, shiny side up, on the cocktail.

Punt e Mes

Punt e Mes, an Italian liqueur, is like a cross between sweet vermouth and Campari. It translates to "point and a half" in the Piedmont dialect and is so named because the makers considered the flavor to be one point of sweetness and half a point of bitterness. If you can't find it, substitute sweet vermouth. If you do invest in a bottle—which of course I think you should!—try it in place of sweet vermouth the next time you make a Negroni or Manhattan to add an extra kick of bitterness and body to those classics.

XOLITO

tequila and grapefruit with sweet vermouth and cherry

When I was a kid, I loved making breakfast in bed for my folks on weekend and summer mornings. It was my secret way of getting them out of bed so we could start the day and have some fun. I made a full spread, with buttermilk, coffee, eggs, toast, and chocolate sprinkles (believe it or not, they're a very Dutch thing) and a "rusk" of butter mixed with grapefruit marmalade to smear on toast. I never really cared much for the rusk: I mean, when you're a little kid, the thinking is: Why smear marmalade on your toast when you can top it with chocolate sprinkles instead? But as I grew older, my taste buds changed. (I've read that our taste buds change every five years.) I grew fond of marmalade, grapefruit marmalade in particular. I make my own grapefruit marmalade, which I stir into this drink instead of fruit juice. The grapefruit flavor is really intense and refreshing.

This cocktail is a cross between a blood and sand and a greyhound, which is vodka and grapefruit juice. I wanted the cocktail to have the name of a dog because of the greyhound connection, but I wanted it to be an unusual breed of dog because of the unusual mix of ingredients in the drink. A xolito is more commonly known as a Mexican hairless dog; it was just the right dog for this cocktail.

Makes 1 cocktail

GLASS
Double old fashioned

COCKTAIL
1½ ounces tequila blanco
2 bar spoons (2 teaspoons) Grapefruit Marmalade (page 169)
¾ ounce Cherry Liqueur (page 252)
¾ ounce Sweet Vermouth (page 240)
1 ounce fresh lemon juice (about 1 lemon)

GARNISH
4 or 5 strands of grapefruit rind from the marmalade

Combine the cocktail ingredients in a shaker and fill with 2 heaping cups of ice cubes. Cover the shaker and shake hard for 7 seconds. Dump the cocktail, including the ice, into a double old fashioned glass. To garnish, lay the grapefruit strands on the cocktail, some sticking up, some lying down, like the ruff of a lion.

Grapefruit Marmalade

I use Ruby Red grapefruits to make this marmalade. I love their rosy champagne color, they're easy to find, and they have nice flavor. The leftover marmalade is great spooned on toast, vanilla ice cream, or plain Greek yogurt. And of course, if you do not feel inspired to make this, you can totally buy it in the store, but it will not have the beautiful strands of grapefruit peel you get when you make it yourself.

Makes about 1½ cups

3 grapefruit (preferably Ruby Red)
½ cup water
2 cups sugar
½ cup fresh lemon juice (about 4 lemons)

Peel the grapefruit with a vegetable peeler. Thinly slice the rinds lengthwise. Juice the grapefruit and measure out 1 cup for the marmalade. Reserve the rest for another use.

Combine the rinds, grapefruit juice, and water in a small saucepan and bring to a boil over medium-high heat. Reduce the heat to medium-low and simmer for 5 minutes to soften the rind strips. Add the sugar and lemon juice and simmer for 30 minutes, until the liquid is thick and jammy. Turn off the heat and let the marmalade cool to room temperature. Transfer to a jar and refrigerate for up to 2 months.

MOSCOW MARGARITA (AKA DANIELEWSKI)

tequila and roasted beets with lime and ras el hanout

Mark Z. Danielewski, arguably one of the most important novelists of his generation, has been a regular at Lucques for years, but more important, a regular at my bar for years. He comes in wearing his hipster hat, a scruffy, way-more-than-five-o'clock beard, and often a T-shirt with a cat print on it. He sits at the bar in a seat that many regulars like, where the light just misses you and the shadow gives you an easy hug. You can see all the restaurant from this spot: couples and parties coming in and going out, people holding hands, breaking up, living life. You see the host being friendly, while overhearing the barman's conversation with the next customer. "What can I get you tonight? Something to eat, something to drink, or both?" In this corner, Mark starts most nights with his cocktail, then a bold glass of wine. He orders and eats his steak frites, no French fries, extra salad. We talk about Muay Thai and tai chi, about girls, writers, novels, and movies. When no one is around, politics and religion are thrown into the conversation mix as well.

One day Mark comes to me and says, "Christiaan, I want to have my birthday party here at the bar. I would love it if everyone has the same experience that I have here with you." Of course it was flattering, but it wasn't something we had done before. "Mark, we love you a lot, but we do first-come, first-served at the bar. I can always ask, though." (Never say no.) What I didn't know then, but I know now, is that he had a lot of pull in the restaurant. When I asked my manager, the answer was yes.

The plan was that Mark would rent out all ten seats at the Lucques bar, treat everyone to dinner, and then have more friends come for drinks. He asked me to make a celebratory cocktail for the party, with tequila. With any tequila-based drink, it's really easy to fall back on the formula for a margarita: tequila, lime, sweetness, and some twist. But I wanted this one to be special, and somehow I got the idea to add roasted beet to the mix. I remember going to the sous chef at the time, Jason Kim, and asking him, "Can you show me how to roast beets?" He did. I added it to the drink. And it turned out to be a winner. When I served this almost fluorescent red-purple drink, other customers at the restaurant started asking: "What is that?" "Can I have one of those?" It's been in regular rotation on the menu ever since.

Russia is the world's largest producer of beets, which is how this drink got its name. One medium beet makes enough for eight cocktails. If you find store-bought roasted beets, you can totally use them, as long as they are not seasoned with anything more than salt and pepper. I know that it's a lot to have your oven on for just one beet. You can also roast the whole bunch and turn the rest into a salad, with a simple olive oil and vinegar dressing with ras el hanout added. It would be a great thing to serve after your Moscow Margaritas.

(CONTINUED)

GLASS

Double old fashioned

COCKTAIL

½ ounce Roasted Beet (about ⅛ medium beet; recipe follows), cooled to room temperature

2 ounces tequila blanco

1 ounce fresh lime juice (about 1 lime)

¾ ounce Ras el Hanout Syrup (page 269)

GARNISH

A lime wheel

Muddle the beet in a short shaker with 1 ice cube until it becomes a slurry. Add the rest of the cocktail ingredients. Fill the shaker with ice cubes, cover, and shake hard for about 7 seconds. Fill a double old fashioned glass with ice cubes and use a Hawthorne strainer to strain the cocktail into the glass. To garnish, cut the lime wheel three-quarters of the way through from one edge toward the center. Stretch the lime wheel out so it becomes a spiral and lay it on top of the cocktail.

Roasted Beet

The cooks at Lucques make huge baking sheets full of beets at a time. I don't need that many, so I put the beets in a small *cazuela,* a Spanish word for "baking dish," which is the word the guys in the kitchen, and thus I also, use. With this recipe, I was also introduced to the term *fork tender.* I mix drinks for a living; I had never heard that term before, but that's when you know the beets are done: when they're fork tender. If you are roasting an entire bunch of beets, add extra olive oil, salt, and pepper and make sure to use a baking dish or baking sheet large enough to fit the beets in a single layer; everything else about the recipe is the same.

Makes 1 beet

1 medium beet (about 5 ounces)

1 tablespoon extra virgin olive oil

⅛ teaspoon kosher salt

A generous amount of freshly ground black pepper

3 tablespoons water

Adjust the oven racks so one is in the middle position and preheat the oven to 350°F.

Put the beet in a small *cazuela*, or baking dish, and toss with the olive oil, salt, and pepper. Pour the water into the bottom of the pan and cover with aluminum foil. Bake until the beet is fork tender, about 45 minutes. Remove the beet from the oven and set aside to room temperature. Slip the skin off and discard it. Chop the beet to use in multiple cocktails.

PEACH FEVER

tequila with tonic, Bénédictine, lime, and peach

When I make a cocktail, I start with the one or two ingredients I want to work with—in this case yellow peaches and tonic—and then I add one more ingredient at a time until I get to a cocktail that really works. After muddling some peach and adding some tonic, I thought tequila would go nicely with the peaches, so I added that, and I was right. Tequila goes well with lime, so I added a bit of lime juice. At that point, it was a good drink. But I wanted a *great* drink. I felt like the cocktail could use another layer of flavor, and the Bénédictine turned out to be just the thing. Tonic was originally used to fight malaria, and since malaria is often associated with fever, I couldn't resist calling my drink Peach Fever.

I make this in the summer, inspired by the super delicious stone fruit grown by a young farmer named Steven Murray. Steve is an amazing guy—speaks multiple languages and spends the majority of his time traveling the world in search of seeds. I am the lucky recipient of his discoveries. His farm in Bakersfield, California, grows and sells every kind of stone fruit imaginable, but for this I use good old-fashioned peaches. Search out the best peaches you can find in your area, and make this only in the summer, when peaches are in season.

Makes 1 cocktail

GLASS
Tom Collins

COCKTAIL
1½ ounces ripe peach, unpeeled (about ¼ small peach)
1½ ounces tequila blanco
¾ ounce Tonic Syrup (page 272)
¾ ounce Bénédictine (see page 86)
1 ounce fresh lime juice (about 1 lime)

GARNISH
3 thin peach slices

Muddle the peach in a short shaker until it becomes a slurry. Add the rest of the cocktail ingredients. Fill the shaker with ice cubes to the rim, cover, and shake hard for 7 seconds. Fill a Tom Collins glass with ice cubes. Using a Hawthorne strainer, strain the cocktail over the ice. To garnish, fan the peach slices out on top of the drink.

CA SOUR

Opuntia and poached pear with Velvet Falernum and Red Wine Bitters

A sour is a cocktail formula that consists of sweet, sour, and spirit. Pisco and whiskey sours are the most common. To make this California sour, I use a prickly pear spirit called Opuntia. Prickly pear is a cactus that grows all over the deserts of southern California. I pair it with pear juice in this cocktail as a kind of play on words. I put this cocktail in the tequila section even though Opuntia is technically a brandy because it is made from the *fruit* of the cactus, not the cactus. And, of course, if you cannot find this, use tequila blanco instead. The Red Wine Bitters floated on the cocktail creates a beautiful red layer on top, so it looks like the colors of a southern California sunset.

Makes 1 cocktail

GLASS
Double old fashioned

COCKTAIL
1½ ounces Opuntia
1 ounce Poached Pear Juice (recipe follows)
¾ ounce fresh lime juice (less than 1 lime)
½ ounce Velvet Falernum (page 242)

GARNISH
Red Wine Bitters (page 262)

Combine the cocktail ingredients in a shaker and fill it with ice cubes. Cover and shake hard for 7 seconds. Fill a double old fashioned glass with crushed ice cubes and, using a Hawthorne strainer, strain the cocktail into the glass. To garnish, slowly pour the bitters to float on top of the cocktail (you will use about 2 bar spoons or 2 teaspoons).

Poached Pear Juice

Pears are available year-round, but they have almost no flavor unless they are in season, which is during the fall. I poach the pears before juicing them, which draws out their flavor and also prevents the juice from turning brown.

Makes about 16 ounces (2 cups)

½ pound soft ripe pears (preferably Bartlett), cored and chopped (about 1½ cups)
1 cup dry white wine (such as chardonnay)
¼ cup sugar
2 short cinnamon sticks
2 dried bay leaves

Put all the ingredients in a saucepan and bring the liquid to a boil over medium-high heat. Reduce the heat to low and simmer for 15 minutes, until the pears are tender. Turn off the heat and let the mixture cool for 10 minutes. Remove and discard the cinnamon sticks and bay leaves. Transfer the remaining ingredients to a blender and puree. (If you put ingredients in a blender while they are still very hot, the heat will expand and explode out of the blender.) Strain the puree through a chinois or cheesecloth and discard the solids. Transfer the puree to a labeled bottle or jar and close; it will keep, refrigerated, for up to 2 weeks.

Let's say that you, the Home Barman, want to start a whiskey company, and you come to me. Let's pretend I am the Money Guy.

Home Barman: "Christiaan, I have a great idea. I want to start a whiskey company. I heard there is a high demand, and I think I can make something really nice."

Money Guy: "Dear Reader, I love whiskey. Let's get into business. How much money do you need? But more important: When do you think I can get my money back? Because I love whiskey. But I love my money more."

Home Barman: "Oh. No worries. We will ferment it. Distill it. And put it in barrels for, say, four years, maybe six, after which we will bottle it and bring it to market. So maybe seven years?"

Money Guy: "Dear Home Barman: Like I said, I love whiskey. But I love my money more. I don't want to wait seven years to see my money again. Maybe we should think about a vodka project instead."

I tell you this little story to show you how and why there is a shortage of American whiskey right now.

About ten years ago, maybe fifteen, American spirit lovers around the world became interested in American whiskey, particularly bourbon. Where once aged scotch was the coveted, status-wielding sipping beverage, suddenly, twenty-three-year-old Pappy Van Winkle bourbon was the bottle to get your hands on. Whiskey bars specializing in artisan whiskeys popped up in big cities across the country and in Europe.

Shows like *Mad Men* made drinking American whiskey look glamorous. And suddenly American whiskey was the talk of the town. And hard to come by. As demand grew, product grew scarce. So hundreds of start-up small-batch whiskey producers entered the scene. But there is no shortcut to an aged product. All you can do is wait. In the meantime, prices went up. And that's where we are right now. With a seemingly endless demand for whiskey and a still rapidly growing craft-whiskey-producing scene.

Today whiskey is the second-largest-selling spirit in America, after vodka. Sellers of whiskey claim they can't keep whiskey, in particular premium whiskey, on their shelves. Not only has American whiskey surpassed aged scotch as a favorite, status-wielding sipping beverage, but classic whiskey-based cocktails, including the old fashioned, Manhattan, whiskey sour, Mint Julep, Sazerac, hot toddy, and Boulevardier are all the rage. At my bars I sell a ton of whiskey cocktails, which is why I included a lot of whiskey cocktail recipes in this book. Many of my whiskey cocktails are based on those classics, particularly the old fashioned, and that is not a coincidence: the old fashioned is a simple, three-ingredient cocktail (2 ounces whiskey, 1 sugar cube, 3 dashes bitters, and an optional splash of soda water, stirred and served in a double old fashioned glass over ice) that highlights the flavor of the whiskey. Because I love how whiskey tastes, when I use it in cocktails, I like to stick with a similarly simple formula.

TYPES OF WHISKEY

Whiskey, America's national spirit, is a category of grain spirits made with either barley, rye, corn, or wheat. The grains are distilled and then typically aged in wood, usually oak, barrels. There are many different types of whiskey within this category, but the most common types are rye, bourbon, malted whisky, and moonshine.

MOONSHINE, also known as "white whiskey," "corn whiskey," "white lightning," and "white dog," is unaged whiskey, often made of corn. It is also a term used for any distilled spirit produced without a license; it was so named because the moonshiners made their juice at night, under the moonlight, to avoid being discovered. Moonshine isn't a sipping alcohol. Moonshine is one-dimensional and rough around the edges. I use it in cocktails when I want to add aggressive raw flavor.

BOURBON. Where moonshine is like a delinquent young kid, bourbon is beautiful, elegant, and wise. It is made from at least 51 percent corn and aged for a minimum of two years in charred new American white oak barrels. The majority of the bourbon produced comes from the South, specifically Kentucky. You can make bourbon anywhere but you will have to call it something else—Baby Bourbon, Washington Bourbon, West of Kentucky Bourbon. But if you call it "straight bourbon" it has to be from Kentucky. Bourbon accounts for two-thirds of the total distilled spirits exported from the United States.

RYE WHISKEY is made from at least 51 percent rye; the remainder is made up of corn, wheat, and malted barley or a combination. It is aged for a minimum of two years in charred new American white oak barrels. The rye grains produce a spirit that is less sweet and spicier than bourbon. Where bourbon is associated with the South, historically, rye whiskey was produced in the Northeast, with Pittsburgh being the epicenter. Rye production came to a halt during Prohibition and has only recently been resurrected with the worldwide enthusiasm for craft cocktails and artisanal spirits.

MALTED WHISKY is a grain spirit made from malted barley in copper pot stills, the majority of which is produced in Scotland. (Outside of the United States and Ireland, whiskey is spelled without the *e*. Some American brands, including Makers Mark, have also dropped the *e*.) The most famous style of malted whisky is scotch, and it is one of the most famous spirits worldwide. Scotch is drier than American whiskey, and depending on what area it is from, it can have a strong smoky flavor. There are two basic types of scotch: single malt scotch, and blended scotch. Single malt scotch is distilled exclusively from malted barley, made in a copper pot still at one distillery, after which it is aged in oak for a minimum of three years. Blended scotch can come from a blend of malted and unmalted grains. Single malt scotch is meant only for sipping, and it can be quite expensive. To make cocktails, I use only blended scotch. I think it's ironic that, with its fancy, even pretentious image, most scotch is aged in barrels that were already used for something else: used bourbon barrels, sherry barrels, and port barrels, each of which imparts a unique flavor to the scotch.

STOCKING YOUR BAR

AMERICAN BORN ORIGINAL MOONSHINE (51.5% abv) has the unmistakable grassy flavor of an unaged spirit. Its high alcohol content makes it awesome in cocktails, because you do not need a lot of the spirit. It is bottled in what looks like a big old canning jar with a screw-on aluminum lid and a Wild West type of label. The packaging is gimmicky to my taste, but I'm willing to overlook that because of the price at which this quality moonshine is being delivered.

RITTENHOUSE RYE (50% abv) is one of the few remaining whiskeys bottled in "bond," which means it is government regulated to be aged a minimum of four years, bottled at 100 proof, with one distiller, one distillery, and in the course of one season. Named after Rittenhouse Square in Philadelphia, a city that has a rich history of American rye production, Rittenhouse is very reasonably priced, especially considering the quality of the product. It is the rye I reach for most often when making a mixed drink, but you could also sip it.

SAZERAC RYE, 6-YEAR (45% abv) was named after the classic New Orleans cocktail, which in turn was named after the cognac Sazerac de Forge & Fils. It is a Kentucky whiskey. It is warm on the nose and has a full-bodied flavor that stands up to complementing flavors when it is used in cocktails. I also like this whiskey neat. Its harder-to-find big brother, 18-year Sazerac Rye, makes an awesome sipping spirit, but it is way too fine to use in cocktails.

WILLETT RYE, 3-YEAR (55.5% abv) is made by a family that has been bottling whiskey for over a hundred years. For most of those years, like many small whiskey makers, they bought the whiskey distillate from a large producer and then aged it themselves. These days the family has stepped up their game; they now start from scratch, distilling the grains and then aging the juice themselves. I love this rye, which has the flavor of baking spices and a hint of vanilla. It is a bit young and, because of that, has a slightly aggressive, grassy quality. I like it in cocktails and also to drink neat.

ELIJAH CRAIG SMALL BATCH BOURBON (47% abv) is one of the brands owned and produced by Heaven Hill Distillery, the second-largest producer of aged bourbon in the United States. For the money, it is one of the better bourbons you can find. This is my go-to bourbon for mixing. (Heaven Hill also brings you Parker's Heritage Collection, which comes out once a year. Each year it is different; they are all worth seeking out for the whiskey lover.)

BUFFALO TRACE BOURBON (45% abv) was purchased in 1992 by the Sazerac company, one of the great bourbon makers in the United States. Just about every whiskey that comes out of this distillery, from the Eagle Rare bourbon, Blanton's Single Barrel bourbon, Antique Collection whiskey, and the legendary Pappy Van Winkle lineup, wins awards. And while those make great sipping spirits, Buffalo Trace, a full-bodied whiskey with flavors of vanilla, toffee, and caramel, is the one you'd want to use for mixing cocktails. Although there is no formal age statement on the bottle, the distiller claims that this juice is aged between eight and ten years.

OLD WELLER ANTIQUE 107 BOURBON (53.5% abv) is a find; it is super inexpensive and, oh, so good. Some call it the "poor man's Pappy," referring to the award-winning Pappy Van Winkle whiskey, as it is said to have the same "mash bill" (mix of grains) as that of the coveted twenty-three-year-old whiskey. Old Weller 107 does not have an age statement, but it is supposedly aged for about seven years. It has great vanilla, honey, caramel, and hints of oak flavors. It is not too pricey to use in cocktails, but it's also good enough to drink neat.

FAMOUS GROUSE BLENDED SCOTCH WHISKY (40% abv), economical and easy to find, is said to be the most drunk scotch in Scotland. It is made from a blend that includes respected single malts Highland Park and Macallan. It hits all the notes you want from a scotch that are imparted from the barrel, including toffee, pepper, and sherry. It's a great bang for the buck.

PIG'S NOSE BLENDED SCOTCH WHISKY (40% abv) is relatively inexpensive, easy to find, and has all the flavor qualities for which scotch is known and loved: vanilla, pine, honey, a little oak, and light smoke. This is made by master distiller Richard "the Nose" Paterson, who also created one of my favorite sipping whiskies, Dalmore. The latter one would be a great addition to your bar, specifically the 18-year.

BALVENIE CARIBBEAN CASK 14-YEAR SINGLE MALT SCOTCH WHISKY (43% abv). Your bar is not complete without a sipping single malt. I could have picked many for this one, but one of my favorites is made by the Balvenie distillery. This distillery has been racking up awards for I don't know how many years. While some are more exciting than others, there is not a bad one in its lineup. The cool thing about this 14-year single malt is that it has been finished in Caribbean rum casks. Something you don't find a whole lot, or at all, but it brings super-smooth layers to an already complex single malt.

KENTUCKY SOUR

bourbon and cola with lemon and egg white

A traditional sour is made with whiskey, lemon juice, simple syrup, and egg white. I substitute house-made Cola Syrup for the simple syrup to add more layers of flavor. The result is a very intense, bold-flavored drink. I use bourbon in place of rye, which is traditional in a sour, because with so many flavors going on in this drink I thought it could use a "bigger"-flavored spirit. This cocktail is also good straight up; if you prefer it that way, strain it into a coupe glass. If you are not up for the task of making the cola syrup, I recommend maple syrup.

Pictured on page 228.

Makes 1 cocktail

GLASS
Double old fashioned

COCKTAIL
2 ounces bourbon
1 ounce fresh lemon juice (about 1 lemon)
¾ ounce Cola Syrup (page 271)
½ ounce egg white (about ½ egg)

GARNISH
Angostura bitters

Combine the cocktail ingredients in the short side of a Boston shaker. Put a tall shaker tin on top, flip the shaker around so the tall tin is on the bottom, and dry-shake (shake without ice) hard for 7 seconds. Pour the cocktail into the short shaker and fill to the rim with ice cubes. Put the tall tin on top, flip the shaker again so the tall tin is on the bottom, and shake hard a second time for 7 seconds. Using a Hawthorne strainer, strain the cocktail into the short shaker and discard the ice; don't clean the shaker. Put the tall shaker on top, flip so the tall tin is on the bottom, and dry-shake hard one last time for 7 seconds. Fill a double old fashioned glass with ice cubes and fine-strain the cocktail into the glass. To garnish, drizzle a line of bitters across the top of the drink.

CARDOON

rye whiskey and Cynar with ginger and amber ale

Talk about crowd pleasers! This is my best-selling whiskey cocktail, along with the Kingbird (page 188). Its defining ingredient is Cynar, an Italian amaro, or bitter liqueur. Cynar contains thirteen ingredients, including various plants and herbs, but the dominant ingredient is artichoke; since the cardoon is a variety of artichoke, I gave this cocktail the name Cardoon. Cynar is really intense, but a small amount of it in this cocktail adds an extra layer of herby, grassy flavor without being overwhelming.

I use beer instead of egg white, which is preferable to me in cocktail making, since it adds flavor as well as a creamy and frothy texture. Beer is a natural complement to whiskey because both are made from grains: In essence, when you distill beer, you get whiskey. Amber beer is a medium-bodied beer; I use it in this drink because a lighter-bodied beer would disappear amid the bold flavors in this drink. There are many great amber beers on the market with the craft beer revolution that has happened here. Some I particularly like are Rare Vos Ommegang Brewery, Lagunitas, and Fat Tire.

Makes 1 cocktail

GLASS
Coupe

COCKTAIL
1 ounce rye
1 ounce Cynar
1 ounce fresh lemon juice (about 1 lemon)
¾ ounce Ginger Syrup (page 186)
1 ounce amber ale

Combine the cocktail ingredients in the short side of a Boston shaker. Put the tall shaker tin on top, flip the shaker around so the tall tin is on the bottom, and dry-shake (shake without ice) hard for about 7 seconds, until the tins feel like they are pulling apart from the pressure of the CO_2 in the beer expanding. Pour the cocktail into the short shaker and fill to the rim with ice cubes. Put the tall tin on top, flip the shaker again so the tall tin is on the bottom, and shake hard a second time for 7 seconds. Using a Hawthorne strainer, strain the cocktail into the short shaker. Discard the ice, put the tall tin on top, flip so the tall tin is on the bottom, and dry-shake hard one last time for 7 seconds. Fine-strain the cocktail into the glass.

(CONTINUED)

Ginger Syrup

This recipe is nothing more than simple syrup with the spicy zing of fresh ginger added, so it's very versatile. You can use it in any recipe calling for simple syrup, such as the Fire and Smoke (page 154).

Makes about 12 ounces (1½ cups)

1½ cups sugar
¾ cup water
2 ounces fresh ginger, peeled and roughly chopped (about ½ cup)

Combine the sugar and water in a medium saucepan and heat it over medium-high heat, stirring occasionally, until the sugar dissolves, about 2 minutes. Turn off the heat and set the syrup aside to room temperature. (If you combine the sugar syrup with the ginger when the syrup is warm, the syrup will turn brown. If you wait for it to cool, it turns out a pretty white color. Also, if you put ingredients in a blender while they are still very hot, the heat will expand and explode out of the blender.) Transfer the syrup to a blender. Add the ginger and blend until the ginger is pulverized. Strain through a chinois or cheesecloth and discard the solids. Transfer the syrup to a labeled bottle or jar and close; it will keep, refrigerated, for up to 3 weeks.

AMERICAN POET

bourbon and green Chartreuse with Orange Bitters and Luxardo

In my earliest days as a barman, when I wanted to "invent" a new drink, I would start from scratch. I would ask myself questions like what kind of cocktail, what flavor profile, what direction do I want to go? And if I wanted to add layers, I would try different things and fail the majority of the time. One day I was in this process with a cocktail, and a waiter came in and had a big book with him, *The Flavor Bible*. "Did you ever read this?" he asked. I hadn't. What the book does is match flavors. Say you want to work with peaches, it will give you fifty things that go well with peaches. This was a revelation to me. Not long after that, one of my favorite winemakers, Jeff Fisher of Habit Wine, gave me a contemporary cocktail book. That's when the wheels really started turning. The cocktail book showed riffs on old-school cocktails, how they changed them up by adding and taking away and switching out the traditional ingredients. This drink was the first cocktail that I made after reading those two books. It's a play on a cocktail called the last word, which is made with equal parts gin, Chartreuse, Luxardo, and lime juice (¾ ounce of each ingredient, shaken with ice and fine-strained into a coupe glass). I tweaked the recipe a bit, changed proportions, replaced and added some different liquors, but the essence, the soul, is still the same. I use bourbon instead of gin, which gives the cocktail a deeper, softer, rounder, flavor; if you're making this for someone who likes milder-flavored alcohol, substitute vodka for the bourbon. It makes an interesting, delicious alternative to the usual vodka cocktail.

Makes 1 cocktail

GLASS
Coupe or Martini

COCKTAIL
1½ ounces bourbon
½ ounce green Chartreuse (see page 235)
½ ounce Luxardo maraschino cherry liqueur
¾ ounce fresh lime juice (less than 1 lime)
3 dashes of Orange Bitters (page 260)

GARNISH
An orange twist

Combine the cocktail ingredients in a shaker and fill it with ice cubes. Cover and shake hard for 7 seconds. Hold a Hawthorne strainer and your cocktail in one hand to hold back the ice and the fine strainer in the other to double-strain the cocktail into a coupe (or Martini) glass. To garnish, rub the outside of the orange twist on the inside rim of the glass. Squeeze the orange twist over the cocktail to release the oils and drop the twist, shiny side up, on the cocktail.

KINGBIRD

bourbon and maple with cassia bark, sassafras, and chicory

The old fashioned has become a bit of a hipster cocktail lately. Everyone loves it, and when I make a riff on one, which this is, it sells like crazy. The magical "twist" here is the spice blend in the Kingbird Tincture, which consists of sassafras, cassia, and chicory. I turned these three flavors into a simple bitters. The sassafras leaves have a kind of green tea quality; sassafras root is what gives root beer its distinctive flavor. Cassia is related to cinnamon and has a similar, if rougher, taste. And the chicory, aka the "poor man's coffee," is like a soft, less aggressive expression of coffee, and it is also a bit peppery.

Like the classic old fashioned, this is the kind of drink that a cocktail lover might sip all evening, in lieu of wine with dinner. In case you were wondering what's behind the name, the kingbird is a bird that feeds on the berries of the sassafras tree.

Makes 1 cocktail

GLASS
Double old fashioned

COCKTAIL
2 ounces bourbon
2 bar spoons (2 teaspoons) pure maple syrup
¼ ounce (2 bar spoons) Kingbird Tincture (page 268)

GARNISH
An orange twist
A lemon twist

Combine the cocktail ingredients in a mixing glass and stir with a bar spoon for 10 to 15 seconds, until the glass feels cold. Rub the inside of a double old fashioned glass with the outside of the orange and lemon twists. Place an ice ball in the glass or fill it with ice cubes. Using a julep strainer, strain the cocktail over the ice. To garnish, squeeze the orange and lemon twists over the cocktail to release the oils and drop the twists, shiny side up, on the cocktail.

COWBOYS AND INDIANS

moonshine and Suze with Luxardo and peach

I have a collection of comic books stretching four shelves on my entry room wall, so you could say I'm more than a little bit obsessed. Half of those are about cowboys and Indians, which have that magical, pioneering quality that is especially appealing to a European, where there is just nothing like it. Naturally, being obsessed with cocktails and *naming* of cocktails, I had to give a cocktail the name Cowboys and Indians, and this peach and white whiskey cocktail seemed like just the one. It's made with moonshine, which is a very American thing. Peaches are such a special summer fruit. They are so good when they are in season, but once they're gone from the farmers' markets, there's nothing to do but wait until the next year. I love stone fruit from Tenerelli Farms, a farm that sells at the Santa Monica farmers' market. They grow white peaches, yellow peaches, nectarines—every kind of stone fruit you can imagine. This cocktail is equally mouthwatering made with nectarine.

Makes 1 cocktail

GLASS
Tom Collins

COCKTAIL
2 ounces ripe peach, unpeeled
(about ¼ medium peach), cut into quarters
1½ ounces moonshine (white whiskey)
¾ ounce Luxardo maraschino cherry liqueur
1 ounce fresh lemon juice (about 1 lemon)
2 bar spoons (2 teaspoons) Suze (see page 86)

GARNISH
3 half-slices peach
3 sage leaves

Muddle the peach in a shaker until it's a slurry. Add the remaining cocktail ingredients, fill the shaker with 2 heaping cups of ice cubes, cover, and shake hard for 7 seconds. Dump the cocktail, including the ice, into a Tom Collins glass. To garnish, fan the peach slices on the cocktail and stick the stems of the sage leaves into the cocktail.

ENGINE

rye whiskey and Jelinek Fernet with blood orange, egg, and absinthe

My grandfather from my mother's side was the hospitality man in our family—he owned and ran a restaurant for most of his adult life. He died when I was young, so most of what I know about him are stories that my mom told me. One of the things I do remember is that he would drink a cognac with an egg whisked into it in the morning—every morning. When my mom was college age and began to hang out and drink with her folks, she would share that raw egg experience with her dad. Before he opened his restaurant, my grandfather used to work as a waiter for Compagnie Internationale des Wagons-Lits, the company that ran the catering business on the Orient Express. He worked a route from Amsterdam to Basel on what was known as the Engadine Express. That's where this cocktail got its name. The whole egg in a cocktail is known as a "flip"; it makes the drink foamy the same way egg white, which is more common in cocktails, does; it also adds a rich, eggy flavor. I added a few more ingredients to the cocktail to make a raw egg cocktail more appealing.

Makes 1 cocktail

GLASS
Coupe

COCKTAIL
1 large egg
1 ounce rye
1 ounce Jelinek Fernet or another Italian amaro
½ ounce absinthe
1 ounce fresh blood orange juice
or other orange juice
½ ounce fresh lemon juice (less than ½ lemon)

GARNISH
Ground cinnamon

Whisk the egg to combine the yolk and white. Combine ½ ounce of the whisked egg (you'll need only a third of the whisked egg; save the rest for another use, like breakfast) with the rest of the cocktail ingredients in the short side of a Boston shaker. Cover with the tall shaker, turn the shakers upside down, and dry-shake (shake without ice) hard for about 7 seconds, until you feel the pressure build. Pour the cocktail into the short shaker and fill with ice cubes. Cover with the tall shaker, turn upside down, and shake hard for 7 seconds. Using a Hawthorne strainer, strain the cocktail into the short shaker. Discard the ice and cover the short shaker with the tall shaker. Turn upside down and dry-shake hard for 7 seconds one final time. Fine-strain the cocktail into a coupe glass, and sprinkle ground cinnamon on top.

FIVE-CARD CASH

bourbon and saffron with honey and Chinese five-spice

Cocktails used to be more straightforward than they are today. If you asked for a whiskey cocktail, you got whiskey with bitters and sugar added to it or what today is known as an old fashioned. For this cocktail, I started with the old fashioned template, which is booze, sugar, and bitters, and added saffron and Chinese five-spice blend to give the cocktail an exotic flavor. The saffron also gives this cocktail a remarkable golden hue. I make it with Kentucky whiskey, so I gave it the name of the Kentucky lottery. I like the alliteration of the name, like Cool Hand Luke. The "five" is a reference to the Chinese five-spice. The five-spice tincture takes a week to make, so plan accordingly when you're considering this recipe. The good news is that it lasts for six months, so once you make it, you'll have it on hand to make this for the months ahead.

Makes 1 cocktail

GLASS
Double old fashioned

COCKTAIL
2 ounces bourbon

2 bar spoons (2 teaspoons) Five-Spice Tincture (page 263)

2 bar spoons (2 teaspoons) Honey Saffron Syrup (recipe follows)

GARNISH
A lemon twist

A grapefruit twist

Combine the cocktail ingredients in a mixing glass, fill with ice cubes, and stir with a bar spoon until the glass is cold, 10 to 15 seconds. Rub the outside of the lemon and grapefruit twists on the inside rim of a double old fashioned glass and fill the glass with ice cubes. Using a julep strainer, strain the cocktail into the glass. To garnish, squeeze the lemon and grapefruit twists over the cocktail to release the oils and drop the twists, shiny side up, on the cocktail.

Honey Saffron Syrup

This syrup is a beautiful fiery red color.

Makes about 6 ounces (¾ cup)

Small pinch of saffron

¾ cup orange blossom honey

¼ cup hot water

Put the saffron in a small saucepan and toast it over medium heat, shaking the pan so it doesn't burn, for 1 to 2 minutes, until you can smell the saffron. Add the honey and water and heat over medium-high heat, stirring until the honey dissolves into the water. Turn off the heat and set aside to cool slightly. Transfer the syrup to a blender and blend on medium speed for 1 minute to pulverize the saffron. (If you put ingredients in a blender while they are still very hot, the heat will expand and explode out of the blender.) Cool to room temperature. Transfer the syrup to a labeled bottle or jar and close; it will keep, refrigerated, for up to 1 month.

TENDERFOOT

rye whiskey and ginger with green Chartreuse, Orgeat, and egg white

Tenderfoot is the title of a comic book that was among the many my dad gave me as a boy, when he passed his entire comic book collection to me. This being a whiskey drink and the comic book being about the Wild West, the name seemed to fit. Plus, I feel myself like a "tenderfoot." Even though I run three bar programs and have had a lot of success in that, I feel like the new guy on the block, like that kid from Amsterdam who has never poured a drink fancier than Bacardi and Coke or vodka OJ. This cocktail is frothy from the egg white and green from the Chartreuse, but the defining ingredient is the fresh ginger. It's a really bright, refreshing, and pretty drink.

To obtain fresh ginger juice, pass a small piece of ginger through a juicer or grate it with a Microplane grater and push it through a strainer. One 1-inch piece of ginger will yield about 1 teaspoon of juice.

Makes 1 cocktail

GLASS
Tom Collins

COCKTAIL
1½ ounces rye whiskey
½ ounce Orgeat (page 274)
½ ounce green Chartreuse (see page 235)
1 ounce fresh lime juice (about 1 lime)
⅛ teaspoon fresh ginger juice
½ ounce egg white (about ½ egg)

GARNISH
2 thin cucumber slices
A fresh mint sprig

Combine the cocktail ingredients in the short side of a Boston shaker. Put a tall shaker tin on top, flip the shaker around so the tall tin is on the bottom, and dry-shake (shake without ice) hard for 7 seconds. Pour the cocktail into the short shaker and fill to the rim with ice cubes. Put the tall tin on top, flip the shaker again so the tall tin is on the bottom, and shake hard a second time for 7 seconds. Using a Hawthorne strainer, strain the cocktail into the short shaker and discard the ice; don't clean the shaker. Put the tall shaker on top, flip so the tall tin is on the bottom, and dry-shake hard one last time for 7 seconds. Fill a Tom Collins glass with fresh ice cubes and fine-strain the cocktail into the glass. To garnish, fold the cucumbers and skewer with a bamboo pick and lay it on top of the drink or lay the cucumber slices directly on the drink. Stick the mint sprig into the cocktail, leaving only the leaves visible.

LEE-ENFIELD

rye whiskey and walnut with lemon and pale ale

We host a lot of "cookbook dinners" at Lucques. The way it works is that the kitchen picks a few dishes from the book whose author we are hosting to cook and serve. I pick a cocktail from the book, and the author comes in, signs copies, and talks about the book while the customers enjoy the meal and drinks we've prepared. We were doing one such dinner for a cookbook called *French Roots* by Jean-Pierre Moullé, the former executive chef of Chez Panisse, and his wife, Denise Lurton Moullé. There were not a whole lot of cocktails in the book, but flipping through it I came across a recipe that called for walnut wine. I loved the idea of it, but it asked for green walnuts, and it was not the season for them. That idea led to this cocktail, which starts with walnut liqueur, which I made from dried walnuts. The cocktail is shaken with beer, and it's really refreshing and like a whiskey and beer sour, with a really nice walnut flavor. It's the rare drink that I opted not to garnish. The foamy layer of beer on top is all it needs. The drink is named after a rifle that is made of walnut wood. (I'm not the first to name a cocktail after a rifle; of course, there is the classic French 75.) This cocktail has a deep flavor and creamy texture from the shaken beer. Try it instead of just cracking a beer on a hot summer night.

This cocktail is made with pale ale, which has all the notes of an IPA (India pale ale), but it is lighter and less bitter. I look for those made by small producers, such as Craftsman Brewing Company here in Los Angeles (Pasadena, specifically), Eagle Rock, Strand Brewing Company, and the more widely available Sierra Nevada pale ale. Choose one that you like or that is produced near where you live.

Makes 1 cocktail

GLASS
Double old fashioned

COCKTAIL
1 ounce rye
1 ounce fresh lemon juice (about 1 lemon)
¾ ounce Walnut Liqueur (page 247)
1½ ounces pale ale

Combine the cocktail ingredients in the short side of a Boston shaker. Put the tall shaker on top, flip it around, and dry-shake (shake without ice) hard for 7 seconds, until the shakers feel like they are pulling apart from the pressure of the CO_2 in the beer expanding. Pour the ingredients into the short shaker, fill it to the rim with ice cubes, and shake hard for 7 seconds. Using a Hawthorne strainer, strain the cocktail again into the short shaker. Discard the ice, close the shaker again, and dry-shake hard one last time for 7 seconds. Fill a double old fashioned glass with ice cubes and strain the cocktail into the glass.

MOONRAKER

moonshine with poached apple, tamarind, and wheat beer

I developed this cocktail for an event we did for a very-high-end event production company, Bureau Betak. They create the craziest, most mind-blowing fashion events you can imagine. Whether it's in the middle of a desert or in an empty warehouse in downtown Los Angeles, every element of every event is taken to the next level. For this event, they hired an orchestra to play on top of a roof at the intersection of Santa Monica Boulevard and Highland Avenue, smack in the middle of Hollywood. Helicopters flew overhead, dropping guys who zip-lined down from the sky to the roof wearing survival gear. It was wild! For the cocktail, I wanted to make something that felt truly American, so I started with the idea of moonshine, which is 100 percent American, and from there apple was a natural because what's more American than apple pie? The cocktail is shaken with beer, so it has a big finger of foam on top. Tamarind has a sour quality, which contrasts great with the apple. The rich, reddish color of the tamarind, topped with the foamy beer, also made for a sleek, aesthetically pleasing cocktail worthy of the event.

Wheat beer is made of malted wheat instead of the usual malted barley. It has a more structured profile than conventional beer. I use it often in cocktails because it doesn't overpower the other ingredients. Some brands I like are Weihenstephaner, Modern Times, Blanche de Bruxelles, and Sierra Nevada kellerweis.

Makes 1 cocktail

GLASS
Double old fashioned

COCKTAIL
1 ounce moonshine (white whiskey)
1 ounce Poached Apple Juice (page 99)
1 ounce fresh lemon juice (about 1 lemon)
¾ ounce Tamarind Syrup (page 197)
1 ounce wheat beer

Combine the cocktail ingredients in the short side of a Boston shaker. Put the tall shaker on top, flip it around, and dry-shake (shake without ice) hard for 7 seconds, until the shakers feel like they are pulling apart from the pressure of the CO_2 in the beer expanding. Pour the ingredients into the short shaker, fill it to the rim with ice cubes, and shake hard for 7 seconds. Using a Hawthorne strainer, strain the cocktail again into the short shaker. Discard the ice, close the shaker again, and dry-shake hard one last time for 7 seconds. Fill a double old fashioned glass with ice cubes and use the Hawthorne strainer to strain the cocktail into the glass.

Tamarind Syrup

Tamarind is a tree indigenous to tropical Africa that grows pods containing seeds of fruit, which has a tangy, sweet, and tart flavor. It is often sold as a paste and used a lot in many different cuisines, including Indian, East Asian, Mexican, and South American cuisines, so it's pretty easy to find at specialty and ethnic grocery stores. I make a syrup from it, which makes it easy to add to cocktails. When you're warming the paste in water, it goes through a stage where it doesn't look very appealing, and you wonder, How is this going to taste good? Trust me; it tastes *great*.

Makes about 6 ounces (¾ cup)

1¾ ounces (about ¼ cup) tamarind paste
¾ cup sugar
¾ cup water

Combine the tamarind paste, sugar, and water in a small saucepan and heat over medium-high heat to dissolve the tamarind, breaking the tamarind up with a fork or cocktail muddler to help the process along. Turn off the heat and let the syrup cool to room temperature. Strain the mixture through a chinois or cheesecloth into a labeled bottle or jar and close; it will keep, refrigerated, for up to 1 month.

RAOUL DUKE

bourbon and cherry with lemon and Galliano L'Autentico

Several years ago, Sony Pictures invited me to design a cocktail menu for the film *Passengers*. It was a super-big-budget film with lots of huge stars. I made five different cocktails: one for each character. This particular one was for Jennifer Lawrence's character, Aurora. Originally the cocktail recipes were meant to be packaged with a DVD of the film, but that never happened; they ended up being served at a celebratory party at the Avalon Hotel in Beverly Hills after the film won two Oscars. They also printed the recipes to make a little book, which they handed out, along with a jigger and strainer, to the press. After the smoke had cleared and the film work was done, I took this libation, switched the name around, and now it lives on the menus of the Lucques group.

Raoul Duke is the fictional character in Hunter S. Thompson's autobiographical novel *Fear and Loathing in Las Vegas*. Thompson is from Kentucky, and so is bourbon, so naming a bourbon cocktail after him seemed appropriate. I love this cocktail but because people aren't that familiar with Galliano, a bright yellow, vanilla-forward Italian liqueur, it isn't the easiest sell. But it's a very refreshing cocktail, with tons of flavor from the bourbon, the sourness of the cherries of the Cherry Liqueur, and the vanilla and licorice flavors of the Galliano.

Makes 1 cocktail

GLASS
Coupe

COCKTAIL
1 ounce bourbon
¾ ounce Galliano L'Autentico
¾ ounce Cherry Liqueur (page 252)
1 ounce fresh lime juice (about 1 lime)

GARNISH
A lemon twist
An orange twist

Combine the cocktail ingredients in a shaker. Fill the shaker with ice cubes, cover, and shake hard for 7 seconds. Fine-strain the cocktail into a coupe glass. To garnish, rub the outside of the orange twist and lemon twist on the inside rim of a coupe glass. Squeeze the orange and lemon twists over the cocktail to release the oils and drop the twists, shiny side up, on the cocktail.

Pictured, left to right: Glasgow Kiss (page 200) and Raoul Duke, both made with Cherry Liqueur (page 252)

GLASGOW KISS

scotch and red Lillet with cherry and absinthe

This refreshing scotch-based cocktail is a riff on a corpse reviver #2, a cocktail made of gin, white Lillet, Cointreau, and absinthe. It makes a great first drink for late afternoon or evening. I wanted to give the cocktail a name that referenced the scotch, so I asked a Scottish friend, who suggested I call it the Glasgow Kiss. I loved the sound of it, and when I asked him what it meant, he told me a it referred to a head butt, like something one guy would do to another in a bar brawl. Of course, he said, when the cops showed up ten minutes later, they would all be friends again and having another drink together. Then I liked the name even more.

Pictured on page 199.

Makes 1 cocktail

GLASS
Coupe or Martini

COCKTAIL
1 ounce blended scotch whisky
1 ounce red Lillet
1 ounce Cherry Liqueur (page 252)
1 ounce fresh lemon juice (about 1 lemon)
¼ ounce absinthe

GARNISH
A lemon twist

Combine the cocktail ingredients in a shaker, fill the shaker with ice cubes, cover, and shake hard for 7 seconds. Rub the outside of the lemon twist on the inside rim of a coupe (or Martini) glass. Fine-strain the cocktail into the glass. To garnish, squeeze the lemon twist over the cocktail to release the oils and drop the twist, shiny side up, on the cocktail.

Batch of Glasgow Kisses

This cocktail works well as a "batch" drink because it contains a lot of ingredients. This way you do all your pouring in advance and then, when you get home from work and want a drink or want to serve a cocktail to a guest in the week ahead, all you have to do is pour the "mix" into a glass of ice, give it a lemon twist, and you're ready to go.

Makes one 1–liter bottle

GLASS
Coupe or Martini

COCKTAILS
7 ounces blended scotch whisky
7 ounces red Lillet
7 ounces Cherry Liqueur (page 252)
7 ounces fresh lemon juice (about 6 lemons)
4 ounces water
1¾ ounces absinthe

GARNISH
7 lemon twists

Combine the cocktail ingredients in a 1-liter bottle. Close and give the bottle a gentle shake to combine the ingredients. Refrigerate until chilled, at least 2 hours, and for as long as 1 week.

To serve, remove the bottle of cocktail mix from the refrigerator and shake to recombine the ingredients. For each cocktail, rub the inside rim of a coupe (or Martini) glass with the outside of a lemon twist and fill the glass with ice cubes. Pour 4½ ounces of the cocktail into the glass. Squeeze the lemon twist over the cocktail to release the oils and drop the twist, shiny side up, on the cocktail.

WATCHMEN

rye whiskey and dry vermouth with port and bitters

I had a nephew from my first marriage, a young kid I adored named Jeremy. He was barely one when I met him and not even nineteen when he passed. The first time I met him, he pulled himself up on the bed where I was sleeping so he could climb into bed with me. The last time I saw him, we were eating ice cream with my boys around the corner from where I live. He and I hung out a lot when I was married to his aunt. His mom was going to school at the time. Jem's dad worked all day long. So I would hang out with him during the day. I'd take him to school or have him ditch class so we could go to a movie. I think I was twenty-five. I didn't always know what to do with a kid, so I took him to the places that I loved. We went to museums, concerts, nice restaurants. Of course, being a comic book fan myself, I had to introduce him to comic books. Until then, I limited my comic book obsession to European comic books. But they weren't for sale here, so I extended my love of comic books to include American comics, which I bought for him. One of my favorites was *The Watchmen*. Since there are some similarities in this drink to the classic Manhattan, I thought of Dr. Manhattan, a character in *The Watchmen*, and gave this cocktail its name. It couldn't be easier to make: it's just booze and a twist—no juice in sight. The port gives the drink a subtle sweetness and warmth. You'll love sipping on this on a cold fall or winter afternoon.

Makes 1 cocktail

GLASS
Coupe

COCKTAIL
1½ ounces rye whiskey
¾ ounce port
¾ ounce Dry Vermouth (page 238)
4 dashes of Classic Bitters (page 258)

GARNISH
An orange twist

Combine the cocktail ingredients in a mixing glass, fill the glass with ice cubes, and stir with a bar spoon for 10 to 15 seconds, until the glass is cold. Rub the outside of the orange twist on the inside rim of a coupe glass. Using a julep strainer, strain the cocktail into the glass. Squeeze the orange twist over the cocktail to release the oils and drop the twist, shiny side up, on the cocktail.

TANGIER

bourbon and ras el hanout with Classic Bitters

Tangier, temporary home to Orwell, Matisse, Tennessee Williams, and the Rolling Stones. Written famously about by Paulo Coelho in *The Alchemist*, but also writers like Allen Ginsberg, Jack Kerouac, and William S. Burroughs have used this city as a backdrop in their novels. Arguably one of the most exciting cities in North Africa, Tangier seems like such a mysterious place, a melting pot where so many free thinkers and artists came together, like the spices I use in my ras el hanout.

Translating literally as "head of the market," ras el hanout has as many recipes as there are grandmothers. It's a spice blend commonly used in North Africa, so the name of this drink seems appropriate. When I make a new syrup that I think will go well with whiskey, I like to check its potency by using it in place of the classic sugar cube in an old fashioned. My thinking is that if the flavor of the syrup shines through in the old fashioned (and isn't overwhelmed by the whiskey), then I've made a syrup that I'm going to be happy using behind my bar.

Makes 1 cocktail

GLASS
Double old fashioned

COCKTAIL
2 ounces bourbon
¼ ounce Ras el Hanout Syrup (page 269)
4 dashes of Classic Bitters (page 258)

GARNISH
An orange twist
A lemon twist

Combine the cocktail ingredients in a mixing glass, fill it halfway with ice cubes, and stir for 10 to 15 seconds, until the glass feels cold. Fill a double old fashioned glass with ice cubes and use a julep (or Hawthorne) strainer to strain the cocktail into the glass. To garnish, rub the outside of the orange twist and lemon twist on the inside rim of the glass. Squeeze the orange and lemon twists over the cocktail to release the oils and drop the twists, shiny side up, on the cocktail.

THUNDERER

bourbon and honey with grapefruit, ginger, and chile de árbol

This easy-to-make cocktail was one of the earlier drinks I created for the bar menu at our Brentwood restaurant, Tavern. It is made with a honey syrup infused with fresh ginger and chiles de árbol, so you get those flavors and that heat in the cocktail. I added grapefruit to make it tangy. The cocktail is named for the pistol used by Billy the Kid. I used to watch the movie *Young Guns*, about the adventures of Billy the Kid, over and over again; I still dream of riding a horse through the desert and sipping whiskey at night around a campfire. This cocktail is the product of that Wild West fantasy. It's the perfect drink in the winter, when citrus is in season and when you're nursing a cold.

Makes 1 cocktail

GLASS
Coupe

COCKTAIL
1½ ounces bourbon

1 ounce fresh grapefruit juice (about ¼ grapefruit, preferably Ruby Red)

¾ ounce fresh lemon juice (less than 1 lemon)

½ ounce Honey Árbol Ginger Syrup (recipe follows)

GARNISH
4 thin slices chiles de árbol

Combine the cocktail ingredients in a shaker. Fill the shaker with ice cubes, cover, and shake hard for 7 seconds. Use a Hawthorne strainer to strain the cocktail into a coupe glass. Garnish with the chile de árbol slices.

Honey Árbol Ginger Syrup

Makes about 8 ounces (1 cup)

¾ cup orange blossom honey

¼ cup boiling water

2 ounces fresh ginger, peeled and roughly chopped (about ½ cup)

½-inch piece of chile de árbol, plus more to taste

Put the honey and water in a blender and stir until the honey dissolves. Add the ginger and chile and blend on high speed until the ginger is pulverized. Strain through a chinois or cheesecloth and discard the solids. Let the syrup cool to room temperature. Transfer to a small jar or bottle and refrigerate for up to 1 month. If you have some leftover syrup, be sure to try the Pistolero (page 158) as well.

Pictured, left to right: Thunderer and Pistolero (page 158), both made with Honey Árbol Ginger Syrup

Brandy is misunderstood. People take it too seriously. The impression of brandy is that it is an upper-class, snobby kind of thing to drink on a night out when you're all dressed up, and you drink it from a big snifter in front of a grand fireplace. And, sure, that's a great way to enjoy brandy. But it doesn't have to be limited to that. And you don't have to be fancy and upper crust to enjoy it. In Europe, especially in the Netherlands, where I am from, it's very common to enjoy a snifter of brandy as an after-dinner drink, and not just on special occasions.

Brandy is a liquor made from fermented fruit, typically grapes. Basically, it's distilled wine. Technically brandy can be made from any fruit. Apple brandy, and in particular Calvados, is the one you're most likely to have heard of and the one I use most often. But there are also smaller productions of brandy that are made from raspberries, pears, cherries, and other fruit. Most brandy is aged in oak barrels, though some American brandies are aged in charred oak, and some brandies aren't aged at all. In fact, the word *brandy* is derived from the Dutch word for burned wine, *brandewijn*. The reason the Dutch call it burned is that in the process of distilling it the fermented fruit is warmed up. Wine is a fermented fruit. Beer is a fermented grain. If you warm that up, like burning it, it makes alcohol, like hard liquor.

I was introduced to brandy in the form of "vieux," or "Dutch cognac." Vieux is a grain liqueur with color and flavor added in an effort to imitate French brandy. So the French quickly put an end to the name, which you have to admit was a pretty clever marketing ploy. Even though vieux is just a cheap imitation of brandy, it's what made me feel comfortable with this otherwise kind of unknown liqueur. I saw my parents enjoy it often, after dinner straight up or in a coffee, and I drank my share of vieux in a glass of Coca-Cola.

"Hey, let's have a *vieuxtje* [or 'little vieux']" is a common phrase in the Netherlands, just like "Let's have a mezcalito [or 'little mezcal']" is something you hear often in Mexico. Today with the cocktail and spirits movements, brandy is having a comeback, but it still hasn't reached its full potential. It is still not a "cool" spirit. You're not going to hear anybody in the United States saying, "Let's do a shot of cognac!" or "Hey, let's get together and drink brandy!"

The aged brandy that we know is largely French, but in recent years small producers of American brandy have sprung up all across the United States. What's interesting about these producers is that they're breaking all the rules. In the American tradition, they are not resigned to following a set of rules that somebody made two hundred years ago. They're experimenting within the category of fruit distillates. I like what they are doing, and it's only a matter of time until it catches on.

Although I am definitely a fan of brandy, it is the spirit I use least in cocktails in part because it is the spirit my customers ask for the least. Of course there are some classics to be inspired by, including the sidecar, brandy old fashioned, brandy Alexander, stinger, sangria, and Sazerac. I used a few of these as a jumping-off point for my own cocktails, but for most of my drinks I totally went rogue and mixed the brandy with whatever I felt moved to mix it with at the time.

TYPES OF BRANDY

Brandy is a large category that includes cognac, Armagnac, apple brandy, and pisco, among others.

COGNAC is a type of brandy that must be produced in the French commune of Cognac, in the region of Nouvelle-Aquitaine. It is the champagne of brandies. There are countless makers of cognac, from mass producers including Rémy Martin and Hennessy, to small, artisan producers. If you were looking to spend lots of money on liquor, this would be the category where you could easily do that. For the purpose of cocktail making, there are two types of cognac to consider, VS, which is aged for three to four years, and VSOP, which is aged for five to six years. Cognac and cognac-based cocktails are not the most frequently requested drinks at my bar, but I like to have a bit of everything.

ARMAGNAC, home of the oldest brandy in France, is a town next to Cognac, and like cognac, a true Armagnac must be made from grapes grown in that region. The main difference between cognac and Armagnac is that cognac is double-distilled in a pot still, where Armagnac is single-distilled in a column still. This single distillation turns this spirit for me into a rougher, more beautiful, robust, and pure spirit to explore.

APPLE BRANDY, as you might guess, is brandy made from apples instead of grapes. It is made all over the world, and it has a different name depending on where it's made. The most widely known apple brandy is Calvados, from Normandy, France, which is aged a minimum of two years. In America, apple brandy, called *applejack*, is made by a process called "freeze distilling." The way it works is the fermented apple juice is frozen; the water content freezes, leaving the alcohol behind, which results in a product with a concentrated alcohol content. (Traditional distilling, by contrast, relies on the alcohol content to evaporate, rather than freezing off the impurities.) The term *jacking* came from the fact that the distillers were "jacking up" the alcohol content through the freeze distillation process. Applejack is exclusively American; it was popular during the colonial period and extinct until the recent cocktail revival; now there are several smaller producers from New York to Wisconsin to California.

UNAGED BRANDY, sometimes called *clear brandy*, includes pisco, grappa, and eau de vie. These brandies have none of the refined, warm qualities we associate with brandy. The only thing these have in common with brandies like cognac and Armagnac is that they are made from distilled fermented fruit, so I include them here. These brandies are rough around the edges and closer in spirit and flavor to moonshine (white whiskey). You can find some unaged brandies, particularly pisco, that have a little more nuance. Peru and Chile both claim pisco as their own; it's a topic both take very seriously.

ABSINTHE was originally made from a high-proof distilled grape spirit, so I took the liberty to include it here. Even though there are absinthes using grape as a base, today the majority of the "absinthe" consumed is actually made from a grain spirit and flavored with anise and fennel, the dominant flavors of absinthe. To call it absinthe, it must contain wormwood. There are tales about absinthe being hallucinogenic, but what I believe is that if you drink a bottle of any 120-proof liqueur, you'll be seeing green fairies. For cocktails, I often use absinthe liqueur in its place, which has a more pleasurable price than the real-deal absinthe and is easier to find; you can use absinthe liqueur in any of my recipes where absinthe is called for.

STOCKING YOUR BAR

PISCO ENCANTO (40.5% abv) is made in Peru from four different grape varietals, with Quebranta grapes being dominant. It is very round and complex, with a nice green grape flavor and vanilla hints. The guys from Encanto like to say this pisco was "made by bartenders *for* bartenders." It works awesome in a pisco sour.

MACCHU PISCO (40% abv) is a fairly economical pisco, also made from Quebranta grapes. It is a little rougher around the edges than Encanto, but it is equally good in cocktails.

MAISON ROUGE VS COGNAC (40% abv) is owned by the Hardy family. Under its own label "Hardy Cognac," this family-owned distillery produces brandies that are priced into the thousands of dollars. But we are not talking about those; we are talking about the VS. This is my go-to cognac for making cocktails. It tastes like what cognac should taste like, with flavors of grape, apple, vanilla, and wood, and it is inexpensive. Are there better cognacs? Without a doubt. But for making cocktails, this is everything you want and need.

PARK VS COGNAC (40% abv). One of my favorite cognacs; they have a great lineup besides the VS. In the Los Angeles cocktail scene, this is probably the most popular one and used by many as their go-to cognac. If you want to be a little more luxurious in your cocktail making, this one comes highly recommended. It has flavors of apricot and vanilla, is only slightly more expensive than Maison Rouge, and can double as a sipping cognac.

KELT VSOP COGNAC (40% abv) is most definitely for sipping, not for making cocktails, as it is fairly expensive. Their "gimmick" is that they barrel the cognac and ship the barrels around the world, which takes ninety days. They claim that bouncing on the waves, with the liquid sloshing around in the barrel and surrounded by salty air, gives the cognac the same characteristics it had when it was shipped that way for export hundreds of years ago. I'm a little skeptical. Sea travels aside, this is a great-tasting cognac. It is produced from grapes that come from Grande Champagne, a region known for producing the best cognac.

CHÂTEAU LAUBADE, BAS ARMAGNAC. The brandy chapter would not be complete without a recommendation for Armagnac. Bas Armagnac is one of the three regions of Armagnac. Laubade is one of my favorite castles to produce brandy. They have a variety of vintages, some dating back to as early as 1888. Their Armagnac comes from one vintage and is aged in Gascony oak barrels, so every year they make a new expression. This is not what I would use for cocktails, but it's fun to have on your back bar. From their collection I use only the vintage or "Millésimes" for the Lucques Group.

LECOMPTE CALVADOS (40% abv), the classic French apple brandy, is aged for a minimum of three years in French oak. It has the unmistakable flavor of fresh apples, combined with the warm, sweet note of honey. It is the only Calvados I use in cocktails. If I want to sip on Calvados, I still chose Lecompte, but I splurge on one that has been aged longer.

LAIRD'S APPLEJACK (40% abv) has a low price tag and high proof, making it perfect for mixing into cocktails. Like American whiskey, this brandy is aged in charred new American oak barrels, which sets it apart from its French counterpart, Calvados. Don't tell a French person I said this, but you can use it in cocktails calling for Calvados. One key point, this distiller makes two kinds: one is an apple brandy bottled in bond at 100 proof, and one comes in at 80 proof and is mixed with grain spirit. To get more bang for your buck, use the 100 proof.

LA CLANDESTINE ABSINTHE (53% abv), which is from Switzerland, the birthplace of absinthe, is the one I enjoy, undiluted, at home. It has a super clean flavor. The beverage is clear, but when you add water to it, it turns opaque the way a traditional absinthe should. I wouldn't use an expensive booze like this in a cocktail, but I love it enough that I had to mention it. Save it for sipping.

HERBSAINT ABSINTHE LIQUEUR (45% abv), made in New Orleans, is a high-proof liqueur created to be used in cocktails. Absinthe purists take offense with the fact that this product even carries the name *absinthe* since it does not contain wormwood, a key ingredient in true absinthe. But cocktail making isn't for purists anyway. I add this liqueur to a cocktail when I want the fresh flavors of fennel and anise that absinthe is known for. So technically, it has no reason to be in this chapter, but since I use it as an absinthe, I included it here.

BIENVILLE

Calvados and tonic with Classic and Orange Bitters

Bienville was the former governor of the French Quarters in New Orleans. This cocktail is a play on a Vieux Carré, a cocktail that originated in New Orleans; thus the name. When I was brainstorming it, I started with the classic Vieux Carré recipe and then kept adding this, subtracting that. What I ended up with is a pretty distant play on the original, but the name stuck. I think of this as a predinner cocktail; apple generally has a warm flavor, but the lightness of the tonic and the brightness of the lime make this an excellent choice.

Makes 1 cocktail

GLASS
Double old fashioned

COCKTAIL
1½ ounces Calvados
1 ounce fresh lime juice (about 1 lime)
¾ ounce Tonic Syrup (page 272)
½ ounce Orange Liqueur (page 245)
3 dashes of Orange Bitters (page 260)

GARNISH
A grapefruit twist

Combine the cocktail ingredients in a short shaker and fill to the rim with ice cubes. Cover and shake hard for 7 seconds. Fill a double old fashioned glass with ice cubes (or use an ice ball) and use a Hawthorne and fine strainer to strain the cocktail over the ice into the glass. To garnish, squeeze the grapefruit twist over the cocktail to release the oils and drop the twist, shiny side up, on the cocktail.

Batch of Bienvilles

Makes one 1-liter bottle

GLASS
Double old fashioned

COCKTAILS
12 ounces Calvados
8 ounces fresh lime juice (about 8 limes)
3 ounces water
6 ounces Tonic Syrup (page 272)
4 ounces Orange Liqueur (page 245)
½ ounce Orange Bitters (page 260)

GARNISH
8 grapefruit twists

Combine the cocktail ingredients in a 1-liter bottle and cover. Give it a gentle shake to combine the ingredients. Refrigerate until chilled, at least 2 hours, and for as long as 1 week.

To serve, pour 4 ounces into each of 8 glasses filled with ice cubes. To garnish, squeeze a grapefruit twist over each cocktail to release the oils and drop the twists, shiny side up, on the cocktails.

COMMUNION

pisco with Concord grapes, lime, and Génépi des Alpes

This name was chosen in a roundabout way. Here's the story: Concord grapes were developed in Concord, Massachusetts, in 1849. Twenty years later a doctor named Welch made an invention by which he could use pasteurization to prevent the juice from fermenting. So he used the juice in his church for Holy Communion. Since this cocktail is made with Concord grape juice, the name seemed to fit.

Technically speaking, this cocktail is a derivation of a sour, which means a cocktail that combines sour (in this case lime juice) and sweet (Concord grape). It's super pretty—purple from the Concord grape syrup with a bright green fresh mint sprig on top. Concord grapes are in season in Los Angeles in the fall, so even though this is a fruity, refreshing drink, I also think of it as a fall cocktail, perfect for the warm autumn days we have in southern California in September and October. It's really easy to make. If you have the syrup premade in the fridge, you can shake this up and have a beautiful, delicious cocktail in a few seconds.

Makes 1 cocktail

GLASS
Double old fashioned

COCKTAIL
1½ ounces pisco
½ ounce Génépi des Alpes (see box on page 216)
½ ounce Concord Grape Syrup (page 216)
1 ounce fresh lime juice (about 1 lime)

GARNISH
A fresh mint sprig

Combine the cocktail ingredients in a shaker and fill with ice cubes. Cover and shake hard for 7 seconds. Fill a double old fashioned glass with ice cubes and use a Hawthorne strainer to strain the cocktail into the glass. To garnish, stick the mint sprig into the cocktail so only the leaves are visible.

(CONTINUED)

Concord Grape Syrup

Years ago, before I left for the States, my brothers and I gave my parents a grapevine as a gift. They have a little seating area in their garden, and I thought it would be cool to have grapevines growing all around it. More than a decade later, I visited with my wife and children in the fall, and that grapevine had grown so huge that grapes were everywhere. My dad got the idea to make grape juice with my son River. It was so flavorful. When I got back home, I made a syrup from Concord grapes. It's so good, and such an intense, beautiful grape color and flavor. I start with grapes and make the juice, but I give you both options: starting with grapes or grape juice. At the restaurant, I make it only during the Concord grape season, which is the fall.

Makes about 8 ounces (1 cup)

½ pound Concord grapes
¼ cup water
Sugar

Combine the grapes and water in a small saucepan and bring the liquid to a boil over medium heat. Reduce the heat and simmer the grapes until the skins crack, about 10 minutes. Pass the contents of the saucepan through a chinois or cheesecloth into a glass measuring cup, pressing on the grapes with the back of a ladle or a wooden spoon to extract as much of the liquid as possible. Discard the solids. Take note of the amount of juice. Return the liquid to the saucepan, add an equal amount of sugar, and heat it over medium-high heat, stirring occasionally, until the sugar dissolves, about 2 minutes. Transfer the syrup to a labeled bottle or jar and close; it will keep, refrigerated, for up to 1 month.

Batch of Communions

Makes one 1-liter bottle

GLASS
Double old fashioned

COCKTAILS
12 ounces pisco
8 ounces fresh lime juice (about 8 limes)
4 ounces Génépi des Alpes
4 ounces Concord Grape Syrup (recipe above)
4 ounces water

GARNISH
8 fresh mint sprigs
8 large lime twists

Combine the cocktail ingredients in a 1-liter bottle and cover. Give it a gentle shake to combine the ingredients. Refrigerate until chilled, at least 2 hours, and as long as 1 week. To serve, remove the bottle from the refrigerator. Fill a double old fashioned glass with ice cubes and pour 4 ounces of the cocktail into the glass. Garnish with a fresh mint sprig.

Génépi des Alpes is an Alpine liqueur with a soft, herbaceous flavor similar to but not as intense as absinthe. And unlike absinthe, which comes from the same region, génépi is a liqueur. (When made in France it's spelled Génépy, while in Italy it's Génépi.) I use Génépi when I want to add a green, herbal layer of flavor to a cocktail without having that flavor dominate the drink.

DR. COMMON

absinthe and pistachio with green Chartreuse and egg white

Most barmen use absinthe in very small quantities: a quarter ounce to add a touch of flavor or even less is used to rinse the inside of a glass, as in the classic Sazerac, but for this cocktail, I use it as the base. Absinthe needs to be used with other strong flavors to prevent it from dominating, so I combine it in this recipe with pistachio and Chartreuse. The result is a drink that is really pretty, with a wonderful flavor. This is a drink I would order if I sat at my own bar and I could have two of them. Absinthe was allegedly invented by a guy with the excellent name Dr. Pierre Ordinary. Since *ordinary* can mean the same thing as "common," I switched around those words to name this drink.

Pictured on page 130.

Makes 1 cocktail

GLASS
Coupe

COCKTAIL
1 ounce absinthe
1 ounce fresh lime juice (about 1 lime)
½ ounce green Chartreuse (see page 235)
¾ ounce Pistachio Syrup (page 132)
½ ounce egg white (about ½ egg)

Combine the cocktail ingredients in the short side of a Boston shaker. Put a tall shaker tin on top, flip the shaker around so the tall tin is on the bottom, and dry-shake (shake without ice) hard for 7 seconds. Pour the cocktail into the short shaker and fill to the rim with ice cubes. Put the tall tin on top, flip the shaker again so the tall tin is on the bottom, and shake hard a second time for 7 seconds. Using a Hawthorne strainer, strain the cocktail into the short shaker and discard the ice; don't clean the shaker. Put the tall shaker on top, flip so the tall tin is on the bottom, and dry-shake hard one last time for 7 seconds. Fine-strain the cocktail into a coupe glass.

FIRE STARTER

cognac and apple with green Chartreuse, bourbon, and spiced raisin

As boys, my brothers Melchior and Dimitri and I, along with the boys we grew up with, used to play in the old World War II bunkers left by the Germans in the sand dunes on Terschelling, an island off the coast of the Netherlands, where my family spent summers and long weekends. One day we got the bright idea to light a fire in one of those bunkers. We obviously didn't think it through, since just a few hundred yards away was a 400-year-old lighthouse that overlooks the entire island, so not surprisingly, we got caught just minutes later. Suffice to say that all these years later I am still, at heart, a boy who likes to play with fire. So one evening, after I created this cocktail to go with a fall Sunday Supper, the weekly prix-fixe dinner event at Lucques, I was tasting it with our general manager—and my cocktail soundboard—Matt Duggan. It was that rare cold day in Los Angeles, and we were thinking how great it would be to be sitting next to the fireplace in the center of the room at Lucques. With my eyes focused on that fireplace, I decided to finish this cocktail by—yup—lighting it up in flames! It's a really fun presentation and a delicious and unusual by-the-fireplace sort of cocktail. If you don't have both cognac and bourbon, you can use 1½ ounces of one or the other.

Makes 1 cocktail

GLASS
Double old fashioned

FOR THE GLASS
2 bar spoons (2 teaspoons) green Chartreuse (see page 235)
A fresh rosemary sprig

COCKTAIL
¾ ounce cognac
¾ ounce bourbon
¾ ounce Spiced Raisin Syrup (page 220)
¾ ounce fresh apple juice or store-bought fresh-pressed juice
1 ounce fresh lime juice (about 1 lime)

Pour the Chartreuse into a double old fashioned glass. Put the rosemary sprig in the Chartreuse and make sure the rosemary is covered so it soaks in the Chartreuse.

Combine the cocktail ingredients in a shaker. Fill the shaker with ice cubes, cover, and shake hard for 7 seconds. Light the rosemary sprig on fire (use a long-reach lighter or a long match to avoid burning your hand when the rosemary ignites) and let it burn for 2 or 3 seconds. Dump the contents of the shaker into the glass on top of the fire. (There will be some flames and smoke; definitely a crowd pleaser.) Lift the rosemary and lay it on top of the cocktail.

(CONTINUED ON PAGE 220)

From top to bottom: Combine the cocktail ingredients in a shaker. Light the rosemary sprig on fire. Dump the contents of the shaker into the glass.

Spiced Raisin Syrup

Since brandy is made from grapes, I liked the idea of pairing it with grapes in a cocktail—and what are raisins but dried grapes? I know: the word *raisin* doesn't sound very sexy. But get beyond that and make this anyway, because cooked with the wine and all the delicious spices, this is so good you're going to want to make it again and again. Drizzle leftover syrup on pancakes and vanilla ice cream.

Makes about 5 ounces (⅔ cup)

1 cup black raisins
½ cup fresh orange juice
½ cup dry red wine, such as merlot or cabernet
Rind of ¼ orange (peeled with a vegetable peeler)
Rind of ½ lemon (peeled with a vegetable peeler)
½ cup sugar
½ teaspoon allspice berries
¼ teaspoon black peppercorns
¼ teaspoon juniper berries

Combine all the ingredients in a small saucepan. Heat the liquid over medium-high heat, stirring, until the sugar dissolves, about 2 minutes; be careful that the flame isn't so high that it can travel around the sides of the pan, as the alcohol in the pan will catch fire. Reduce the heat to medium and simmer for 15 minutes to soften the raisins. Turn off the heat and set aside to cool slightly. Transfer the contents of the saucepan to a blender and pulse until the raisins are roughly chopped but not pureed. (If you put ingredients in a blender while they are still very hot, the heat will expand and explode out of the blender.) Pass the mixture through a chinois or cheesecloth, pushing on the solids to extract as much of the liquid as possible, and discard the solids. Transfer the syrup to a jar. The syrup will keep, refrigerated, for up to 1 month.

RIVER'S LICORICE

absinthe with Orgeat, pineapple, and Luxardo

I want my boys to grow up eating licorice like any good Dutch child. So River, being the all-American boy that he is, when I've tried to get him to eat it, he's always hated it. One day River, Opa (grandpa), and I were on the train to Utrecht, Netherlands, where they have an epic train museum. On this day trip I found licorice candies that were in the shape of little cars—shiny red Cadillacs and English double-decker buses. Half of each candy was true black licorice and the other half was some fruity, gummy bear kind of consistency. I handed him a Cadillac—he took one bite of the licorice part and made a face. From that point on, he grabbed the cars, ate the fruity portion, and handed the black licorice portion to me. We got to one car and River said, "Mmmm . . . this is pineapple!" I was so intrigued by the pineapple and licorice combination that when I got back home I set out to make a pineapple-licorice cocktail. This cocktail doesn't have a garnish because the fresh pineapple juice gets foamy when you shake it, so you have a nice little layer of foam on top of the glass. Canned pineapple is not a good substitute.

Makes 1 cocktail

GLASS
Coupe

PREP
10 ounces fresh pineapple

COCKTAIL
1 ounce absinthe
1 ounce fresh pineapple juice
1 ounce fresh lime juice (about 1 lime)
¾ ounce Orgeat (page 274) or store-bought
½ ounce Luxardo maraschino cherry liqueur

To prep the drink, put the pineapple, including the core if it remains, through a juicer. You will have enough juice to make 4 cocktails.

To make the cocktail, combine the cocktail ingredients in the short side of the shaker. Put a tall shaker tin on top, flip the shaker around so the tall tin is on the bottom, and dry-shake (shake without ice) hard for 7 seconds. Pour the cocktail into the short shaker and fill to the rim with ice cubes. Put the tall tin on top, flip the shaker again so the tall tin is on the bottom, and shake hard a second time for 7 seconds. Using a Hawthorne strainer, strain the cocktail into the short shaker and discard the ice cubes; don't clean the shaker. Put the tall shaker on top, flip so the tall tin is on the bottom, and dry-shake hard one last time for 7 seconds. Fine-strain the cocktail into a coupe glass.

MERCANTILE

pisco and Thompson grape with Bénédictine and pecan

For this cocktail I started with an elegant pisco and built a cocktail around it. I added grape juice for sweetness. Then I tasted it. I wanted a toasty flavor, so after some trying and tasting, I landed on pecan syrup. And then I added Bénédictine to get that one last layer of flavor that, for me, takes a cocktail over the edge. That basically describes how I go about building any cocktail.

This cocktail is named for mercantilism, the economic practice that inspired the building of overseas colonies. The Spanish settlers of what is now Peru and Chile planted grapes and developed a wine industry in those places so strong that it came to threaten the Spaniards. Pisco was born out of these traditions, and this cocktail was born out of pisco.

Makes 1 cocktail

GLASS

Double old fashioned

COCKTAIL

1 ounce pisco
½ ounce Bénédictine (see page 86)
½ ounce Pecan Liqueur (page 248)
¾ ounce Fresh Grape Juice (recipe follows)
1 ounce fresh lemon juice (about 1 lemon)

GARNISH

1 Thompson seedless green grape

Combine the cocktail ingredients in a shaker and fill with ice cubes. Cover and shake hard for 7 seconds. Fill a double old fashioned glass with ice cubes and use a Hawthorne strainer to strain the cocktail into the glass. To garnish, slice the grape, skewer a slice, and lay it on top of the cocktail.

Fresh Grape Juice

I've been eating grapes my whole life but never even thought to juice them until I became obsessed with cocktail making. Home-pressed Thompson grape juice is so flavorful and fresh tasting, and with a subtle note of—of all things—vanilla! It's so quick to make, once you try it, like me, you'll be hooked. I tried three different grapes for this drink before landing on Thompson grapes. I needed something that wouldn't be washed away but also wouldn't be overpowering. Thompson grapes it was. The only downside is that the color of the juice fades with time.

Makes about 6 ounces (¾ cup)

1 cup Thompson seedless green grapes (about ½ pound)

Put the grapes in a blender and blend until they are pulverized. Strain the juice through a chinois or cheesecloth. Transfer the juice to a labeled bottle or jar and close; it will keep, refrigerated, for up to 3 days.

FIFTH KINGDOM

cognac and chai with Luxardo, Orgeat, and egg white

I named this cocktail for Kerala, the region known as "the spice garden of India," which was originally divided into five separate kingdoms. Although this has the flavor of chai spice, it is nothing like that milky chai beverage you buy at your favorite coffee shop. The egg white creates a thick finger of foam on top of the drink, which looks pretty and tastes velvety. Chai spice and cognac are, to me, both warm flavors, so I think of this as a fall or winter drink, something to enjoy before or after dinner, but definitely in front of a roaring fire.

Makes 1 cocktail

GLASS
Coupe

COCKTAIL
¾ ounce Chai Cognac (page 244)
¾ ounce rye whiskey
½ ounce Luxardo maraschino cherry liqueur
½ ounce Orgeat (page 274)
1 ounce fresh lime juice (about 1 lime)
½ ounce egg white (about ½ egg)

GARNISH
A fresh mint sprig

Combine the cocktail ingredients in the short side of a Boston shaker. Put a tall shaker tin on top, flip the shaker around so the tall tin is on the bottom, and dry-shake (shake without ice) hard for 7 seconds. Pour the cocktail into the short shaker and fill to the rim with ice cubes. Put the tall tin on top, flip the shaker again so the tall tin is on the bottom, and shake hard a second time for 7 seconds. Using a Hawthorne strainer, strain the cocktail into the short shaker and discard the ice; don't clean the shaker. Put the tall shaker on top, flip so the tall tin is on the bottom, and dry-shake hard one last time for 7 seconds. Fine-strain the cocktail into the glass. To garnish, stick the mint sprig in the foam.

NORMANDY

Calvados and amaro with apple butter and Cynar

I worked with the Dutch opera while making a second attempt at college, with a major in psychology. At one point they needed a martial artist. I was already getting into martial arts, so I told them I'd do it. We traveled to the Salzburger Festspiele, the most recognized theater festival in the world. It was a great experience. At one point during my off time I ended in the Austrian Alps, up on top of a castle, on top of a mountain, eating apple pie with vanilla ice cream. It was the best apple pie I have ever eaten to this day, in part because of the setting, I'm sure. I created this cocktail to re-create that warmth, that feeling of eating warm apple pie. It starts with an apple "caramel" that is a traditional sweet where I come from. The Cynar and amaro add welcome body and contrasting bitterness to the drink. I suggest you make this cocktail in the fall, when apples are in season. I imagine drinking it on a lazy afternoon doing a Sudoku puzzle in front of a fireplace.

Makes 1 cocktail

GLASS
Double old fashioned

COCKTAIL
1 ounce Calvados
½ ounce Averna or another Italian amaro
½ ounce Cynar
1 ounce fresh lemon juice (about 1 lemon)
¾ ounce Brown Sugar Dutch Apple "Stroop" (page 226)

GARNISH
An orange twist

Rub the outside of the orange twist on the inside rim of a double old fashioned glass. Set the glass and twist aside while you make the cocktail.

Combine the cocktail ingredients in a shaker and fill it with ice cubes. Cover and shake hard for 7 seconds. Fill a double old fashioned glass with ice cubes and use a Hawthorne strainer to strain the cocktail into the prepared glass. To garnish, squeeze the orange twist over the cocktail to release the oils and drop the twist shiny side up on the cocktail.

(CONTINUED)

Brown Sugar Dutch Apple "Stroop"

In the Netherlands we have a product called *appel stroop*, which is basically apple caramel. It's the same stuff they make stroopwafels with, which you might have seen at the counter at Starbucks. It's very thick and has an intense apple flavor. It's a commercial product that I have never seen here, but when my boys are in the Netherlands, they can't get enough of it. It's like apple crack. I re-created it and use it in cocktails. It is a thin, drizzling consistency. Use leftover syrup as we use it in the Netherlands: drizzled on pancakes, vanilla ice cream, or buttered rye bread.

Makes about 8 ounces (1 cup)

2 sweet apples, such as Gala or Fuji, peeled, cored, and chopped (about 2 heaping cups)
½ cup water
1 cup granulated sugar
¼ cup packed dark brown sugar

Put the apples and water in a small saucepan and cook over medium heat, stirring occasionally, until the apples are very soft but not falling apart, about 30 minutes. Turn off the heat and set aside to cool slightly. Transfer the apples to a blender and blend until they're pulverized. (If you put ingredients in a blender while they are still very hot, the heat will expand and explode out of the blender.) Pass the apple puree through a chinois or cheesecloth back into the saucepan you cooked the apples in.

Add the granulated and brown sugars and warm over medium heat, stirring, until the sugar dissolves, about 2 minutes. Turn off the heat and set aside to cool to room temperature. Transfer the syrup to a jar. The "stroop" will keep, refrigerated, for up to 3 months.

Pictured: the Normandy (page 225)

WIRE BIRD

cognac and cranberry with cola and egg white

As a bartender I kind of cringe when a customer says: "I'll have a cognac and Coke." I used to think of cognac as something to enjoy as an after-dinner drink. You get a fancy big snifter glass and a nice cognac and you drink it slowly, ideally in front of a fireplace. But here in the States, cognac and Coke, over ice, is a pretty popular cocktail. After making a few dozen of them over the years, I finally thought, There must be *something* good about it. The fact is, although admittedly I kind of looked down on the drink, I'd never actually tasted it. When I did, I could understand why people liked it. There was something refreshing about it. I added fresh cranberry juice and honestly, I loved it. (Fresh pineapple juice also works great, but it *has* to be fresh to cut through the alcohol.) I shake it with egg whites to make the drink foamy, which softens the experience and makes a more elegant drink.

The wire bird, also known as the St. Helena plover, is the state bird of St. Helena, the island where Napoleon went into exile. Legend has it that Napoleon took a few barrels of Courvoisier (cognac) with him into exile, so that's where this cocktail got its name.

Makes 1 cocktail

GLASS
Coupe

COCKTAIL
1½ ounces cognac
1 ounce Cranberry Juice (page 230)
or fresh pineapple juice
1 ounce fresh lemon juice (about 1 lemon)
¾ ounce Cola Syrup (page 271)
½ ounce egg white (about ½ egg)

GARNISH
Angostura bitters

Combine the cocktail ingredients in the short side of a Boston shaker. Put a tall shaker tin on top, flip the shaker around so the tall tin is on the bottom, and dry-shake (shake without ice) hard for 7 seconds. Pour the cocktail into the short shaker and fill to the rim with ice cubes. Put the tall tin on top, flip the shaker again so the tall tin is on the bottom, and shake hard a second time for 7 seconds. Using a Hawthorne strainer, strain the cocktail into the short shaker and discard the ice; don't clean the shaker. Put the tall shaker on top, flip so the tall tin is on the bottom, and dry-shake hard one last time for 7 seconds. Fine-strain the cocktail into a coupe glass. To garnish, drop a few drops of bitters over the top and use a straw to draw a swirl through the drops.

(CONTINUED)

Pictured, left to right:
Kentucky Sour (page 183)
and Wire Bird, both made
with Cola Syrup (page 271)

Cranberry Juice

To be honest, I never thought there was anything wrong with store-bought cranberry juice—not something I would necessarily use in a cocktail, but hey, it's fine. After making my own grape juice, I decided to try making my own cranberry juice just to see what the results were like. The juice turned out so flavorful and with such glorious color that I could never go back to store-bought.

Makes about 18 ounces (2¼ cups)

10 ounces fresh or frozen cranberries
(about 3 scant cups)

2 cups water

⅓ cup sugar

Combine the cranberries and water in a medium saucepan and bring to a boil over high heat. Reduce the heat to medium-low and simmer until the cranberry skins have popped, about 6 minutes. Turn off the heat. Pass through a chinois or cheesecloth into a glass measuring cup, pushing the fruit through. Scrape the thick goo that will accumulate on the outside of the chinois or cheesecloth and add it to the juice. Discard the solids.

Return the juice to the saucepan and add the sugar. Heat the liquid over medium-high heat, stirring, until the sugar dissolves, about 2 minutes. Turn off the heat and let the juice cool to room temperature. Transfer the juice to a labeled bottle and close; it will keep, refrigerated, for up to 2 weeks.

CURRENCY

applejack and pomegranate molasses with Pedro Ximénez

Pomegranate molasses is a thick, reduced pomegranate juice, used often in Middle Eastern cooking. It has a sweet, tart, really distinct flavor; it's the defining ingredient in this cocktail. (You can find it at Middle Eastern markets and specialty food stores.) I first made this cocktail with gin, but it always left me thinking that it needed to be rounder to have more flavor. I started making it with applejack, which is distilled apple cider. That did it for me: the sweetness of the apple, along with the tartness of the pomegranate molasses and the nuttiness of the sherry, all came together into this perfect cocktail.

Makes 1 cocktail

GLASS
Double old fashioned

COCKTAIL
1½ ounces applejack brandy
½ ounce Pedro Ximénez sherry
1 ounce fresh lemon juice (about 1 lemon)
¾ ounce Pomegranate Molasses
Syrup (recipe follows)

Combine the cocktail ingredients in a shaker. Fill the shaker with ice cubes, cover, and shake hard for 7 seconds. Fill the glass with ice cubes and use a Hawthorne strainer to strain the cocktail into a double old fashioned glass.

Pomegranate Molasses Syrup

If you happen to have simple syrup on hand, make this by stirring equal parts pomegranate molasses and simple syrup. If not, this is a recipe for making the syrup from scratch.

Makes about 6 ounces (about ¾ cup)

¼ cup plus 2 tablespoons sugar
¼ cup pomegranate molasses
¼ cup water

Combine the ingredients in a small saucepan and heat over medium-high heat, stirring or swirling the pan constantly, until the sugar dissolves, about 2 minutes. Transfer the syrup to a labeled bottle or jar and close; it will keep, refrigerated, for up to 2 months.

I know, you're supposed to love all your babies the same, but I'll come right out and say it: this chapter, which includes vermouth, infused liqueurs, bitters, complex (not so simple) syrups, and other infusions, is my favorite. As a bar guy, this is where I get to "geek out." These are the products of hours and weeks and sometimes months of tinkering, tasting, researching, and tinkering and tasting some more. When I land on a final recipe, when at last I hit the note that I want in replicating a favorite, it's a real "Hallelujah!" moment.

This chapter is divided into five sections. **VERMOUTHS** make up the fortified and infused section, sweet and dry, and are probably my pride and joy. **LIQUEURS** are spirits infused with other flavors, fruits, nuts, and sugar, such as Chai Cognac, Strawberry Liqueur, and Pecan Liqueur. **BITTERS** can be more complex than liqueurs and infused with more ingredients, including many herbs, spices, and roots. They are intensely flavored and, yes, bitter. My favorite is Apertivo, which is my version of Campari. **TINCTURES,** also called *alcohol infusions,* are generally very simple, consisting of neutral-flavored vodka infused with one or very few ingredients. **SYRUPS** do not contain or have very little alcohol. They allow you to sweeten a cocktail and add flavor at the same time.

The recipes in this chapter are a little more involved, or at least require more ingredients, but they're worth the effort, as they enable you to add many flavors in one drop or jigger, which makes for cocktails that are more layered and complex.

Replicating, or making my versions of the classics, such as Aperitivo and vermouth, was probably the most difficult thing I've done as a barman and also the most rewarding. To do so, first I tasted what I wanted to replicate. For instance, when I set about to replicate Campari, although I'd tasted it hundreds of times, now I was *really* tasting it. I wanted to notice all the flavor that went into the mix that I know as the taste of Campari. Grapefruit, hints of rhubarb, and the unmistakable bitterness of gentian root. Various spices. I made batch after batch, adding these and other ingredients in different amounts until I had created a beverage that tasted to me like Campari. From such experiences, I learned more than I ever could have imagined about the nuances of the original liqueurs I was re-creating, and through that knowledge I gained a better understanding of the role of those liqueurs in classic cocktails as well as my own cocktails.

If all this tinkering sounds intimidating, the good news is that you don't have to do what I did. All you have to do is follow these recipes. You'll notice that in many of them the ingredient lists are long and the ingredients themselves uncommon. Finding them is an experience in Internet foraging, but it's all there at your fingertips (or in a well-stocked brick-and-mortar spice store if you have access to one). Once you get the ingredients, these concoctions are surprisingly easy to make. And for each one, the formula is more or less the same: boil, refrigerate, and strain. Put it in a clean bottle and add it to your cocktail-making collection. Enjoy.

STOCKING YOUR BAR

Making drinks at home is easy, especially if you have a bar stocked with the basics, at least one spirit from each category (I go into those spirits in each chapter) as well as the following liqueurs and bitters that you may need repeatedly to mix up your favorite classic and artisan cocktails.

GREEN CHARTREUSE (55% abv) is a French herbal liqueur made by Carthusian monks in the Alps. The legend behind it is that only two monks at a time are allowed to know the recipe, and these two monks cannot travel together, so if something happens to the monk in his travels, the recipe lives on in the other monk. There are many different versions of Chartreuse, the most common being green Chartreuse and yellow Chartreuse. I suggest you keep green Chartreuse on your bar for use in many of these and other classic cocktails such as the Last Word (see box). If you have some extra space, I also like to keep a bottle of green Chartreuse VEP, which is aged fifteen years as opposed to the four years that standard green Chartreuse is aged; besides being three times older, it is also three times more expensive. This one is not for cocktails; just use it as a digestive.

LUXARDO MARASCHINO CHERRY LIQUEUR (32% abv) Don't let the name fool you; this Italian liqueur is nothing like the fluorescent red maraschino cherries that are used as a garnish in mediocre bars. It doesn't have that cloying sweetness of those cherries, and, in fact, it's not even red. The clear, dry liqueur is made by distilling Marasca cherries (a variety grown exclusively

on the coast of Croatia) *and* their pits. This is an integral part of many classic cocktails that you would never guess contained a liqueur made of cherries, including the Last Word, the Hemingway Daiquiri, the Martinez, and the Aviation.

Classic Cocktails Using Luxardo Maraschino Cherry Liqueur

LAST WORD: ¾ ounce gin, ¾ ounce fresh lime juice, ¾ ounce Luxardo, and ¾ ounce green Chartreuse shaken with ice and fine-strained into a coupe glass, with a twist of lime.

HEMINGWAY DAIQUIRI: 1½ ounces light rum, ¾ ounce fresh grapefruit juice, ¾ ounce fresh lime juice, and ½ ounce Luxardo, shaken and fine-strained into a coupe glass.

MARTINEZ: 2 ounces sweet vermouth, 1 ounce Old Tom gin, 1 bar spoon (1 teaspoon) Luxardo, and a dash of angostura bitters, combined in a mixing glass filled with ice, fine-strained into a coupe glass, and garnished with a lemon twist.

AVIATION: 2 ounces London dry gin, 1 ounce fresh lemon juice, and ¾ ounce Luxardo combined in a shaker filled with ice, shaken hard, and fine-strained into a coupe glass coated with crème de violette.

HEERING ORIGINAL CHERRY LIQUEUR (21.8% abv), aka "Cherry Heering," is a cherry liqueur made in Denmark. It is made by macerating cherries, combining them with neutral grain spirits, adding sugar, and aging the mix in oak for five years. The result is a bright red liqueur with a deep cherry flavor. It is best known for its role in the classic cocktail the blood and sand.

Cherry Heering was the flavor profile I had in mind when I was working on my own recipe for Cherry Liqueur (page 252). I like them both: of course, there is nothing like homemade, but on the other hand, there is the convenience of a quality store-bought product.

CAMPARI (25% abv) is an Italian liqueur with a beautiful, ruby-red color and a bitter, herbal flavor. I use it throughout these cocktails and also make my own version, Aperitivo (page 256; you can substitute Campari for any recipe calling for house-made Aperitivo). A very popular aperitivo in Italy consists of Campari mixed with soda and garnished with an orange slice, but Campari is most famously used in the Negroni, which is equal parts Campari, sweet vermouth, and gin.

SWEET VERMOUTH (16% to 18% abv) is a fortified wine infused with wormwood (the name *vermouth* comes from the German word for wormwood) and other ingredients including herbs, roots, botanicals, spices, and sugar. It is complex and layered, with the dominant flavor profile being burned sugar, dried fruit, citrus, and allspice. The majority of sweet vermouth is vermouth rosso or "red vermouth," because of its color. (It also sometimes referred to as "Italian vermouth.") The most common uses of sweet vermouth are in the Manhattan, Rob Roy, Negroni, and blood and sand cocktails. Some brands of sweet vermouth that I like are Dolin, Carpano Antica, Noilly Prat, and Alessio. But, of course, my favorite is my own Sweet Vermouth (page 240).

DRY VERMOUTH (16% to 18% abv), like sweet vermouth, is a fortified, infused wine. Also known as "French vermouth," dry vermouth differs from sweet vermouth in that it has less residual sugar. It is made with various alpine herbs and has a very soft, elegant flavor. The most famous use of dry vermouth is in a classic Martini, although in the modern Martini the vermouth barely touches the drink. I make my own Dry Vermouth (page 238); my preferred storebought brands are Dolin and Noilly Prat.

ORANGE LIQUEUR (40% abv) is best known for its role in the margarita, cosmopolitan, sidecar, and Long Island iced tea. I make my own Orange Liqueur (page 245), but if you must buy it, Grand Marnier is my favorite; it is made of orange rinds and has an intense orange flavor without being overly sweet.

CLASSIC BITTERS (44.7% abv). When I think of "classic" bitters, I think of angostura, which is the one that you will find on every bar in America and that is used in many classic cocktails, including the old fashioned, Manhattan, and the more contemporary Trinidad sour. Angostura is great, don't get me wrong, but in the last ten years many small companies have started producing bitters; it's really fun to try the different brands, as each one contains a unique blend of ingredients that gives the bitters a unique personality. I worked long and hard to create my Classic Bitters (page 258). The bitters I also keep behind my bar and recommend you do, too, are angostura (regular and orange), Regan's, Fee Brothers, and Peychaud's. Every bar needs bitters. In general bitters are seen as a nonpotable alcohol because they are used in such small amounts, but they are indeed potable, and I happen to have known many barmen who do a shot of straight angostura bitters before their shift.

AMARO (16% abv to 40% abv) means "bitter" in Italian, and the word is used to describe a category of bitter herbal Italian liqueurs that includes sweet vermouth, Fernet, and Cynar, among others. Amaros are typically enjoyed after dinner as a digestive aid, but I also use them to add a layer of flavor in cocktails. There are truly countless varieties of amaro from Italy; each village has its own amaro, and they're all slightly (or very) different. I suggest you keep at least two on your bar. Some I like are Nonino, Averna, Montenegro, and Meletti.

ORGEAT is a sweet almond syrup enhanced with orange flower water. I make my own (page 274), but the store-bought version will also do the trick. The important thing is that you have it on hand. It adds so many layers of flavor. It's also an integral part of classic cocktails including the mai tai, Trinidad especial, and Japanese Cocktail. If you buy this in the store or online, look for brands by Small Hands or Liquid Alchemist.

DRY VERMOUTH

wormwood and white wine with citrus, angelica root, coriander, licorice, and brandy

Dry vermouth is a fortified wine flavored with botanicals. It is a key ingredient in a classic Martini (2 ounces gin and 1 ounce dry vermouth, stirred and served in a Martini glass), and the upside-down Martini (2½ ounces vermouth and 1 ounce gin, stirred and served in a Martini glass), which was Julia Child's favorite cocktail. I also use dry vermouth in the Watchmen (page 201). I started making my own, along with Compound Gin (page 254), because I thought, How cool would it be to make something as straightforward as a Martini but with both components house-made? Making it turned out to be more difficult than I thought, not the least reason of which is that there are no good recipes to work from. It was like reinventing the wheel. After a *lot* of tinkering and many batches that went down the drain, literally, I finally landed on this, which is pretty easy to make and really, really delicious. You can find wormwood in spice stores and online.

Makes about 1 liter

Rind of ¼ grapefruit (peeled with a vegetable peeler)
Rind of ¼ orange (peeled with a vegetable peeler)
½ teaspoon dried wormwood
½ teaspoon shredded licorice root
¼ teaspoon dried lavender
1 small sage leaf
½ teaspoon juniper berries
½ teaspoon chamomile
1 thin slice fresh cucumber
1 bay leaf
3 cups dry white wine (such as chardonnay)
½ cup amontillado sherry
¾ cup pisco
1 teaspoon sugar

Cut a roughly 12-inch square piece of cheesecloth and put in on your work surface. Put the grapefruit rind, orange rind, wormwood, licorice root, lavender, sage leaf, juniper berries, chamomile, cucumber, and bay leaf in the center. Close the bundle by bringing the corners toward the middle and tie a knot in it to seal it closed.

Combine all the ingredients, including the cheesecloth bundle, in a large saucepan. Heat over medium-high heat, stirring, until the sugar dissolves, about 2 minutes; be careful that the flame isn't so high that it can travel around the sides of the pan, as the alcohol in the pan will catch fire. Reduce the heat to medium-low and simmer for 10 minutes. Turn off the heat and set aside to cool to room temperature. Cover and refrigerate overnight. Remove the cheesecloth bundle and squeeze to extract the liquid; discard the bundle. Transfer the vermouth to a labeled bottle and close. It will keep, refrigerated, for up to 2 months.

Pictured: ingredients for Dry Vermouth

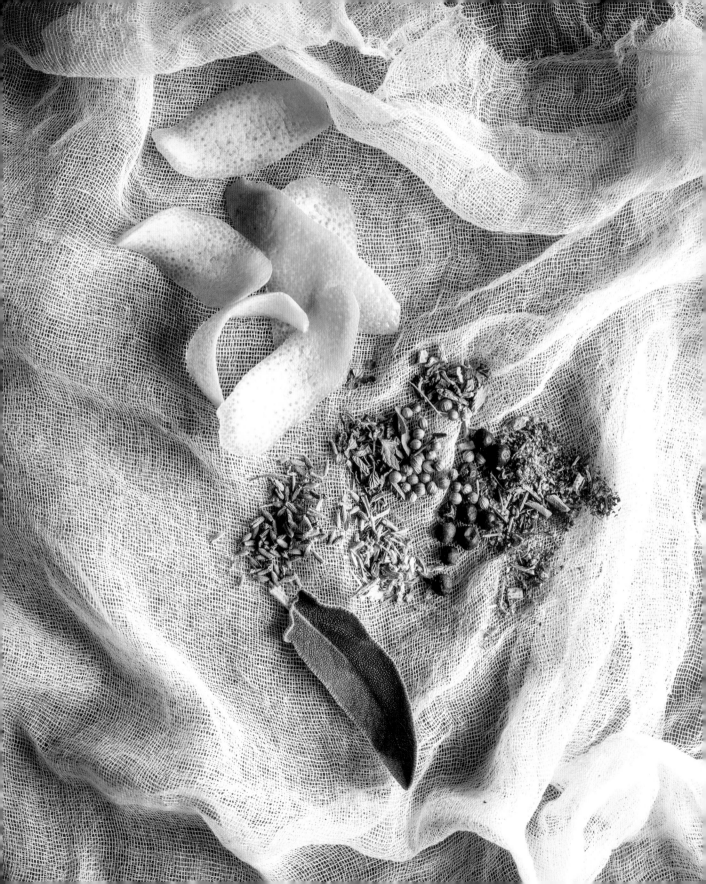

SWEET VERMOUTH

wormwood and white wine with burned sugar, sage, rosemary, orange, and dried fruit

Sweet vermouth is different from dry vermouth in that it has more sugar added to it. Sweet vermouth is often referred to as "Italian vermouth" or vermouth rosso because it is often reddish brown in color. This takes only an hour to make, and it's so good. To get all the rich, warm flavor notes that I wanted in this, I start with burned sugar, and I use dried fruits, port wine, brandy, and a variety of spices, including black cardamom, which you can find in Indian and other specialty grocery stores or online. You can use this in any cocktail where sweet vermouth is called for, such as a classic Manhattan (2 ounces rye, 1 ounce sweet vermouth, 2 to 3 dashes angostura bitters, served up) or a blood and sand (¾ ounce blended scotch, ¾ ounce sweet vermouth, ¾ ounce Cherry Heering, ¾ ounce orange juice, served up). I also use this in the Cat's Paw (page 82), the Spring Negroni (page 88), the Mocambo (page 121), and the Xolito (page 168).

Makes about 48 ounces (6 cups)

4 cups sauvignon blanc (or another dry white wine, such as pinot grigio)

1¼ cups sugar

¼ cup plus 2 teaspoons dried currants

2 pitted prunes

1 tablespoon plus 1 generous teaspoon chopped fresh rosemary leaves

2 tablespoons plus 1 teaspoon chopped fresh sage leaves

3 teaspoons fresh thyme leaves

Rind of 1½ oranges (peeled with a vegetable peeler)

½ tablespoon dried wormwood

¼ teaspoon sassafras root

½ cup inexpensive port

¼ teaspoon black peppercorns

½ teaspoon shredded cinchona bark

1 teaspoon burdock root

10 black cardamom pods

½ teaspoon anise

7 ounces pisco

Bring the wine to a boil over medium-high heat in a small saucepan; be careful that the flame isn't so high that it can travel around the sides of the pan, as the alcohol in the pan will catch fire Reduce the heat so the wine is barely simmering until you're ready to add it to the sugar.

Meanwhile, put the sugar in a heavy-bottomed medium saucepan (a light-colored pan is ideal so you can see the sugar turn color as it cooks) and cook over medium-high heat, swirling the pan but not stirring, until the sugar is melted and dark amber color, tilting and swirling the pan so the sugar cooks evenly, about 3 minutes. Gradually add the wine, stirring constantly with a long wooden spoon as you add it; be careful as the mixture will be very hot, and a lot of steam will rise from the pan. (If the sugar clumps up, which will happen if the wine is added too quickly, cook it for a minute or two until it melts.) Add the rest of the ingredients, reduce the heat to medium-low, and simmer for 30 minutes. Turn off the heat and set aside to cool to room temperature. Cover and refrigerate overnight or for at least 12 hours. Remove the mixture from the refrigerator, strain it through a chinois or cheesecloth, and discard the solids. Transfer the vermouth to two labeled bottles and close. (I reuse wine or liquor bottles for this.) It will keep, refrigerated, for up to 2 months.

Pictured: ingredients for Sweet Vermouth

VELVET FALERNUM

Velvet Falernum is a spiced almond concoction originally from Barbados. That I know of, there isn't an artisan Velvet Falernum you can buy in a store, so I make my own. Velvet Falernum is made as a liqueur and a nonalcoholic syrup. Mine is a liqueur, meaning it has a rum base. It has so many layers of flavor to it: in addition to the dominant flavors of almonds, vanilla, cloves, and allspice, it is brightened up by fresh ginger and fresh lime. Velvet Falernum is essential in rum punch and other tiki-type drinks. I use it in the Evening Storm (page 113) and the CA Sour (page 175).

Makes about 16 ounces (2 cups)

½ cup raw almonds

¾ cup light rum

¾ cup water

2½ ounces fresh ginger, peeled and finely chopped (about 1 cup)

1½ teaspoons whole cloves

1½ teaspoons allspice

Rind of 2 limes (peeled with a vegetable peeler)

¼ vanilla bean

1½ cups sugar

⅛ teaspoon almond extract

Adjust the oven racks so one is in the middle position and preheat the oven to 350°F.

Bring a small saucepan of water to a boil over high heat. Add the almonds and plunge them into the boiling water to blanch for 1 minute. Strain and set aside to cool to room temperature. Put the almonds in a clean dishcloth, close the cloth, and rub the nuts together in the cloth to rub off the skins; discard the skins.

Spread the almonds on a baking sheet and toast for about 5 minutes, shaking the pan once during that time, until the almonds are fragrant. Remove from the oven.

Transfer the almonds to a blender. Add the rum, water, ginger, cloves, allspice, and lime peel. Using a small sharp knife, split the vanilla bean down the middle. Scrape the seeds out of the bean and add as well. Blend the mixture until the nuts look like rough coffee grind. Transfer the mixture to a container and let it sit overnight.

Transfer the mixture to a medium saucepan and add the sugar and the almond extract. Heat over medium-high heat, stirring often, until the sugar dissolves, about 4 minutes. Set aside to cool to room temperature. Strain the mixture through a chinois or cheesecloth into a labeled bottle or jar and close; it will keep, refrigerated, for up to 1 month.

ESPRESSO RUM

dark rum and espresso with vanilla, black cardamom, and lavender

This espresso-infused rum is my version of coffee liqueur, the most common of which is Kahlúa. I use decaf espresso because most people enjoy this as an after-dinner drink and I don't want to keep them up all night. Drizzle any leftover rum over vanilla ice cream or stir it into your afternoon coffee.

You can buy black cardamom pods at Indian and other specialty food stores or online, and sassafras root at spice stores, Indian groceries, or online sources. Black cardamom pods have a totally different flavor from green cardamom pods.

Makes about 16 ounces (2 cups)

1 cup inexpensive dark rum

1 cup water

¾ cup plus 1 tablespoon sugar

1 tablespoon plus 1 teaspoon ground decaf espresso

¼ teaspoon dried lavender flowers

¼ teaspoon sassafras root

2 black cardamom pods

½ vanilla bean

Combine everything but the vanilla bean in a medium saucepan over medium-high heat. Use a small paring knife to split the vanilla bean down the middle. Use the knife to scrape the seeds out of the bean and add the seeds and bean to the pot. Heat the liquid, stirring often, until the sugar dissolves, about 2 minutes; be careful that the flame isn't so high that it can travel around the sides of the pan, as the alcohol in the pan will catch fire. Turn off the heat and set aside to cool to room temperature. Strain the rum through a doubled piece of cheesecloth and discard the solids. Transfer the rum to a labeled bottle or jar, close; it will keep, refrigerated, for up to 3 months.

CHAI COGNAC

cognac and chai with mint, lemon, and orange

I love the flavor combination of chai spice blend, and it's a great complement to cognac. When I first thought about the combination, I knew it would be delicious, but it turned out to be even more special than I imagined. I add mint, which gives the cognac a bright, fresh aftertaste that contrasts really nicely with the warm flavors of the chai and cognac.

Makes about 8 ounces (1 cup)

Rind of 1 lemon (peeled with a vegetable peeler)
Rind of 1 orange (peeled with a vegetable peeler)
1 cup cognac or brandy
1 tablespoon loose-leaf chai tea
1 tablespoon sugar
¼ cup fresh mint leaves (about 30 leaves)

Put all the ingredients in a small saucepan and heat over medium-high heat, stirring, until the sugar dissolves, about 2 minutes; be careful that the flame isn't so high that it can travel around the sides of the pan, as the alcohol in the pan will catch fire. Turn off the heat and let the cognac cool to room temperature. Transfer to a jar, cover, and refrigerate overnight to infuse the liquor with the seasonings. Pass the cognac through a chinois or cheesecloth and discard the solids. Transfer the cognac to a labeled bottle or jar and close; it will keep, refrigerated, for up to 6 months.

ORANGE LIQUEUR

I thought about calling this the four musketeers, four of a kind, or anything along those lines. I had a group of four friends: Hessel (boy), Hessel (girl), Thijs (boy), and me. We all did theater together, all got in trouble together. I remember racing against traffic on our one-way village street in our mothers' cars. I remember us trying (and failing) to hot-wire a car in Antwerp. Thijs's father imported Grand Marnier into the Netherlands, and whenever it was my buddy's birthday we were invited by his dad to have dinner in some fancy restaurant. The highlight would be after dessert when he would order French coffees—coffee with Grand Marnier and whipped cream.

When I started running the bar program at Lucques and the other restaurants, I was determined to make as many cocktail components from scratch as I could, rather than relying on the common versions that you find in stores. This was one of the first liqueurs that I developed, which is basically my version of Grand Marnier. For this, I wanted to make sure you could taste the fruit; I wanted it to taste like orange, not like orange extract. I use a combination of vodka, for its mild flavor, and brandy, for the warmth it adds to the overall flavor profile. I always have a bottle in my well, for making margaritas and cosmos. Use the syrup to make a classic margarita, cosmo, or white lady, which is 2 ounces gin, 1 ounce fresh lemon juice, and ¾ ounce Orange Liqueur, served straight up, with an orange wheel.

Makes about 16 ounces (2 cups)

3 oranges
½ grapefruit (preferably Ruby Red)
¼ vanilla bean
1 cup vodka
1 cup brandy
2 cups sugar

Using a vegetable peeler, peel the oranges and grapefruit half and put the rinds in a medium saucepan. Tear off and discard the white pith from both fruit. Cut the orange and grapefruit half each in quarters and add them to the saucepan. Using a paring knife, scrape the seeds out of the vanilla bean and add the seeds and the pod to the saucepan. Add the vodka, brandy, and sugar and heat the mixture over medium-high heat until the sugar dissolves; be careful that the flame isn't so high that it can travel around the sides of the pan, as the alcohol in the pan will catch fire. Turn off the heat and set aside to cool to room temperature. Transfer to a 2-quart container with a lid. Cover and refrigerate for 1 week to infuse the vodka with the flavors. Remove the mixture from the refrigerator and strain through a chinois or a fine-mesh strainer. Discard the solids. Transfer the orange liqueur to a bottle. It will keep, refrigerated, for up to 3 months.

WALNUT LIQUEUR

When I was a kid, walnuts were not my thing. I thought there was only one kind, the kind that dries out your mouth when you eat them. My mom used to serve walnuts with cheese and some jam when people came over and I would eat everything but the nuts. But life happens and you learn to taste different things. So when I started buying produce for the bars, I found myself at the Rancho La Vina stand, where a walnut farmer from Santa Barbara asked, "Would you like to taste some walnut oil?" Walnut oil? It sounded kind of strange. And then I tasted it. I didn't know oil could be this good, a bit fancy but very good.

I bought some walnuts to play with at the restaurant. On the drive back, I thought about what I could match them with. Apples, pears, prunes, honey, maybe some vanilla? I was already making my Orgeat and my pecan syrup, so how difficult could it be to make a walnut syrup? What if I used brandy instead of vodka to pull out the flavor of the nuts? The process turned out to be slightly more difficult, the flavor profile of walnuts a little more subtle, so I had to figure it out, play around a bit. But in the end it was delicious.

Makes about 16 ounces (2 cups)

1½ cups shelled walnut halves (about 5½ ounces)
½ cup inexpensive vodka
½ cup inexpensive brandy
½ cup water
1½ cups sugar

Put the walnuts, vodka, brandy, and water in a blender and blend to roughly chop the walnuts. Transfer the mixture to a covered container and refrigerate overnight. Put the walnuts, vodka, brandy, and water in a blender to roughly chop the walnuts. Transfer the mixture to a covered container and refrigerate overnight. Remove the nut mixture from the refrigerator, add the sugar, and heat over medium-high heat, stirring occasionally, until the sugar dissolves, about 4 minutes; be careful that the flame isn't so high that it can travel around the sides of the pan, as the alcohol in the pan will catch fire. Set aside to cool to room temperature. Strain the liqueur through a chinois or cheesecloth into a labeled bottle or jar and close; it will keep, refrigerated, for up to 1 month.

PECAN LIQUEUR

Pecans are one of the few nuts native to the United States. I wasn't familiar with them until I moved here, and now I love them. I use this liqueur in cocktails where I want that toasty, nutty, fall feeling, including the McIntosh (page 98) and the Mercantile (page 223). Drizzle the liqueur over vanilla ice cream or use it in place of simple syrup in a classic whiskey sour.

Makes about 9 ounces (1 cup plus 2 tablespoons)

1 cup raw pecan halves
¾ cup water
¾ cup inexpensive brandy
1½ cups sugar

Adjust the oven racks so one is in the middle position and preheat the oven to 350°F.

Spread the pecans on a baking sheet and toast them in the oven until they are lightly browned and fragrant, shaking the pan once during that time so they toast evenly, about 10 minutes. Remove the nuts from the oven and set them aside to cool to room temperature.

Combine the pecans, water, and brandy in a blender. Turn on the machine and pulse until the pecans are crushed; you don't want to process them so long that they become a paste or juice. Transfer the mixture to a small jar or pint-size deli container. Cover and refrigerate for 24 hours.

Remove the mixture from the refrigerator and transfer it to a small saucepan. Add the sugar and heat over medium-high heat, stirring until the sugar dissolves, about 4 minutes; be careful that the flame isn't so high that it can travel around the sides of the pan, as the alcohol in the pan will catch fire. Set aside to cool to room temperature. Strain through a chinois or cheesecloth and discard the solids. Transfer the liqueur to a labeled bottle or jar and close; it will keep, refrigerated, for up to 1 month.

GUAVA LIQUEUR

At the Santa Monica farmers' market I find three different varieties of guava. Pineapple guava is not my favorite; I don't recommend these. Pink guava works, but in my opinion the best variety is the Mexican Beaumont guava, a white, creamy-looking guava, which I get from Garcia Farms. I don't do anything to the guava, like peel or seed it. I just cut it up and throw it in a blender. This liqueur is delicious. Use this in place of the Strawberry Liqueur in Il Lavoro (page 136) and the G & G (page 101) to add a more unusual, fragrant fruity flavor to the drink. Juniper berries are available in grocery stores, spice stores, and online.

Makes about 6 ounces (¾ cup)

5 ounces chopped fresh guava (about 1 small guava)
¼ cup plus 1 tablespoon brandy
¼ cup plus 1 tablespoon vodka
¼ cup water
¼ teaspoon juniper berries
¼ teaspoon dried lavender flowers
2 tablespoons orange blossom honey
1 tablespoon sugar

Combine the ingredients in a small saucepan and bring to a boil over medium-high heat; be careful that the flame isn't so high that it can travel around the sides of the pan, as the alcohol in the pan will catch fire. Reduce the heat to medium-low and simmer for 5 minutes. Turn off the heat and set aside to cool to room temperature. Strain the liquid through a chinois or cheesecloth and discard the solids. Transfer the liqueur to a labeled bottle or jar and close; it will keep, refrigerated, for up to 2 months.

STRAWBERRY LIQUEUR

strawberry and brandy with lavender and turmeric

Gaviota strawberries are a variety that was invented in Oxnard, California, a strawberry-growing region between Los Angeles and Santa Barbara. There's a patent on them, owned by the University of California. Gaviota strawberries are low in acid and high in flavor, and they are the most delicious strawberries you'll ever eat. When you bite into one, you think, "That's what a strawberry is supposed to taste like!" I've bought strawberries at Whole Foods when I couldn't get these, but these are my preference. I spiced up this liqueur to give it more dimensions of flavor, so it didn't just taste like something you'd put on ice cream (although it does make an excellent vanilla ice cream topping for grown-ups). I use it to make the Il Lavoro (page 136) and the G & G (page 101). Use this liqueur in place of orange liqueur to add an exciting new dimension to your next margarita (2 ounces tequila, 1 ounce lime juice, 1 ounce of this liqueur, on the rocks or straight up in a salt-rimmed glass).

Makes about 8 ounces (1 cup)

5 ounces hulled and quartered strawberries
¼ cup plus 1 tablespoon inexpensive brandy
¼ cup plus 1 tablespoon inexpensive vodka
¼ cup water
⅛ teaspoon black peppercorns
⅛ teaspoon dried lavender
⅛ teaspoon ground turmeric
¼ cup plus 2 tablespoons sugar

Combine all the ingredients in a small saucepan and bring to a boil over medium-high heat; be careful that the flame isn't so high that it can travel around the sides of the pan, as the alcohol in the pan will catch fire. Reduce the heat to medium-low and simmer for about 5 minutes, until the strawberries lighten in color. Turn off the heat.

Pass the syrup through a chinois or cheesecloth, pushing on the fruit with a ladle or a wooden spoon to extract as much liquid as you can from them. Scrape off the puree that will accumulate on the outside of the strainer and add it to the liquid. Discard the solids.

Let the syrup cool to room temperature. Transfer the liqueur to a labeled bottle or jar and close; it will keep, refrigerated, for up to 3 months.

Ingredients for Guava Liqueur (page 249) and Strawberry Liqueur: (1) strawberries, (2) guavas, (3) black peppercorns, (4) dried lavender, (5) ground turmeric, (6) juniper berries, (7) orange blossom honey

CHERRY LIQUEUR AND BRANDIED CHERRIES

brandy and cherries with orange rind, vanilla, lemon, lavender, and cassia bark

In Dutch, we have a saying "Swat two flies with one hit." That's what this is: a two-for-the-price-of-one recipe. From a cup and a half of cherries, you get 2 cups of cherry liqueur better than any you'll buy in a store—and you get a pint of brandied cherries that will take your Manhattan game to the next level. I started by wanting to make cherry liqueur, which I discovered would benefit by using the cherry pits in addition to the cherries themselves.

Make the cherries first, and what you have left, and what is in the canning jar, is your cherry liqueur. I use the liqueur in the Xolito (page 168), Glasgow Kiss (page 200), and Raoul Duke (page 198). Or use it in place of orange liqueur in a cosmopolitan or Hemingway Daiquiri (2 ounces light rum, ¾ ounce lime juice, ¾ ounce grapefruit juice, ½ ounce cherry liqueur, shaken with ice cubes, strained into a coupe glass, and garnished with a lime wheel).

Because it calls for cherries *and* their pits, you can only make this when cherries are in season. If you see cherries at the market, jump on them! You blink and cherry season is gone. I use Tartarian cherries, but any sweet cherries, such as Rainier or Bing, will also work.

Makes about 16 ounces (2 cups) Brandied Cherries and about 16 ounces (2 cups) Cherry Liqueur

1 pound sweet cherries, such as Tartarian, Rainier, or Bing (about 3 cups)

2 cups brandy

1⅓ cups water

1 ounce fresh lemon juice (about 1 lemon)

2 whole star anise

6 whole cloves (¼ teaspoon)

¼ teaspoon dried lavender

1 ounce black cardamom pods

Wide rind from 1½ oranges (peeled with a vegetable peeler)

¾ ounce cassia bark

5 cups sugar

½ vanilla bean

Pit the cherries. Reserve ¼ cup of the pits and discard the rest. Set half of the cherries aside while you make the liqueur

Put the other half in a large saucepan with the remaining ingredients except for the vanilla bean. Split the vanilla bean lengthwise with a small sharp knife. Use the knife to scrape the seeds out of the bean and add the bean and seeds to the pan. Add the pits and heat over medium-high heat until the sugar dissolves, about 2 minutes; be careful that the flame isn't so high that it can travel around the sides of the pan, as the alcohol in the pan will catch fire. Let it simmer on low heat for about 15 minutes. Strain the liqueur through a chinois or cheesecloth and press with a ladle or wooden spoon to extract as much flavor and juice of the cherries as you can; discard the solids.

Put the remaining half of the pitted cherries in a pint jar. Pour enough hot cherry liqueur into the jar to cover the cherries, leaving ½ inch of space at the top free of liquid. Let the cherries and liqueur cool to room temperature. Pour the remaining liqueur into a 1-pint bottle. Both will keep, refrigerated, for up to 3 months.

COMPOUND GIN

juniper and Meyer lemon with orange, cucumber, and rose

When I was very green and just learning to buy liquor, a salesman came in and tried to sell me on his gin. "We make a completely local gin," he said. I asked him where they had their distillery, and he told me, "Well, we buy a neutral grain spirit from Iowa and infuse it and do a second distillation here, in downtown Los Angeles." They lost me at Iowa. That didn't sound too local to me.

Infusing alcohol with spices rather than distilling it with spices is called compound gin. Although I wasn't interested in their product, they gave me the idea to start making my own compound gin right here at the restaurant. I infuse mine with juniper berries, Meyer lemon, licorice, cucumber, rose petals, and lavender. If you want to experiment with different herbs and botanicals, just make sure that juniper berries make up half the total amount of additions, since juniper is what makes gin taste like gin. I use the gin in the Compound (page 85) and the G & G (page 101). But you can use this gin whenever American gin is called for.

Makes one 750-ml bottle

3 tablespoons dried juniper berries

1 tablespoon coriander seeds

1 green cardamom pod

1 teaspoon shredded licorice root

1 teaspoon dried rosebuds, torn into small pieces

1 teaspoon dried lavender

2 thin cucumber slices

2 thinly sliced Meyer lemon wheels

One 750-ml bottle inexpensive vodka

2 ounces 151-proof grain spirit (optional)

Put the juniper berries, coriander seeds, cardamom, licorice root, rosebuds, and lavender in a mortar and pestle and give them a quick crack—nothing too serious. Put the cucumber, Meyer lemon, and cracked spices in a quart-size jar. Add the vodka and grain spirit. Close the jar and set aside at room temperature for 3 to 5 days to infuse the vodka with the flavors. Give the bottle a good shake once a day; you may want to start tasting it after day 3 to make sure you don't take the gin past its prime, as it becomes too bitter. Pass the liquid through a chinois or cheesecloth and discard the solids. Transfer the gin to a 750-ml bottle. The gin will keep at room temperature for up to 1 year.

Pictured: ingredients for Compound Gin

APERITIVO

grapefruit and gentian with cinchona, cassia, and black cardamom

Campari is a popular Italian aperitivo (*apéritif* in French and often the word used in English) and the base of many Italian cocktails, the most popular being the Negroni. Making my own Campari was a super "bar geek" sort of thing. First because there's nothing at all wrong with store-bought Campari. But I wanted to make something more natural, something more round, something less aggressive, and absolutely something without artificial coloring. (Originally Campari was colored with a natural dye extracted from crushed beetles; today it is colored with an artificial red dye.) Unlike many liqueurs, whose flavors are widely known, the mix of flavors in Campari is a mystery. What does it taste like? You get the bitter gentian root, the bittering agent in all Italian amaros, right in your face; the rest of the flavors are very subtle and soft. I tinkered with this for a long time to get something that I was happy with. It wasn't easy, but I was obsessed. This has beautiful flavors and isn't quite as bitter as Campari. I color it with beet. but the beet is optional. Note that if you don't use it, you will have an almost colorless aperitivo.

Makes about 1 liter (4 cups)

2¼ ounces orange rind in wide strips (peeled with a vegetable peeler from about 3 oranges)

1½ ounces grapefruit rind in wide strips (peeled with a vegetable peeler from about 1 grapefruit)

1½ teaspoons shredded rhubarb root

1 gram cassia bark

1 tablespoon gentian root

1½ teaspoons cinchona bark

1 teaspoon black cardamom pods (about 3)

1 teaspoons angelica root

¼ teaspoon dried lavender

2½ cups grain vodka

1½ cups sugar

1¼ cups water

¾ ounce peeled raw purple beet (one 1-inch cube; optional)

Cut a 12-inch-square piece of cheesecloth and put it on your work surface. Put the orange rind, grapefruit rind, rhubarb root, cassia bark, gentian root, cinchona bark, cardamom pods, angelica root, and lavender in the center. Close the bundle by bringing the corners toward the middle and tie a knot with the cheesecloth to seal it closed.

Combine the vodka, sugar, and water in a medium saucepan. Add the cheesecloth bundle and heat the liquid over medium-high heat until the sugar dissolves, about 2 minutes; be careful that the flame isn't so high that it can travel around the sides of the pan, as the alcohol in the pan will catch fire. Reduce the heat to medium-low and simmer for 15 minutes. Turn off the heat and set aside to cool to room temperature.

If you are using the beet, add it to the pot. Cover and refrigerate overnight or for at least 12 hours to steep the flavors further. Remove the pot from the refrigerator and remove and discard the cheesecloth bundle and the beet. Transfer the aperitivo to a labeled bottle and close; it will keep, refrigerated, for up to 3 months.

Classic Recipes Using Campari

There are many great cocktails that start with Campari. Use this homemade version to make:

NEGRONI: 1 ounce each gin, sweet vermouth, and Campari, stirred and served over ice cubes in a double old fashioned glass with an orange twist.

SPAGLIATO: Built in an old fashioned glass over fresh ice cubes with 1 ounce each Campari, sweet vermouth, and prosecco and garnished with an orange twist.

BOULEVARDIER: 1 ounce each bourbon, Campari, and sweet vermouth, stirred and served in a double old fashioned glass over ice cubes with an orange twist.

OLD PAL (the favorite of my recipe tester, Adam Ohler): 1 ounce each rye whiskey, Campari, and dry vermouth, stirred and served over ice cubes in a double old fashioned glass with a lemon twist.

CLASSIC BITTERS

cinnamon and sassafras with cardamom, cloves, and chicory

Bitters are made from alcohol infused with aromatic plant extracts such as cinchona bark (quinine), gentian root, wormwood, and angostura bark and root. Cocktail bitters are still manufactured by a handful of companies today, each with its own closely guarded recipe. In general angostura is the most popular, and it's great, but, naturally, I wanted to make one of my own, with exactly the flavor profile that I wanted, and the pride of knowing it's house made. Bitters are generally used in very small quantities, a dash here, a quarter ounce there, or a thin layer floated on top of a cocktail. There is a reason I call this Classic Bitters. It's the bitters I make that most closely resembles angostura, which is *the* classic bitters. If you're going to make just one bitters in this book, make this. I use it in the Rule Breaker (page 79), the Black on Black (page 116), the CA Sour (page 175), the Tangier (page 203), the Watchmen (page 201), the Bienville (page 213), and the Wire Bird (page 229). I even went a little bit wild and used bitters as a main ingredient in the Hilo (page 100). This bitters has the flavor of a classic such as angostura, but it doesn't have the deep reddish brown color. When I am using the bitters to float on or stain a drink, I use angostura. Also, if you do not feel up for the task of making this, you can totally use angostura in the recipes.

Pictured: ingredients for Classic Bitters

Makes one 1-liter bottle

2 cups 151-proof grain alcohol (such as Everclear)
¼ ounce cassia bark
1 tablespoon plus 1 teaspoon dried lavender
2½ teaspoons sassafras bark
2 teaspoons sassafras leaves
2 teaspoons chicory root
2 teaspoons cardamom pods
1¾ teaspoons coriander seeds
1½ teaspoons whole cloves
1½ teaspoons angelica root
1 teaspoon gentian root
¾ teaspoon cinchona bark
1⅔ cups boiling water
¼ cup pure maple syrup

Put the grain spirit in a 1-liter jar. Add everything else except the water and maple syrup. Close the jar and put it in the refrigerator for 1 week; try to remember to shake it every day.

At the end of 7 days, strain the liquid through a chinois or cheesecloth into a clean bottle or jar; do not discard the herbs and spices. Put the steeped alcohol in the refrigerator.

Return the herbs and spices to the jar you steeped the alcohol in. Pour the boiling water into the bottle and close it. Refrigerate for 1 week. Again, don't forget to shake daily; this helps to extract as much flavor as possible.

At the end of the second week, strain the tea through a chinois or cheesecloth into a large glass measuring cup or bowl and discard the herbs and spices. Add the steeped alcohol and the maple syrup and stir to combine. Strain the bitters through cheesecloth and discard the solids. Transfer the bitters to a labeled bottle and close; it will keep, refrigerated, for up to 1 year.

ORANGE BITTERS

blood orange and cardamom with gentian, angelica, and fennel

Every time I see the guys in the kitchen cleaning blood oranges, I am amazed by how beautiful a sight it is: the insides of the oranges are this gorgeous bloody magenta color, and the outsides are bright orange. Suzanne makes beautiful appetizers with it. One day I saw one of our prep cooks, Abraham, cutting the rind off the oranges with a knife. I asked him to save the rind for me, not knowing what I would do with them. He took me seriously and every day started giving me 8 quarts of blood orange rinds! I turned them into blood orange bitters. When Abraham cuts off the rind, a small sliver of the fruit is still attached, which adds a layer of sweetness to the flavor of the bitters. These bitters take 2 weeks to make, because the flavors need to steep into the alcohol, so make it not when you need it but when you see blood oranges at the market or when you feel like tinkering around in the kitchen with something that I guarantee will be beautiful and delicious. If blood oranges are not available, you can totally use regular oranges. It doesn't get that pretty red hue, but you'll still get a nice flavor. I use these bitters in the American Poet (page 187). A couple of dashes would also add a nice layer of flavor to a classic Martini (½ ounces gin and ½ ounce dry vermouth, stirred and served in a Martini glass) or a Sazerac (¼ ounce absinthe, 1 sugar cube, 1½ ounces rye whiskey or cognac, and 3 dashes of these bitters).

Makes about 24 ounces (3 cups)

9 blood oranges or navel oranges (about 4 pounds)
2 cups 151-proof grain alcohol (such as Everclear)
2 tablespoons green cardamom pods
1 teaspoon angelica root
1 teaspoon cinchona bark
½ teaspoon gentian root
½ teaspoon whole cloves
½ teaspoon fennel seeds
2 ounces Simple Syrup (page 59)

Adjust the oven racks so one is in the center and preheat the oven to 250°F. Put a baking rack on a sheet pan.

Cut off the bottoms and tops off the oranges; do not discard. Working one at a time, put the oranges upright on a cutting board and cut down along the sides of the oranges to remove the rind, including the piths and a minuscule layer of fruit. Repeat, cutting off the remaining orange rinds in the same way. (Reserve the oranges for another use; juice them or cut them into supremes and toss them into salads.)

Lay the orange rinds in a single layer on the baking rack and place them in the oven until they are light brown and dried out, about 40 minutes. Remove them from the oven and set aside to cool to room temperature. Measure the orange rinds to get 2 cups.

Combine the rinds with the rest of the ingredients except the simple syrup in a 2-quart container. Cover and refrigerate for 1 week; try to remember to shake it every day.

Remove the mixture from the refrigerator and strain it through a chinois or cheesecloth; do not discard the solids. Transfer to a covered container.

Bring 1½ cups water to a boil over high heat. Turn off the heat, add the contents of the strainer (the solids) to the pot, and set aside to cool to room temperature. Transfer to a covered container.

Place both covered containers in the refrigerator for 1 week. Remove both concoctions from the refrigerator. Strain the "tea" through a chinois or cheesecloth and discard the solids.

Pour the spice-infused alcohol, the spice-infused water, and the simple syrup into a labeled bottle or jar; close and give it a shake to combine the ingredients. The bitters will keep, refrigerated, for up to 1 year.

RED WINE BITTERS

red wine and port with angostura bitters

This red wine bitters is made by combining red wine with port and bitters, so it's what you might call semi-homemade. Originally I went all out and made a red wine bitters from scratch, adding all the ingredients that are *in* bitters rather than adding the bitters. But then one Friday night at Lucques we had a full bar with diners at the bar, behind which was a row of people waiting for a table, also drinking, plus I had all the orders coming in for cocktails for people sitting at tables. The orders and tickets kept coming in—a few glasses of wine, some bubbles, a cocktail, more cocktails, more wine, and then—a CA Sour. I reached for the red wine bitters. My squeeze bottle was out. Frantically, I came up with this version just by mixing components that I had behind the bar: red wine, port, simple syrup, and bitters. When you're in a pinch, you come up with ideas that work really well and that also work really well for the home bartender for the same reason: they're quick and easy and made with what you have on hand. It's a great way to use up that little bit of red wine you have left in the bottle after a dinner.

Makes about 5 ounces (⅔ cup)

¼ cup plus 2 tablespoons dry red wine
(such as cabernet sauvignon)
3 tablespoons inexpensive port
½ ounce Simple Syrup (page 59)
½ ounce angostura bitters

Put all the ingredients in a bottle or jar. Cover, give the bottle or jar a shake, and the Red Wine Bitters is ready to go. It will keep, refrigerated, for up to several months.

FIVE-SPICE TINCTURE

Buddha's hand and peppercorns with star anise, fennel, cloves, and cinnamon

A tincture refers to an extraction of flavors with alcohol. For this recipe, I make my own five-spice blend.

Makes about 16 ounces (2 cups)

1 Buddha's hand or 1 Meyer lemon
1 tablespoon black peppercorns
6 whole star anise
2 tablespoons whole cloves
2 tablespoons fennel seeds
3 tablespoons ground cinnamon
2 cups 151-proof grain alcohol (such as Everclear)
1½ cups boiling water

Put the Buddha's hand (or Meyer lemon) in a wide-mouthed 1-liter jar. Add the spices and grain spirit, close the jar, and refrigerate for 1 week; try to remember to shake the jar once a day. Strain the concoction through a chinois or cheesecloth into a 1-liter bottle. Remove and discard the Buddha's hand (or lemon) and reserve the remaining contents of the strainer. Label the bottle and put it in the refrigerator.

Return the spices to the jar you steeped the alcohol in. Pour the boiling water over the spices and set aside to cool to room temperature. Close the jar and place it in the refrigerator to steep the spices for a week. Strain the tea in a chinois or cheesecloth and discard the solids. Add the tea to the bottle with the alcohol.

The tincture will last, refrigerated, for up to 6 months.

Pictured: Buddha's hands

CHILE DE ÁRBOL TINCTURE

This is a spicy tincture that I use to add to cocktails. Use it in cocktails the way you would Tabasco sauce to your food, whenever you want to add a tiny dash or really fiery heat. You can find chiles de árbol in most grocery stores; they're often sold in cellophane packets where the Hispanic seasonings are sold. I use this when people ask for a spicy margarita, which is often—you really get the heat without the over-powering flavor of jalapeño, which is typically used to add the spice to a spicy margarita. I pour it into an old Tabasco sauce bottle, so I can use it in the same small "dash" portions.

Makes about 8 ounces (1 cup)

4 dried chiles de árbol
1 cup vodka

Slice the chiles open lengthwise. Put them in a jar along with the vodka. Close and set aside for 4 to 7 days, depending on how spicy you want it, shaking the jar daily. Strain the mixture through a chinois or fine-mesh strainer. Transfer to a labeled bottle, close, and store in the refrigerator for up to 6 months. If you want to speed up the process, put the ingredients in a blender and blend on high speed for 30 seconds. Strain through a chinois or cheesecloth.

Tinctures, left to right: Licorice (page 266), Chile de Árbol, Five-Spice (page 263)

LICORICE TINCTURE

Licorice, the candy that you are familiar with, is made from a wooden stick, called *licorice wood*. It's sweeter than sugar. In the Netherlands, kids grow up chewing on licorice wood the same way kids eat candy here. We call it *zoet hout*, or "sweet wood," and since many Americans have an aversion to licorice I often use the Dutch name on menus. I'm afraid people won't order it if they see the word *licorice*, but I know they'll like the cocktail once they do, because the licorice flavor is subtle. This tincture is super easy to make—it's just vodka and licorice wood. You can buy licorice (it's sold as both "licorice root," and "sweet wood") at herb stores. I use this infusion in the Holland Gin Rebel (page 87) and the Fire and Smoke (page 154).

Makes about 8 ounces (1 cup)

1 cup vodka
1 stick licorice root or 2 tablespoons shredded licorice root

Put the vodka and licorice root in a jar. Close the jar and set it aside for 1 week, shaking the jar daily. Pass the vodka through a chinois or cheesecloth and discard the solids. Transfer the vodka to a labeled bottle or jar and close; it will keep, refrigerated, for up to 6 months.

SARSAPARILLA TINCTURE

Sarsaparilla root is the key ingredient that gives root beer its distinct flavor. You can find it in spice stores or from online sources. If I have the option, I like to use Indian sarsaparilla, which is more flavorful than the Mexican variety. I love the warm, caramelly essence of this tincture. When I make it for the restaurants, I put the vodka and sarsaparilla in a jar, cover it with a lid, and put it aside for a week, shaking it daily, to get a slow infusion of the sarsaparilla flavor. However, I know that home bartenders don't usually want to wait for a week to make their cocktails, so as a shortcut you can do a quick blend of the sarsaparilla root and vodka; then it only needs to steep for an hour. This makes a lot more tincture than you need for one recipe, but it lasts for 6 months, and it's a great tincture to have around when you're inventing your own cocktails and want to add another layer to the mix.

Makes about 8 ounces (1 cup)

1 cup vodka
1 ounce dried sarsaparilla root (preferably Indian)

Put the vodka and sarsaparilla in a jar and set it aside to steep for 1 week, shaking it daily. Strain the vodka through a chinois or cheesecloth and discard the solids. Transfer the tincture to a labeled bottle or jar and close; it will keep, refrigerated, for up to 6 months

KINGBIRD TINCTURE

If you're playing around with new cocktail inventions of your own, this tincture is a great addition to your bar, because it won't overpower a cocktail; it will just add another layer of flavor. I made it following a trip to a spice store. They had a wall full of little glass jars full of different spices, roots, teas. It was like a witch's spice rack. I was in heaven. After a good amount of tasting and smelling, I picked three spices I thought might work well together—sassafras, cassia, and chicory—and went back to the restaurant and used them to make this tincture. It was delicious the very first time I made it; it turned out exactly as I had imagined it tasting. That almost never happens, and when it does, it's really exciting.

At the restaurant I let the flavors steep in the vodka over the course of a week, shaking the jar once a day. If you don't want to wait, you can blend the ingredients in a blender and then strain them, which results in an almost identical product. You can buy chicory root in health food stores. You can find cassia and sassafras in spice stores or online. If you can't find sassafras, substitute whole chamomile flowers, which you can find in tea shops.

Makes about 8 ounces (1 cup)

1 cup grain vodka
½ ounce chicory root
½ ounce cassia bark or 1 short cinnamon stick
½ ounce sassafras leaves

Combine all the ingredients in a jar. Close the jar and set it aside to steep for 1 week, shaking the jar daily. Pass the mixture through a chinois or cheesecloth and discard the solids. Transfer the tincture to a labeled bottle or jar and close; it will keep, refrigerated, for up to 6 months.

RAS EL HANOUT SYRUP

ras el hanout and lemon with orange, lime, and sugar

Ras el hanout is a North African spice blend. It literally translates as "head of the shop" in Arabic, every shop owner has his or her own recipe, and people's recipes changed based on what ingredients a spice trader had left with him after going to market. I use the spice blend to flavor this simple syrup, which is one of the most beautiful and elegant syrups I make. The flavor of the peppercorns shines through lightly, behind those of the turmeric and citrus rind.

It is a staple for the Lucques bar; I use it in the Moscow Margarita (page 171), and in the Tangier (page 203). You can swap this spiced syrup for the Cola Syrup to make the Kentucky Sour (page 183), in place of the maple syrup in the Kingbird (page 188), or use it in place of simple syrup in a traditional pisco sour (1½ ounces pisco, 1 ounce fresh lemon juice, ½ egg white, ¾ ounce Ras el Hanout Syrup, triple shaken, strained into a coupe glass, and garnished with a lemon wheel). To be honest, I would use it in many more cocktails than I do except that in a restaurant you have to be careful not to be repetitive.

Makes about 12 ounces (1½ cups)

1 teaspoon allspice berries

1 teaspoon black peppercorns

1 teaspoon ground cinnamon or 1 short cinnamon stick, broken up

1 teaspoon whole cloves

1 teaspoon coriander seeds

1 teaspoon ground ginger

1 teaspoon freshly grated nutmeg

1 teaspoon ground turmeric

1 cup sugar

1 cup water

Rind of 1 orange (peeled with a vegetable peeler)

Rind of 1 lemon (peeled with a vegetable peeler)

Rind of 1 lime (peeled with a vegetable peeler)

Put the spices in a spice grinder and grind to a fine powder. Add 1 tablespoon of the ground spices to a small saucepan and reserve the remainder for another use, such as to make Ras el Hanout Whipped Cream (page 57).

Add the remaining ingredients to the saucepan with the spices and heat over medium-high heat, stirring occasionally, until the sugar dissolves, about 2 minutes. Reduce the heat to medium-low and simmer for about 15 minutes, stirring occasionally, until the liquid is slightly syrupy. Turn off the heat and set aside to cool to room temperature. Strain the syrup through a chinois or cheesecloth, pushing with the back of a ladle or wooden spoon to extract as much flavor as you can from the citrus rinds. Discard the solids. Transfer the syrup to a jar or bottle. It will keep, refrigerated, for up to 2 weeks.

COLA SYRUP

kola nut and ginger with cinnamon, lemon, orange, lavender, lime, and sugar

Several years ago I was working with St. George Spirits, and their distiller Lance Winters was in Los Angeles to launch their gin line. He is a bit of a mad scientist, and one day we were going back and forth about my syrups and his syrups, telling each other what we were creating, and I said, "What would be really cool is if you could make your own cola syrup and use it to make sodas behind the bar." He told me, "Well, I happen to have a recipe." Lance was nice enough to share that recipe with me. Of course, I had to make a small addition, but really it was quite perfect the way it was. Making sodas from this syrup turned out to be nothing but a dream: people who order cola want it to have the exact flavor of the brand that they like, and telling them it's made from house-made syrup isn't going to change their minds. So instead I use the syrup to make cocktails, including one of our most popular, the Companion (page 80). Kola nut is an African fruit originally used to flavor cola, which is where that soda got its name. You can find it ground at spice stores and online, as well as from health food and apothecary stores. You can find citric acid at cooking supply stores and online, but also at supermarkets, especially during canning season (look for it near the canning jars and tools).

Makes about 20 ounces (2½ cups)

1½ cups granulated sugar

2 cups water

½ cup dark or light brown sugar

Rind of 1½ oranges (peeled with a vegetable peeler)

Rind of 1½ limes (peeled with a vegetable peeler)

Rind of 1 lemon (peeled with a vegetable peeler)

¼ teaspoon ground cinnamon

¼ teaspoon freshly grated nutmeg

1 whole star anise

1 black cardamom pod

¾ teaspoon ground kola nut

¾ teaspoon lavender

½ teaspoon sarsaparilla

½ ounce fresh ginger, peeled and roughly chopped

¼ teaspoon citric acid

¼ vanilla bean

Combine all the ingredients in a large saucepan and stir occasionally while bringing it to a boil over high heat. Reduce the heat to medium-low and simmer the concoction for 15 minutes to thicken it slightly. Turn off the heat and let the syrup cool to room temperature. Cover and set aside overnight or for at least 12 hours for the mixture to steep. Strain the syrup through a chinois or fine-mesh strainer and push on the solids with the back of a ladle or a wooden spoon to extract as much flavor from them as possible. Discard the solids. Pour the syrup into a labeled bottle and close; it will keep, refrigerated, for up to 1 month.

Pictured: ingredients for Cola Syrup

TONIC SYRUP

lemongrass and grapefruit with cinchona and gentian root

It may seem surprising, but I really don't go out to a lot of bars to see what other bartenders are doing. For one, I have a wife and two small children, so when we go out, we prefer casual, unpretentious places where the kids can run around and make noise and my wife and I can relax with a cheap beer or an inexpensive glass of wine. The second reason I don't go to a lot of artisan bars is that I do not want to be influenced by trends. I want to find my inspiration from within, and from the cooks I work around, and not to worry about what other people are doing. That being said, one day I was at the bar at the Eveleigh restaurant on Sunset Boulevard, in Hollywood, and the barman, Dave Kupchinsky, had made premixed, bottled gin and tonics to sell. Seeing that simple mixture in those bottles, I just knew right then and there: I had to create a tonic syrup.

Tonic syrup is a play on tonic water, which is a carbonated water used to make gin and vodka tonics. Tonic water was originally developed as a way to ingest quinine, which was used to prevent malaria; the quinine, which is very bitter, was mixed with lemon, lime, and soda to make it palatable. This syrup has the same flavor characteristics as tonic water but concentrated. I use this syrup in the Peach Fever (page 173), Christiaan's G&T (page 103), and the Bienville (page 213). The ingredients I use in my tonic are pretty standard; many recipes don't use grapefruit peel, and others pick and choose from the additions listed below so they have shorter ingredient lists. I used it all, because each contributes a specific flavor, but I didn't stray far from tradition.

Makes about 16 ounces (2 cups)

Rind of ⅓ grapefruit (peeled with a vegetable peeler)
Rind of 1 lime (peeled with a vegetable peeler)
Rind of 2 lemons (peeled with a vegetable peeler)
¾ cup finely chopped lemongrass
1⅓ cups sugar
2 cups water
1½ teaspoons citric acid
½ teaspoon cinchona bark
¼ teaspoon gentian root

Combine all the ingredients in a medium saucepan and heat over medium-high heat until the sugar dissolves, about 2 minutes. Reduce the heat to medium-low and simmer for 15 minutes to thicken the liquid slightly. Turn off the heat and set aside to cool to room temperature. Strain the syrup through a chinois or fine-mesh strainer and discard the solids. Transfer the syrup to a labeled bottle or jar and close; it will keep, refrigerated, for up to 1 month.

Pictured: ingredients for Tonic Syrup

ORGEAT

almonds and sugar with orange flower water

Orgeat is a syrup classically made with almonds, orange water, and rose water. It's often paired with fruit and is an integral part of the famous mai tai and the lesser-known Trinidad sour. To make orgeat, I basically start by making a "milk" of toasted almonds and some extract.

Normally I would use apricot kernels, which taste like almonds on crack, but they are famously used to make cyanide, so naturally people think they're poisonous. However, toasting them and boiling them takes care of those worries. To be on the safe side we will be using almond extract. If you don't have orange flower water or rose water, this is not the end of the world. I have used the rind of half an orange in this recipe while cooking the sugar before, or I haven't used it at all.

I use this syrup in the Brixton Sour (page 97), the Monk's Dream (page 161), the Shangri-La (page 164), the Fifth Kingdom (page 224), River's Licorice (page 221), and the Tenderfoot (page 193). If you want to play around with it, add a splash to any cocktail that features apples, pears, apricots, grapes, orange, or cherries instead of whatever syrup is called for.

Makes about 16 ounces (2 cups)

½ cup raw almonds
2 cups water
2 cups sugar
½ teaspoon orange flower water or rose water
⅛ teaspoon almond extract

Adjust the oven racks so one is in the middle position and preheat the oven to 350°F.

Bring a small saucepan of water to a boil over high heat. Add the almonds and plunge them into the boiling water to blanch for 1 minute. Strain and set aside to cool to room temperature. Put the almonds in a clean dishcloth, close the cloth, and rub the nuts together in the cloth to rub off the skins; discard the skins.

Spread the almonds out on a baking sheet and toast for about 5 minutes, shaking the rack once during that time, until the almonds are fragrant. Remove from the oven and set aside to cool to room temperature.

Combine the almonds and water in a blender and blend until the almonds look a little bigger than coffee grind. Transfer to a labeled jar, close, and let it sit overnight. Put the mixture in a medium saucepan; add the sugar, orange blossom water, and almond extract. Heat over medium-high heat, stirring occasionally, until the sugar dissolves. Set aside to cool to room temperature. Strain the puree through a chinois or cheesecloth into a labeled bottle or jar and close; it will keep, refrigerated, for up to 1 month.

AQUAVIT SYRUP

caraway and dill with cardamom, fennel, coriander, and sugar

Aquavit is like the gin of Scandinavia. Where juniper berries are the prominent flavoring agent in gin (which, like me, is Dutch in origin), aquavit gets its flavor from caraway, which is the seed that gives rye bread its characteristic flavor. I took the same flavor profile that is used to make aquavit and used it to make this syrup, so I can add those flavors to cocktails where other booze is used. Use leftovers of this syrup to make genever sours (2 ounces genever, 1 ounce fresh lemon juice, and 1 ounce Aquavit Syrup). I made this less sweet than I make most of my syrups because that way I could use more of the syrup and get more of the aquavit flavor without making the drink too sweet.

Makes about 12 ounces (1½ cups)

1 teaspoon caraway seeds
1 teaspoon fennel seeds
½ teaspoon coriander seeds
¼ teaspoon cumin seeds
1 green cardamom pod
1 whole star anise
1 cup sugar
1 cup water
Rind of ½ lemon (peeled with a vegetable peeler)
A fresh dill sprig

Toast the caraway, fennel, coriander, cumin, cardamom, and star anise in a small saucepan over medium heat until the spices smell fragrant, shaking the pan so the spices toast evenly, about 1 minute. Add the remaining ingredients and bring to a boil over medium-high heat. Reduce the heat to medium and simmer for 15 minutes to thicken the liquid slightly. Turn off the heat and let the liquid cool to room temperature. Strain through a chinois or fine-mesh strainer and discard the solids. Transfer the syrup to a labeled bottle or jar and close; it will keep, refrigerated, for up to 3 weeks.

ACKNOWLEDGMENTS

I not going to be "that guy" at the awards show who forgets to thank his wife until the music comes on and he is kicked off the stage. So I start by thanking my beautiful wife, Melissa, who puts up with me working over seventy hours a week and who took up even more slack while I was working on this book. Melissa, you are the spine of our family. You gave me the courage to keep on going even when we didn't really know where we were going and when buying a $3.50 bottle of wine from Trader Joe's was a weekly splurge. And thank you for giving me the most amazing gift of all, our two boys, River and Leaf, whose passion for life gives me the energy to work even harder. Thank you to my brothers, Melchior and Dimitri, and my parents, Albert and Mieke. Mama and Papa, thank you for giving me the building blocks and drive to excel in life and for teaching me, "The day starts with tying your shoes." And, "You are a man at night; you are a man in the morning." And thank you to my parents-in-law Janie and Dennis, for giving me the hand of your daughter, the puzzle piece that made my life complete.

Thank you to the restaurant family I was so lucky to fall into, especially to Caroline Styne and Suzanne Goin. Your faith and trust in me helped me be creative and allowed me to find the role and career I have today. And thank you for supporting me in my quest to publish a cocktail book.

Thank you to my book team, starting with my agent, Janis Donnaud, who believed in me from the first time we spoke. She guided me from my first messed up, do-it-yourself proposal to one that she could and did actually sell. My

photographer, Ed Anderson, for believing in a first-time author and showing me how to step up my game. And for bringing Valerie Aikan-Smith to the project; the two of you had a vision that shines through the pages of this book. My editor, Melanie Tortoroli, for your knowledge, patience, and firm hand. The team at Norton, especially Anna Oler and Susan Sanfrey, and copyeditor Chris Benton. My dear friend and recipe tester Adam Ohler, thank you for taking the time to try out all the recipes. None of these words, recipes, stories, or explanations would be here on paper without my cowriter, Carolynn Carreño, whose neverending questions helped me take my recipes from the scribbles that a barman could make sense of to recipes that will allow you to create my cocktails at home.

And back to the restaurant: Thank you to Lucques general manager, Matt Duggan, aka "the Ax," whose expertise, knowledge, work ethic, and neverending support has always made me push myself just a little further. Ignacio Murillo: a few words can't possibly express how grateful I am for his hard work and dedication; I can say without exaggeration that the entire bar program wouldn't work without him. Jessica Goin, head of Lucques catering, who had the faith in me to put me in front of the biggest party planners, celebrities, and former and current heads of state, pushing me to the top of this competitive business. And her team, who just lets me show up and shine: Chris, Matthew, Arthur, and Ozzie, thank you. Aaron Cook, who shoots the photos for my press releases, who laid out my book proposal, and who always pushes me to bigger things. And the party planners who gave me my first steps on the main stage in front of their singular clients: Debbie Geller, Yifat Oren, David Rodgers, Mitie Tucker, Anchor Street Events, Bourgeois Events, Bad Cat Events, and LALAL.

And thanks to those in the industry who support me and others in my craft: Eric Alperin and Gordon Bellaver from Penny Pound Ice, who delivered ice for our photo shoot so beautiful that I saw my own cocktails in a whole different light. Joe Keep from Barkeeper Silverlake, the go-to store in Los Angeles for anything related to the professional bar. Joe, thank you for your never-ending help and passion for bartending—not just for me but for the entire Los Angeles cocktail community. Thank you, John McPherson, who first pushed me to write a book years before I did. You are always ahead of the game. Thank you to Jeff Holmes, for always helping me create new logos.

When I started this book, I wanted all my artist friends to be part of it. Ari Mickelson, my homie and photographer extraordinaire, was the first one I approached. He shot the pictures for my proposal, which helped me sell my book. Thank you for your vision, your help, and your friendship. This book wouldn't be here without you.

Lucques has had many sous chefs and chefs de cuisine throughout the years, every one of whom has had a different impact on my growth, including Jason Winters, who planted the first seed that I should make my own bitters. Jason Kim, Javier Espinoza, Rodolfo and Abraham Aguado. And the past and current bar crews for Lucques, A.O.C., Tavern, and Lucques Catering. You know who you are, and I salute you. And especially Ben Wilson, whose drawings unfortunately never made it into these pages.

But the group I want to thank above all are my regular customers, those who visit me day after day, night after night, those of you who are eager to try all my new cocktails, liqueurs, syrups, and bitters, and who have seen me morph into the barman I am today. Thank you for your continued support.

Proost, en gezondheid!

SOURCES

Amazon
www.amazon.com

Bar Keeper Silverlake
www.barkeepersilverlake.com
614 North Hoover Street
Los Angeles, CA 90004
323-669-1675

Bevmo
www.bevmo.com

The Boston Shaker
www.thebostonshaker.com

Cocktail Kingdom
www.cocktailkingdom.com

Herbs of Mexico (spices)
http://herbsofmexico.com
3903 Whittier Boulevard
Los Angeles, CA 90023
323-815-8867

The Hour
www.thehourshop.com
1015 King Street
Alexandria, VA 22314
703-224-4687

Libbey (glasses)
https://retail.libbey.com

Small Hand Foods
www.smallhandfoods.com

Star West Botanicals
www.starwest-botanicals.com

INDEX

Note: Page references in *italics* indicate photographs.